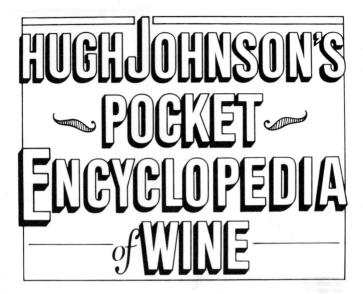

HUGH JOHNSON'S POCKET ENCYCLOPEDIA of WINE

Simon and Schuster/New York

KEY TO SYMBOLS

r.   red
p.   rosé
w.   white   } (in brackets) means relatively unimportant
br.   brown
sw.   sweet
s/sw. semi-sweet
dr.   dry
sp.   sparkling

★   plain, everyday quality
★★   above average
★★★   well known, highly reputed
★★★★ grand, prestigious, expensive
☐   usually particularly good value in its class

80 81 etc.
    recommended years which may be currently available.
80' etc. Vintage regarded as particularly successful for the property
    in question.
80 etc. years in **bold** should be ready for drinking (the others should
    be kept). Where both reds and whites are indicated the red is
    intended unless otherwise stated.
    N.B. German vintages are codified by a different system.
    See note on p. 76.
D.Y.A. drink the youngest available
NV   vintage not normally shown on label

    Cross-references are in SMALL CAPS

    See p. 5 for extra explanation

    A quick-reference vintage chart for France and Germany
    appears on p. 176.

Hugh Johnson's Pocket Encyclopedia of Wine
© 1977 by Mitchell Beazley Publishers Limited
Text © 1977, 1978, 1979, 1980, 1981, 1983 by Hugh Johnson
Revised editions published 1978, 1979, 1980, 1981, 1983
© 1983 Mitchell Beazley Publishers
All rights reserved
including the right of reproduction
in whole or in part in any form
Published by Simon and Schuster
A Division of Simon & Schuster, Inc.
Simon & Schuster Building
Rockefeller Center
1230 Avenue of the Americas
New York, New York 10020

ISBN 0–671–49667–0
Library of Congress Catalog Card Number 77–79242
Designed by Florianne Henfield
Assistant Editor Kathie Gill
Printed in Hong Kong by Mandarin Offset International (H.K.) Ltd.

Contents

Introduction

This wine encyclopedia, which is identical in content to my pocket guide, has been specially designed in this more substantial format for those who are looking for a shelf or desk reference book on wine with up-to-date vintage information in the greatest detail available anywhere.

The organization of the information is planned to be of particular help when you are choosing a bottle of wine – whether you are just starting out or an old hand with a short memory. All you need to establish is what country a wine comes from. Look up the principal words on the label in the appropriate country's section, and you will find enough potted information to let you judge whether this is the wine you want.

Specifically, you will find information on the colour and type of wine, its status or prestige, whether it is usually particularly good value, which vintages are good and which are ready to drink— and often considerably more . . . about the quantity made, the grapes used, ownership and the rest. Hundreds of cross-references help you go further into the matter if you want to.

The introduction to each national section will help you to establish which label-terms are the ones that count. In many cases you will find you can look up almost all the words on the label: estate, grape, shipper, quality-rating, bottling-information. . . .

How to read an entry

The top line of most entries consists of the following information in an abbreviated form.

1. Which part of the country in question the wine comes from. (References to the maps in this book.)
2. Whether it is red, rosé or white (or brown/amber), dry, sweet or sparkling, or several of these.
3. Its general standing as to quality: a necessarily rough and ready guide based principally on the following ascending scale:

        *   plain, everyday quality
       **   above average
      *** well known, highly reputed
    **** grand, prestigious, expensive

   So much is more or less objective. Additionally there is a subjective rating: a box round the stars of any wine which in my experience is usually particularly good (which means good value) within its price range. There are good everyday wines as well as good luxury wines. The box system helps you find them.
4. Vintage information: which were the more successful of the recent vintages which *may* still be available. And of these which are ready to drink this year, and which will probably improve with keeping. Your first choice for current drinking should be one of the vintage years printed in **bold** type. Buy light-type years for further maturing.

The German vintage information works on a different principle: see the Introduction to Germany, page 76.

Acknowledgements

This store of detailed recommendations comes partly from my own notes and partly from those of a great number of kind friends. Without the generous help and co-operation of every single member of the wine trade I have approached, I could not have attempted it. I particularly want to thank the following for giving me material help with research or in the areas of their special knowledge.

Burton Anderson
The late Martin Bamford
Anthony Barton
Jean Claude Berrouet
Michael Broadbent M.W.
Sheila Cavanagh-Bradbury
Alain de Courseulles
Len Evans
Chris Foulkes
Francis Fouquet
Jean-Paul Gardère
Rosemary George M.W.
Robert Hart M.W.
Peter Hasslacher
Ian Jamieson M.W.
Graham Knox
Matt Kramer
Tony Laithwaite

Michael Longhurst
Tim Marshall
Patrick Matthews
Dr. Franz Werner Michel
Christian Moueix
Reginald Nicholson
David Peppercorn M.W.
Alain Querre
Jan and Maite Read
Dr. Bernard Rhodes
Dr. Bruno Roncarati
Steven Spurrier
Keith Stevens
Serena Sutcliffe M.W.
Hugh Suter M.W.
Bob Thompson
Peter Vinding-Diers
James Walker

A Personal Choice

As this book has grown to the point where its 3,000-odd entries refer to at least twice that number of wines it is not surprising that many readers have asked for a few clues or short-cuts. "Surely there is an inside track" is what they are saying. "Who can possibly find his way around in all that lot?"

As a further means of inspiration and access I list here a selection of entries that have given me particular pleasure over the last year—a personal choice. It is not, I add emphatically, my choice of the world's best buys: just a random list of pleasures which will, if you follow the appropriate alphabetical entries, give you pleasure too.

Next year the list will be different: no repeat entries. I am not trying to establish a new classification—only to pass the word around about where exciting wines are coming from.

These are some ideas for 1984.

France

Auxey-Duresses
Bandol
Bergerac
Besserat de Bellefon
Château Rayas
Clos St Jacques
Côtes Canon-Fronsac
Côtes du Ventoux
Crémant de Loire
Delorme, André
Lirac
Madiran
Montagne-Saint-Emilion
Monthélie
Preiss-Zimmer
Ruinart
Roty, Joseph
Tollot-Beaut

Châteaux of Bordeaux

de Barbe
Boyd-Cantenac
Citran
Clos l'Eglise
Fargues
Fombrauge
Haut-Bailly
Gruaud-Larose (Sarget de)
Guiraud
Labégorce-Zédé
de Malle
Malartic-Lagravière
du Tertre
Verdignan
Vieux-Château-Certan

Switzerland

Hammel

Germany

Deinhard
Friedrich Wilhelm
  Gymnasium
Graach
Landwein
Kesten
Martinsthal
Rhodt
Werner

Italy

Bianco Vergine
Ferrari
Franciacorta Pinot
Galestro
Lugana
Montepulciano, Vino
  Nobile de
Petit Rouge
Rivera

Spain and Portugal

Bodegas Beronia
Penafiel
Buçaco
Camarate
Gaeiras

Austria

Apetlon
Langenlois
Rust

Hungary

Mecsek

Romania

Babeasca
Cotnari

Yugoslavia

Bogdanusa
Faros

Bulgaria

Cabernet

Greece

Kalligas

California

Beringer
Iron Horse
Mark West
Piper-Sonoma
Sebastiani
Vichon

The Pacific North-West

Associated Vintners

Australia

Balgownie
Brokenwood
Basedow
Chateau Tahbilk
Leeuwin
Moss Wood
Yellowglen

New Zealand

Te Mata
Vidal

South Africa

Backsberg
De Wetshof

The 1982 vintage

The French vintage of 1982 was a headline-maker. Bordeaux led the way, with winemakers comparing the fermenting juice to 1961, 1945, 1929 ... even 1870. Champagne was relieved of critical shortage by the biggest vintage of all time. These two were enough to convince the world that all 1982s are excellent. But things are never so simple. Burgundy made a mass of good but not remarkable wine. Germany, on the brink of a superb vintage, was delayed with rain. California had a similar problem ... as always, the truth lies in the fine print, not the headlines.

Grape varieties

The most basic of all differences between wines stems from the grapes they are made of. Centuries of selection have resulted in each of the long-established wine-areas having its favourite single variety, or a group of varieties whose juice or wine is blended together. Red burgundy is made of one grape, the Pinot Noir; red Bordeaux of three or four: two kinds of Cabernet, Merlot, Malbec and sometimes others. The laws say which grapes must be used, so the labels assume it.

So in newer vineyards the choice of a grape is the planter's single most crucial decision. Where he is proud of it, and intends his wine to have the character of a particular grape, the variety is the first thing he puts on the label—hence the useful, originally Californian, term "varietal wine".

A knowledge of grape varieties, therefore, is the single most helpful piece of knowledge in finding wines you will like wherever they are grown. Learn to recognize the characters of the most important. At least seven—Cabernet, Pinot Noir, Riesling, Sauvignon Blanc, Chardonnay, Gewürztraminer and Muscat—have memorable tastes and smells distinct enough to form international categories of wine.

Further notes on grapes will be found on page 146 (for California) and in the sections on Germany, Italy, central and south-east Europe, South Africa, etc.

The following are the best and commonest wine grapes.

Grapes for white wine

Aligoté
> Burgundy's second-rank white grape. Crisp (often sharp) wine, needs drinking young. Perfect for mixing with cassis (blackcurrant liqueur) to make a "Kir". Also grown in the USSR.

Blanc Fumé
> Another name for SAUVIGNON BLANC, referring to the "smoky" smell of the wine, particularly on the upper Loire. Makes some of California's best whites.

Bual
> Makes sweet Madeira wines.

Chardonnay
> *The* white burgundy grape, one of the grapes of Champagne, and the best white grape of California. Gives dry wine of rich complexity. Trials in Australia and eastern Europe are also successful.

Chasselas
> A prolific and widely grown early-ripening grape with little flavour, also grown for eating. Best known as Fendant in Switzerland, Gutedel in Germany. Perhaps the same as Hungary's Leanyka and Romania's Feteasca.

Chenin Blanc
> The leading white grape of the middle Loire (Vouvray, Layon, etc.). Wine can be dry or sweet (or very sweet), but always retains plenty of acidity—hence its popularity in California, where it rarely distinguishes itself. See also Steen.

Clairette
> A dull neutral grape widely used in the s. of France.

Fendant
> See Chasselas

Folle Blanche
> The third most widely grown grape of France, though no-where making fine wine. High acid and little flavour makes it ideal for brandy. Known as Gros Plant in Brittany, Picpoul in the Midi. At its best in California.

Furmint
> A grape of great character: the trade mark of Hungary both in Tokay and as vivid vigorous table wine with an appley flavour. Called Sipon in Yugoslavia.

Gewürztraminer (or Traminer)
> The most pungent wine grape, distinctively spicy to smell and taste. Wines are often rich and soft, even when fully dry. Best in Alsace; also good in Germany, eastern Europe, Australia, California.

Grüner Veltliner
> An Austrian speciality. Round Vienna and in the Wachau and Weinviertel can be delicious: light but lively. For drinking young.

Italian Riesling
> Grown in n. Italy and all over central eastern Europe. Inferior to German or Rhine Riesling with lower acidity, but a good all-round grape. Alias Wälschriesling, Olaszriesling (or often just "Riesling").

Kerner
> The most successful of a wide range of recent German var-ieties, largely made by crossing Riesling and Sylvaner (but in this case Riesling and [red] Trollinger). Early-ripening; flowery wine with good acidity. Popular in RHEINPFALZ.

Malvasia
> Known as Malmsey in Madeira, Malvasia in Italy: also grown in Greece, Spain, eastern Europe. Makes rich brown wines or soft whites of no great character.

Müller-Thurgau
> Dominant variety in Germany's Rheinhessen and Rhein-pfalz; said to be a cross between Riesling and Sylvaner. Ripens early to make soft flowery wines to drink young. Makes good sweet wines. Grows well in Austria, England.

Muscadet
> Makes light, very dry wines round Nantes in Brittany. Recently some have been sharper than they should.

Muscat (many varieties)
> Universally grown easily recognized pungent grape, mostly made into perfumed sweet wines, often fortified (as in France's VIN DOUX NATURELS). Muscat d'Alsace is alone in being dry.

Palomino
> Alias Listan. Makes all the best sherry.

Pedro Ximénez
> Said to have come to s. Spain from Germany. Makes very strong wine in Montilla and Malaga. Used in blending sherry. Also grown in Australia, California, South Africa.

Pinot Blanc
> A close relation of CHARDONNAY without its ultimate nobility. Grown in Champagne, Alsace (increasingly), n. Italy (good sparkling wine), s. Germany, eastern Europe, California. Called Weissburgunder in German.

Pinot Gris
> Makes rather heavy full-bodied whites with a certain spicy style. Known as Tokay in Alsace, Tocai in n.e. Italy and Yugoslavia, Ruländer in Germany.

Pinot Noir

Superlative black grape (see under Grapes for red wine) used in Champagne and occasionally elsewhere for making white wine, or a very pale pink "vin gris".

Riesling

Germany's finest grape, now planted round the world. Wine of brilliant sweet/acid balance, flowery in youth but maturing to subtle oily scents and flavours. Successful in Alsace (for dry wine), Austria, parts of eastern Europe, Australia, California, South Africa. Often called White, Johannisberg or Rhine Riesling.

Sauvignon Blanc

Very distinctive aromatic, herby and sometimes smoky scented wine, can be austere (on the upper Loire) or buxom (in Bordeaux, where it is combined with SEMILLON, and parts of California). Also called Fumé Blanc.

Scheurebe

Spicy-flavoured German Riesling × Silvaner cross, very successful in Rheinpfalz, esp. for Ausleses.

Semillon

The grape contributing the lusciousness to great Sauternes; subject to "noble rot" in the right conditions. Makes soft dry wine. Often called "Riesling" in Australia.

Sercial

Makes the driest wine of Madeira—where they claim it is really Riesling.

Seyval Blanc

French-made hybrid between French and American vines. Very hardy and attractively fruity. Popular and successful in the eastern States and England.

Steen

South Africa's best white grape: lively fruity wine. Said to be the Chenin Blanc of the Loire.

Sylvaner (Silvaner)

Germany's workhorse grape: wine rarely better than pleasant except in Franconia. Good in the Italian Tyrol and useful in Alsace. Wrongly called Riesling in California.

Tokay

See Pinot Gris. Also a table grape in California and a supposedly Hungarian grape in Australia.

Traminer

See Gewürztraminer

Trebbiano

Important grape of central Italy, used in Orvieto, Chianti, Soave, etc. Also grown in s. France as Ugni Blanc, and Cognac as "St Emillion".

Ugni Blanc

See Trebbiano

Verdelho

Madeira grape making excellent medium-sweet wine.

Verdicchio

Gives its name to good dry wine in central Italy.

Vernaccia

Grape grown in central and s. Italy and Sardinia for strong wine inclining towards sherry.

Viognier

Rare but remarkable grape of the Rhône valley, grown at Condrieu to make very fine soft and fragrant wine.

Welschriesling (or Wälschriesling)

See Italian Riesling

Weissburgunder

See Pinot Blanc

Grapes for red wine

Barbera
>One of several good standard grapes of Piemonte, giving dark, robust, fruity and often rather sharp wine. High acidity makes it a good grape for California.

Cabernet Franc
>The lesser of two sorts of Cabernet grown in Bordeaux; the Cabernet of the Loire making Chinon, etc., and rosé.

Cabernet Sauvignon
>Grape of great character; spicy, herby and tannic. The first grape of the Médoc, also makes the best Californian, Australian, South American and eastern European reds. Its wine always needs ageing and usually blending.

Carignan
>By far the commonest grape of France, covering hundreds of thousands of acres. Prolific with dull but harmless wine. Also common in North Africa, Spain and California.

Cinsaut
>Common bulk-producing grape of s. France; in S. Africa crossed with Pinot Noir to make Pinotage.

Gamay
>The Beaujolais grape: light fragrant wines at their best quite young. Makes even lighter wine on the Loire and in Switzerland and Savoie. Known as Napa Gamay in California, Blaufräukisch in Germany.

Gamay Beaujolais
>Not Gamay but a variety of PINOT NOIR grown in California.

Grenache
>Useful grape giving strong and fruity but pale wine: good rosé. Grown in s. France, Spain, California and usually blended.

Grignolino
>Makes one of the good cheap table wines of Piemonte. Also used in California.

Merlot
>Adaptable grape making the great fragrant and rich wines of Pomerol and St-Emilion, an important element in Médoc reds, and making lighter but good wines in n. Italy, Italian Switzerland, Yugoslavia, Argentina, etc.

Nebbiolo (also called Spanna)
>Italy's best red grape, the grape of Barolo, Barbaresco, Gattinara and Valtellina. Intense, nobly fruity and perfumed wine taking years to mature.

Pinot Noir
>The glory of Burgundy's Côte d'Or, with scent, flavour, texture and body unmatched anywhere. Less happy elsewhere; makes light wines of no great distinction in Germany, Switzerland, Austria; good ones in Hungary. The great challenge to the wine-makers of California.

Sangiovese
>The main red grape of Chianti and much of central Italy.

Spätburgunder
>German for Pinot Noir.

Syrah (alias Shiraz)
>The best Rhône red grape, with heavy purple wine, which can mature superbly. Said by some to come from Shiraz in Persia; others say Syracuse in Sicily. Very important as "Shiraz" in Australia.

Tempranillo
>The characteristic fine Rioja grape.

Zinfandel
>Fruity adaptable grape peculiar to California.

Wine & Food

There are no rules and regulations about what wine goes with what food, but there is a vast body of accumulated experience which it is absurd to ignore.

This list of dishes and appropriate wines records most of the conventional combinations and suggests others that I personally have found good. But it is only a list of ideas intended to help you make quick decisions. Any of the groups of recommended wines could have been extended almost indefinitely, drawing on the whole world's wine list. In general I have stuck to the wines that are widely available, at the same time trying to ring the changes so that the same wines don't come up time and time again — as they tend to do in real life.

The stars refer to the rating system used throughout the book: see opposite Contents.

Before the Meal — Aperitifs

The traditional aperitif wines are either sparkling (epitomized by champagne) or fortified (epitomized by sherry). The current fashion for a glass of white wine before eating calls for something light and stimulating, dry but not acid, with a degree of character, such as:

France:
>Alsace Edelzwicker, Riesling or Sylvaner; Chablis; Muscadet; Sauvignon de Touraine; Graves Blanc; Mâcon Blanc; Crépy.

Germany:
>Any Kabinett wine.

Italy:
>Soave; Orvieto Secco; Frascati; Pinot Bianco; Montecarlo; Vernaccia; Tocai; Lugano; Albana di Romagna.

Spain:
>Rioja Blanco Marqués de Caceres or Faustino V, or Albariño, but fino sherry or Montilla is even better.

Portugal:
>Any vinho verde.

Eastern Europe:
>Riesling.

California:
>"Chablis"; Chenin Blanc; Riesling; French Colombard; Emerald Riesling; Fumé Blanc.

Australia:
>Riesling.

South Africa:
>Steen.

England:
>English white.

References to these wines will be found under their national A–Z sections.

First courses

Aïoli
>A thirst-quencher is needed with so much garlic. $\star \rightarrow \star\star$ white Rhône, or Verdicchio, and mineral water.

Antipasto (see also Hors d'oeuvre)
>$\star\star$ dry or medium white, preferably Italian (e.g. Soave) or light red, e.g. Valpolicella, Bardolino or young $\star$ Bordeaux.

Artichoke
> ★ red or rosé.
> **vinaigrette** ★ young red, e.g. Bordeaux.
> **hollandaise** ★ or ★★ full-bodied dry or medium white, e.g. Mâcon Blanc, Rheinpfalz or California "Chablis".

Asparagus
> ★★→★★★ white burgundy or Chardonnay, or Tavel rosé.

Assiette anglaise (assorted cold meats)
> ★★ dry white, e.g. Chablis, Graves, Muscadet, Dão.

Avocado
> **with prawns, crab, etc.** ★★→★★★ dry to medium white, e.g. Rheingau or Rheinpfalz Kabinett, Graves, California Chardonnay or Sauvignon, Cape Stein, or dry rosé.
> **vinaigrette** ★ light red, or fino sherry.

Bisques
> ★★ dry white with plenty of body: Verdicchio, Pinot Gris, Graves.

Bouillabaisse
> ★→★★ very dry white: Muscadet, Alsace Sylvaner, Entre-Deux-Mers, Pouilly Fumé, Cassis.

Caviare
> ★★★ champagne or iced vodka.

Cheese fondue
> ★★ dry white: Fendant du Valais, Grüner Veltliner.

Chicken Liver Pâté
> Appetizing dry white, e.g. ★★ white Bordeaux, or light fruity red; Beaujolais, Gamay de Touraine or Valpolicella.

Clams and Chowders
> ★★ big-scale white, not necessarily bone dry: e.g. Rhône, Pinot Gris, Dry Sauternes.

Consommé
> ★★→★★★ medium-dry sherry, dry Madeira, Marsala, Montilla.

Crudités
> ★→★★ light red or rosé, e.g. Côtes-du-Rhône, Beaujolais, Chianti, Zinfandel.

Eggs (see also Soufflés)
> These present difficulties: they clash with most wine and spoil good ones. So ★→★★ of whatever is going.

Empanadas
> ★→★★ Chilean Cabernet, Zinfandel.

Escargots
> ★★ red or white of some substance: e.g. Burgundy; Côtes-du-Rhône, Chardonnay, Shiraz, etc.

Foie gras
> ★★★→★★★★ white. In Bordeaux they drink Sauternes. Others prefer vintage champagne or a rich Gewürztraminer Vendange tardive.

Gazpacho
> Sangria (see Spain) is refreshing, but to avoid too much liquid intake dry Manzanilla or Montilla is better.

Grapefruit
> If you must start a meal with grapefruit try port, Madeira or sweet sherry with it.

Ham, raw
> See Prosciutto

Herrings, raw or pickled
> Dutch gin or Scandinavian akvavit, or ★★ full-bodied white Mâcon-Villages, Graves or Dão.

Hors d'oeuvre (see also Antipasto)

> ★→★★ clean fruity sharp white: Sancerre or any Sauvignon, Alsace Sylvaner, Muscadet, Cape Stein—or young light red Bordeaux, Rhône or equivalent.

Mackerel, smoked

> ★★→★★★ full-bodied tasty white: e.g. Gewürztraminer, Tokay d'Alsace or Chablis Premier Cru.

Melon

> Needs a strong sweet wine: ★★ Port, Bual Madeira, Muscat, Oloroso sherry or Vin doux naturel.

Minestrone

> ★ red: Grignolino, Chianti, etc.

Omelettes

> See observations under Eggs

Onion/Leek tart

> ★→★★★ fruity dry white, e.g. Alsace Sylvaner or Riesling. Mâcon-Villages of a good vintage, California or Australian Riesling.

Pasta

> ★→★★ red or white according to the sauce or accompaniments, e.g.
> **with fish sauce (vongole, etc.)** Verdicchio or Soave.
> **meat sauce** Chianti, Beaujolais or Côtes-du-Rhône.
> **tomato sauce** Barbera or Sicilian red.
> **cream sauce** Orvieto or Frascati.

Pâté

> ★★ dry white: e.g. Chablis, Mâcon Blanc, Graves.

Peppers or aubergines (egg-plant), stuffed

> ★★ vigorous red: e.g. Bull's Blood, Chianti, Zinfandel.

Pizza

> Any ★★ dry Italian red or a ★★ Rioja, Australian Shiraz or California Zinfandel.

Prawns or Shrimps

> ★★→★★★ dry white: burgundy or Bordeaux, Chardonnay or Riesling. ("Cocktail sauce" kills wine.)

Prosciutto with melon

> ★★→★★★ full-bodied dry or medium white: e.g. Orvieto or Frascati, Fendant, Grüner Veltliner, Alsace Sylvaner, California Gewürztraminer, Australian Riesling.

Quiches

> ★→★★ dry white with body (Alsace, Graves, Sauvignon) or young red according to the ingredients.

Ratatouille

> ★★ vigorous young red, e.g. Chianti, Zinfandel, Bull's Blood, young red Bordeaux.

Salade niçoise

> ★★ very dry not too light or flowery white, e.g. white (or rosé) Rhône, white Spanish, Dão, California Sauvignon Blanc.

Salads

> As a first course: any dry and appetizing white wine. After a main course: no wine.
> N.B. Vinegar in salad dressings destroys the flavour of wine. If you want salad at a meal with fine wine, dress the salad with wine instead of vinegar.

Salami

> ★→★★ powerfully tasty red or rosé: e.g. Barbera, young Zinfandel, Tavel rosé, young Bordeaux.

Salmon, smoked

> A dry but pungent white, e.g. fino sherry, Alsace Gewürztraminer, Chablis Grand Cru.

Soufflés

As show dishes these deserve ✶✶→✶✶✶ wines.

Fish soufflés Dry white, e.g. burgundy, Bordeaux, Alsace, Chardonnay, etc.

Cheese soufflé Red burgundy or Bordeaux, Cabernet Sauvignon, etc.

Taramasalata

Calls for a rustic southern white of strong personality; not necessarily the Greek Retsina.

Terrine

As for pâté, or the equivalent red: e.g. Beaune, Mercurey, Beaujolais-Villages, fairly young ✶✶ St-Emilion, California Cabernet or Zinfandel, Bulgarian or Chilean Cabernet, etc.

Trout, smoked

Sancerre, Pouilly Fumé, or California Fumé Blanc.

Fish

Abalone

✶✶→✶✶✶ dry or medium white: e.g. Sauvignon Blanc, Chardonnay, Verdicchio.

Bass, striped

Same wine as for sole.

Cod

A good neutral background for fine dry or medium whites, e.g. ✶✶→✶✶✶ Chablis, cru classé Graves, German Kabinetts and their equivalents.

Coquilles St. Jacques

An inherently slightly sweet dish, best with medium-dry white wine.

in cream sauces ✶✶✶ German wines.

grilled or fried Hermitage Blanc, Gewürztraminer, California Chenin Blanc, Riesling or Champagne.

Crab, cold, with salad

✶✶✶California or Rheinpfalz Riesling Kabinett or Spätlese.

Eel, smoked

Either strong or sharp wine, e.g. fino sherry or Bourgogne Aligoté.

Haddock

✶✶→✶✶✶ dry white with a certain richness: e.g. Meursault, California Chardonnay.

Herrings

Need a white with some acidity to cut their richness. Burgundy Aligoté or Gros Plant from Brittany or dry Sauvignon Blanc. **Kippers:** a good cup of tea, preferably Ceylon.

Lamproie à la Bordelaise

✶✶ young red Bordeaux, especially St-Emilion or Pomerol.

Lobster or Crab

salad ✶✶→✶✶✶✶ white. Non-vintage champagne, Alsace Riesling, Chablis Premier Cru.

richly sauced Vintage champagne, fine white burgundy, cru classé Graves, California Chardonnay, Rheinpfalz Spätlese, Hermitage Blanc.

Mackerel

✶✶ hard or sharp white: Sauvignon Blanc from Bergerac or Touraine, Gros Plant, vinho verde, white Rioja.

Mullet, red

✶✶ Mediterranean white, even Retsina, for the atmosphere.

Mussels

✶→✶✶ Gros Plant, Muscadet, California "Chablis".

Oysters

>   **→*** white. Champagne (non-vintage), Chablis or (better) Chablis Premier Cru, Muscadet or Entre-Deux-Mers.

Salmon, fresh

>   *** fine white burgundy: Puligny- or Chassagne-Montrachet, Meursault, Corton-Charlemagne, Chablis Grand Cru, California Chardonnay, or Rheingau Kabinett or Spätlese, California Riesling or equivalent.

Sardines, fresh grilled

>   *→** very dry white: e.g. vinho verde, Dão, Muscadet.

Scallops

>   See Coquilles St. Jacques

Shad

>   **→*** white Graves or Meursault.

Shellfish (general)

>   Dry white with plain boiled shellfish, richer wines with richer sauces.

Shrimps, potted

>   Fino sherry or Chablis.

Skate with black butter

>   ** white with some pungency (e.g. Alsace Pinot Gris) or a clean one like Muscadet.

Sole, Plaice, etc.

>   **plain, grilled or fried** An ideal accompaniment for fine wines: * up to **** white burgundy, or its equivalent.
>
>   **with sauce** Depending on the ingredients: sharp dry wine for tomato sauce, fairly sweet for Sole véronique, etc.

Trout

>   Delicate white wine, e.g. *** Mosel.
>
>   **Smoked**, a full-flavoured **→*** white: Gewürztraminer, Pinot Gris, Rhine Spätlese or Australian Hunter white.

Turbot

>   Fine rich dry white, e.g. *** Meursault or its Californian equivalent.

Meat

Beef, boiled

>   ** red: e.g. Cru Bourgeois Bordeaux (Bourg or Fronsac), Côtes-du-Rhône-Villages, Australian Shiraz or Claret.

Beef, roast

>   An ideal partner for fine red wine. *→**** red of any kind.

Beef stew

>   **→*** sturdy red, e.g. Pomerol or St-Emilion, Hermitage, Shiraz.

Beef Strogonoff

>   **→*** suitably dramatic red: e.g. Barolo, Valpolicella, Amarone, Hermitage, late-harvest Zinfandel.

Cassoulet

>   ** red from s.w. France, e.g. Cahors or Corbières, or Barbera or Zinfandel.

Chicken or Turkey, roast

>   Virtually any wine, including your very best bottles of dry or medium white and fine old reds.

Chili con carne

>   *→** young red: e.g. Bull's Blood, Chianti, Mountain Red.

Chinese food

>   ** dry to medium-dry white: e.g. Jugoslav Riesling, Mâcon-Villages, California "Chablis".

Choucroute

>   Lager.

Confit d'Oie
> ★★→★★★ rather young and tannic red Bordeaux helps to cut
> the richness. Alsace Tokay or Gewürztraminer matches it.

Coq au Vin
> ★★→★★★★ red burgundy. In an ideal world one bottle of
> Chambertin in the dish, one on the table.

Corned beef hash
> ★★ Zinfandel, Chianti, Côtes-du-Rhône red.

Curry
> ★→★★ medium-sweet white, very cold: e.g. Orvieto abboccato,
> certain California Chenin Blancs, Jugoslav Traminer.

Duck or Goose
> ★★★ rather rich white, e.g. Rheinpfalz Spätlese or Alsace
> Réserve Exceptionelle, or ★★★ Bordeaux or burgundy.
> **Wild Duck** ★★★ big-scale red: e.g. Hermitage, Châteauneuf-
> du-Pape, Calif. or S. African Cabernet, Australian Shiraz.

Frankfurters
> ★→★★ German or Austrian white, or Beaujolais.

Game birds
> Young birds plain roasted deserve the best red wine you can
> afford. With older birds in casseroles ★★→★★★ red, e.g.
> Gevrey-Chambertin, St-Emilion, Napa Cabernet.

Game Pie
> ★★★ red wine.

Goulash
> ★★ strong young red: e.g. Zinfandel, Bulgarian Cabernet.

Grouse
> See under Game birds

Ham
> ★★→★★★ fairly young red burgundy, e.g. Volnay, Savigny,
> Beaune, Corton, or a slightly sweet German white, e.g. a
> Rhine Spätlese, or Chianti or Valpolicella.

Hamburger
> ★→★★ young red: e.g. Beaujolais, Corbières or Minervois,
> Chianti, Zinfandel.

Hare
> Jugged hare calls for ★★→★★★ red with plenty of flavour:
> not-too-old burgundy or Bordeaux. The same for saddle.

Kebabs
> ★★ vigorous red: e.g. Greek Demestica, Turkish Doluca,
> Hungarian Pinot Noir, Chilean Cabernet, Zinfandel.

Kidneys
> ★★→★★★ red: Pomerol or St-Emilion, Rhône, Barbaresco,
> Rioja, California or Australian Cabernet.

Lamb cutlets or chops
> As for roast lamb, but less grand.

Lamb, roast
> One of the traditional and best partners for very good red
> Bordeaux—or its equivalents.

Liver
> ★★ young red: Beaujolais-Villages, Rhône, Médoc, Italian
> Merlot, Zinfandel.

Meatballs
> ★★→★★★ red: e.g. Mercurey, Madiran, Rubesco, Dão,
> Zinfandel.

Mixed Grill
> A fairly light easily swallowable red; ★★ red Bordeaux from
> Bourg, Fronsac or Premières Côtes; Chianti; Bourgogne Pas-
> setoutgrains.

Moussaka
> ★→★★ red or rosé: e.g. Chianti, Corbières, Côtes de Provence,
> California Burgundy.

Oxtail

    →* rather rich red: e.g. St-Emilion or Pomerol, Burgundy, Barolo or Chianti Classico, Rioja Reserva, California Cabernet.

Paella

    ** Spanish red, dry white or rosé, e.g. Panades or Rioja or vinho verde.

Partridge, pheasant

    See under Game birds

Pigeons or squabs

    →** red Bordeaux, Chianti Classico, Cabernet Sauvignon, etc.

Pork, roast

    The sauce or stuffing has more flavour than the meat. Sharp apple sauce or pungent sage and onion need only a plain young wine. Pork without them, on the other hand, is a good neutral background to very good white or red wine.

Rabbit

    *→*** young red: Italian for preference.

Ris de veau

    See Sweetbreads

Sauerkraut

    Beer.

Shepherd's Pie

    *→** rough and ready red seems most appropriate, but no harm would come to a good one.

Steak and Kidney Pie or Pudding

    Red Rioja Reserva or mature **→*** Bordeaux.

Steaks

    Au poivre a fairly young *** Rhône red or Cabernet.

    Tartare ** light young red: Bergerac, Valpolicella.

    Filet or Tournedos *** red of any kind (but not old wines with Béarnaise sauce).

    T-bone **→*** reds of similar bone-structure: e.g. Barolo, Hermitage, Australian Cabernet.

    Fiorentina (bistecca) Chianti Classico.

    Ostrich South African Pinotage.

Stews and Casseroles

    A lusty full-flavoured red, e.g. young Côtes-du-Rhône, Corbières, Barbera, Shiraz, Zinfandel, etc.

Sweetbreads

    These tend to be a grand dish, suggesting a grand wine, e.g. *** Rhine Kabinett or Spätlese, or well-matured Bordeaux or Burgundy, depending on the sauce.

Tongue

    Ideal for favourite bottles of any red or white.

Tripe

    *→** red: Corbières, Mâcon Rouge, etc., or rather sweet white, e.g. Liebfraumilch.

Veal, roast

    A good neutral background dish for any old red which may have faded, or a *** German white.

Venison

    *** big-scale red (Rhône, Bordeaux of a grand vintage) or rather rich white (Rheinpfalz Spätlese or Tokay d'Alsace).

Wiener Schnitzel

    →* light red from the Italian Tyrol (Alto Adige) or the Médoc: or Austrian Riesling, Grüner Veltliner or Gumpoldskirchener.

Cheese

Very ripe cheese completely masks the flavour of wine. Only serve fine wine with mild cheeses.

Bleu de Bresse, Dolcelatte, Gorgonzola

Need fairly emphatic accompaniment: young ** red wine (Barbera, Dolcetto, Moulin-à-Vent, etc.) or sweet white.

Cream cheeses: Brie, Camembert, Bel Paese, Edam, etc.

In their mild state go perfectly with any good wine, red or white.

English cheeses

Can be either mild or strong and acidic. The latter need sweet or strong wine.

Cheddar, Cheshire, Wensleydale, Stilton, Gloucester, etc. If mild, claret. If strong, ruby, tawny or vintage-character (not vintage) port, or a very big red: Hermitage, Châteauneuf-du-Pape, Barolo, etc.

Goat cheeses

→* white wine of marked character, either dry (e.g. Sancerre) or sweet (e.g. Monbazillac, Sauternes).

Hard Cheese, Parmesan, Gruyère, Emmenthal

Full-bodied dry whites, e.g. Tokay d'Alsace or Vernaccia.

Roquefort, Danish Blue

Are so strong-flavoured that only the youngest, biggest or sweetest wines stand a chance.

Desserts

Apple pie, apple strudel

→* sweet German, Austrian or Hungarian white.

Apples, Cox's Orange Pippins

Vintage port (55, 60, 63 or 66).

Baked Alaska

Sweet champagne or Asti Spumante.

Cakes

Bual or Malmsey Madeira, Oloroso or cream sherry.

Cheesecake

→* sweet white from Vouvray or Coteaux du Layon.

Chocolate cake, mousse, soufflés

No wine.

Christmas pudding

Sweet champagne or Asti Spumante.

Creams and Custards

→* Sauternes, Monbazillac or similar golden white.

Crème brûlée

The most luxurious dish, demanding ***→**** Sauternes or Rhine Beerenauslese, or the best Madeira or Tokay.

Crêpes Suzette

Sweet champagne or Asti Spumante.

Fruit flans (i.e. peach, raspberry)

*** Sauternes, Monbazillac or sweet Vouvray.

Fruit, fresh

Sweet Coteaux du Layon white, light sweet muscat (e.g. California).

Fruit salads, orange salad

No wine.

Nuts

Oloroso sherry, Bual, Madeira, vintage or tawny port.

Sorbets, ice-creams

No wine.

Stewed fruits, i.e. apricots, pears, etc.
>   Sweet Muscatel: e.g. Muscat de Beaumes de Venise, Moscato
>   di Pantelleria.

Strawberries and cream
>   *** Sauternes or Vouvray.

Wild strawberries Serve with *** red Bordeaux poured over them
and in your glass (no cream).

Summer Pudding
>   Fairly young Sauternes of a good vintage (e.g. 70, 71, 75).

Treacle Tart
>   Too sweet for any wine but a treacly Malmsey Madeira.

Trifle
>   No wine: should be sufficiently vibrant with sherry.

Sweet Soufflés
>   Sweet Vouvray or Coteaux du Layon.

Zabaglione
>   Light gold Marsala.

Savoury

Cheese straws
>   Admirable meal-ending with a final glass (or bottle) of a
>   particularly good red wine.

Temperature

Temperature
No single aspect of serving wine makes or mars it so easily as getting
the temperature right. White wines almost invariably taste dull and
insipid served warm and red wines have disappointingly little scent or
flavour served cold. The chart below gives an indication of what is
generally found to be the best and most satisfactory temperature for
serving each class of wine.

	°F / °C	
	68 / 20	
Room	66 / 19	
temperature	64 / 18	Best red wines
	63 / 17	especially Bordeaux
Red Burgundy	61 / 16	Chianti, Zinfandel
	59 / 15	Côtes-du-Rhône
Best white Burgundy	57 / 14	
Port Madeira	55 / 13	Ordinaires
	54 / 12	Lighter red wines
Ideal Sherry	52 / 11	e.g. Beaujolais
cellar Fino sherry	50 / 10	Rosés
Most dry white wines	48 / 9	Lambrusco
Champagne	46 / 8	
Domestic	45 / 7	
fridge	43 / 6	Most sweet white wines
	41 / 5	Sparkling wines
	39 / 4	
	37 / 3	
	35 / 2	
	33 / 1	
	32 / 0	

A little learning ...

The last ten years have seen a revolution in wine technology. They have also heard a matching revolution in wine-talk. Attempts to express the characters of wines used to get little further than terms as vague as "fruity" and "full-bodied". Your modern wine-lover is made of sterner stuff. He is satisfied with nothing less than the jargon of laboratory analysis. Rather than expound the old imagery (which should after all be self-explanatory) I therefore give below a summary of the new hard-edge wine-talk.

The most frequent references are to the ripeness of grapes at picking; the resultant alcohol and sugar content of the wine; various measures of its acidity; the amount of sulphur dioxide used as a preservative, and the amount of "dry extract"—the sum of all the things that give wine its characteristic flavours.

The **sugar** in wine is mainly glucose and fructose, with traces of arabinose, xylose and other sugars that are not fermentable by yeast, but can be attacked by bacteria. Each country has its own system for measuring the sugar content or ripeness of grapes, known as the "**must-weight**". The chart below relates the three principal ones (German, French and American) to each other, to specific gravity, and to the potential alcohol of the resulting wine if all the sugar is fermented out.

Specific Gravity	°O °Oechsle	Baumé	Brix	% Potential Alcohol v/v
1.065	65	8.8	15.8	8.1
1.070	70	9.4	17.0	8.8
1.075	75	10.1	18.1	9.4
1.080	80	10.7	19.3	10.0
1.085	85	11.3	20.4	10.6
1.090	90	11.9	21.5	11.3
1.095	95	12.5	22.5	11.9
1.100	100	13.1	23.7	12.5
1.105	105	13.7	24.8	13.1
1.110	110	14.3	25.8	13.8
1.115	115	14.9	26.9	14.4
1.120	120	15.5	28.0	15.0

Residual sugar is the sugar left after fermentation has finished or been artificially stopped, measured in grammes per litre.

Alcohol content (mainly ethyl alcohol) is expressed as a percentage by volume of the total liquid.

Acidity is both fixed and volatile. **Fixed acidity** consists principally of tartaric, malic and citric acids which are all found in the grape, and lactic and succinic acids, which are produced during fermentation. **Volatile acidity** consists mainly of acetic acid, which is rapidly formed by bacteria in the presence of oxygen. A small amount of volatile acidity is inevitable and attractive. With a larger amount the wine becomes "pricked"—i.e. starts to turn to vinegar.

Total acidity is fixed and volatile acidity combined. As a rule of thumb for a well-balanced wine it should be in the region of 1 gramme/thousand for each 10°Oechsle (see above).

pH is a measure of the strength of the acidity, rather than its volume. A pH above 7 is alkaline; below is acid; the lower the figure the more acid. Wine normally ranges in pH from 2.8 to 3.8. Cold northerly climates with less ripe grapes tend to lower pHs; winemakers in hot climates can have problems getting the pH low enough. Lower pH gives better colour, helps prevent bacterial spoilage, allows more of the SO_2 to be free and active as a preservative.

Sulphur dioxide (SO_2) is added to prevent oxidation and other accidents in wine-making. Some of it combines with sugars, etc., and is known as "bound". Only the "**free SO_2**" that remains in the wine is effective as a preservative. **Total SO_2** is controlled by law according to the level of residual sugar: the more sugar the more SO_2 needed.

France

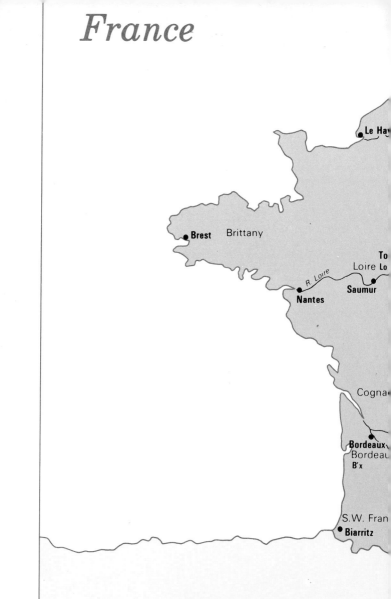

Le Ha

Brest Brittany

To
Loire Lo

R Loire

Nantes Saumur

Cogna

Bordeaux
Bordea
B'x

S.W. Fran
Biarritz

France makes every kind of wine, and invented most of them. Her wine trade, both exporting and importing, dwarfs that of any other country. Tens of thousands of properties make wine over a large part of France's surface. This is a guide to the best known of them and to the system by which the rest can be identified and to some extent evaluated.

All France's best wine regions have Appellations Controlées, which may apply to a single small vineyard or a whole large district: the system varies from region to region, with Burgundy on the whole having the smallest and most precise appellations, grouped into larger units by complicated formulae, and Bordeaux having the widest and most general appellations, in which it is the particular property (or "château") that matters. In between lie an infinity of variations.

Lille

Reims

Strasbourg

Champagne **Champ**

Alsace **Al**

Paris

R. Seine

Chablis

Burgundy

Dijon

B'y

Jura

pper Loire

Beaune

R. Saône

Central France

Geneva

Beaujolais

Savoie

Lyons

ordogne

Clermont-Ferrand

Grenoble

R. Dordogne

R. Rhône

Rhône
Rh

R. Tarn

Nice

Avignon

Provence **Prov**

aronne

Montpellier

Marseille

Toulouse

Midi

Pyrenees **Pyr**

Abbreviations of regional names
shown in bold type are used in
the text.

An Appellation Controlée is a guarantee of origin and of
production method, of grape varieties and quantities produced: not of quality. France does not have a comprehensive
quality-testing system as Germany does. The scale of the
problem is too vast and the French are too French.

Appellations therefore help to identify a wine and indicate
that it comes from a major area. They are the first thing to
look for on a label.

Wine regions without the overall quality and traditions
required for an appellation can be ranked as Vins Délimités
de Qualité Supérieure (VDQS), or (a new third rank created
largely to encourage the improvement of mediocre wines in
the south of France) Vins de Pays. VDQS wines are often
good value, on the Avis principle. Vins de Pays are worth
trying for curiosity's sake.

Recent vintages of the French classics

Red Burgundy

Côte d'Or Côte de Beaune reds generally mature sooner than the bigger wines of the Côte de Nuits. Earliest drinking dates are for lighter commune wines: Volnay, Beaune, etc. Latest for the biggest wines of Chambertin, Romanée, etc. Different growers make wines of different styles, for longer or shorter maturing, but even the best burgundies are much more attractive young than the equivalent red Bordeaux.

1982	Big vintage, pale but round and full. Best in Côte de Beaune.
1981	A small crop, ripe but picked in rain. Light and disappointing.
1980	A difficult, late, wet year, but some respectable wines from the best growers who avoided rot. Better in the Côte de Nuits.
1979	Big generally good ripe vintage with weak spots. S. Côte de Nuits suffered from hail. Not for long storage.
1978	Poor summer saved by miraculous autumn. A small vintage of outstanding quality. The best will live 15 years.
1977	Very wet summer. Better wine than expected, especially in northern côtes. Drink soon.
1976	Hot summer, excellent vintage. As usual great variations, but the best (esp. Côte de Beaune) rich and long-lived—to 1990.
1975	Rot was rife, particularly in the Côte de Beaune. Mostly very poor.
1974	Another big wet vintage; mostly poor, even the best light and lean. Drink up.
1973	Again, vintage rain stretched the crop. Light wines, but many fruity and delicate. Many are already too old.
1972	High acidity posed problems, but the wines are firm and full of character, ageing well. Few need keeping longer now.
1971	Very powerful and impressive wines, not as long-lasting as they first appeared. Most now ready. The best have 5 years ahead.

Older fine vintages: '69, '66, '64, '62, '61, '59 (all mature).

Beaujolais 1982 was a satisfactory vintage. 1981 Crus are admirable. Generally avoid older vintages except 1976 Moulin à Vent.

White Burgundy

Côte de Beaune Well-made wines of good vintages with plenty of acidity as well as fruit will improve and gain depth and richness for some years—anything up to ten. Lesser wines from lighter years are ready for drinking after two or three years.

1982	Fat, tasty whites of low acidity, not for keeping.
1981	A sadly depleted crop with great promise. The best are excellent.
1980	A weak, but not bad, vintage. Drink soon.
1979	Big vintage. Overall good and useful, not great. Drink before '78s.
1978	Very good wines, firm and well-balanced. Keep the best.
1977	Rather light; some well-balanced and good. Drink up.
1976	Hot summer, rather heavy wines; good but not for laying-down.
1975	Hot summer, then vintage rain. Whites did much better than reds. Chablis best, but all now ready.
1974	All now need drinking.
1973	Very attractive, fruity, typical and plentiful. Drink up.
1972	Awkward wines to make with high acidity, even greenness, but plenty of character. All are now ready to drink.
1971	Great power and style, some almost too rich, but the best have good balance. Small crop. Generally ready.

The white wines of the Mâconnais (Pouilly-Fuissé, St Véran, Mâcon-Villages) follow a similar pattern, but do not last as long. They are more appreciated for their freshness than their richness.

Chablis Grand Cru Chablis of vintages with both strength and acidity can age superbly for up to ten years. Premier Crus proportionately less. Drink other Chablis young.

1982 Charming light wines. Good value.
1981 Small, concentrated and fine harvest.
1980 More successful than the rest of Burgundy.
1979 Very big crop. Good easy wines, not for storing.
1978 Excellent wines now approaching their peak.
1977 Reduced quantity, but typical and fresh like 1974. Drink up.
1976 A great vintage, but lacks acidity. Start to drink.

Red Bordeaux

Médoc/red Graves For some wines bottle-age is optional: for these it is indispensable. Minor châteaux from light vintages need only two or three years, but even modest wines of great years can improve for fifteen years or so, and the great châteaux of these years need double that time.

1982 Made in a heat-wave. Some huge rich strong wines. Some with problems.
1981 Admirably consistent despite rain. Not rich, but balanced and fine.
1980 Small, late harvest, ripe but rained-on. Many respectable light wines but few exciting ones. Drink '83–'90.
1979 Abundant harvest of good average quality. Now–'95.
1978 A miracle vintage: magnificent long warm autumn saved the day. Some very good wines. Now–2000.
1977 Pleasant light wine, many better than 1974. Now–'87.
1976 Excessively hot, dry summer; rain just before vintage. Generally very good, maturing rather quickly. Now–'95.
1975 A splendid summer and very fine vintage, with deep colour, high sugar content and some tannin. For long keeping. "Petits Châteaux" are now ready.
1974 Oceans of disappointing light wines, though the best have good colour and have developed some character. Now–'85.
1973 A huge vintage, attractive to drink young and still giving great pleasure. Now–'86.
1972 High acidity from unripe grapes. Do not pay much for '72s. Now.
1971 Small crop. Less fruity than '70 and less consistent. A few châteaux made outstanding wine. Most are ready to drink.
1970 Abundance *and* uniform quality. Big fruity wines with elegance and attractive suppleness. Wines of great distinction for long keeping. Now–2000.
1969/68 Avoid them both.
1967 Never seductive, but characterful in its maturity. Drink soon.
1966 A very fine vintage with depth, fruit and tannin. Classic claret. Now–'90.
Older fine vintages: '62, '61, '59, '55, '53, '52, '50, '49, '48, '47, '45, '29, '28.

St-Emilion/Pomerol
1982 Enormously rich and concentrated wines, perhaps great.
1981 A very good vintage, if not as great as it first seemed.
1980 A poor Merlot year; very variable quality. Choose carefully.
1979 A rival to '78; in most cases even better. Now–'95.
1978 Fine wines, but some lack flesh. Will mature fairly early.
1977 Very wet summer. Mediocre with few exceptions.
1976 Very hot, dry summer and early vintage, but vintage rain made complications. Some excellent; the best great. Now–'95.
1975 Most St-Emilions good, the best superb. Frost in Pomerol cut crops and made splendid concentrated wine. '85–2000.
1974 Vintage rain again. Disappointing light wines. Avoid.
1973 Good summer, big wet vintage. Pleasant wines. Drink up.
1972 Poor summer but fine for the late vintage. Many unripe wines, but some are pleasant enough. Drink now, if at all.
1971 Small crop: fine wines with length and depth, on the whole better than Médocs but generally now ready.
1970 Glorious weather and beautiful wines with great fruit and strength throughout the district. Very big crop. Now–'90s.
1969/68 Avoid them both.
1967 Large and generally very good; better than Médoc. Now.
1966 Ripe, powerful, round. Maturing well. Now–'90.
Older fine vintages: '64, '61, '59, '53, '52, '49, '47, '45.

Ajaccio   Corsica r. p. or w. dr. ∗ NV
>   The capital of Corsica and its strong plain wines.

Aligoté
>   Second-rank burgundy white grape and its sharp wine, often
>   agreeably fruity and with considerable local character when
>   young. Bouzeron (A.C.) makes the best.

Aloxe-Corton   B'y. r. or w. ∗∗∗ **69 71 72 76 77** 78 **79 80**
>   Northernmost village of CÔTE DE BEAUNE: best v'yds.: CORTON
>   (red) and CORTON-CHARLEMAGNE (white). Village wines
>   lighter but often good value.

Alsace   Al. w. or (r.) ∗∗ **71 75 76 78 79 80** 81 82
>   Aromatic, fruity dry white of Germanic character from
>   French Rhineland. Normally sold by grape variety (RIESLING,
>   GEWÜRZTRAMINER, etc.). Matures well up to 5, even 10, years.

Alsace Grand Cru ∗∗∗
>   Appellation restricted to the best named v'yds.

Alsace Grand Vin or Réserve
>   Wine with minimum 11° natural alcohol.

Ampeau, Robert
>   Leading grower and specialist in MEURSAULT.

Anjou   Lo. (r.) p. or w. (sw. dr. or sp.) ∗→ ∗∗∗ **71 73 75 76 78 79 80** 81 82
>   Very various Loire wines, incl. good CABERNET rosé, luscious
>   COTEAUX DU LAYON. Maturity depends on style.

Appellation Controlée
>   Government control of origin and production of all the best
>   French wines (see France Introduction).

Apremont   Savoie w. dr. ∗∗ D.Y.A.
>   One of the best villages of SAVOIE for pale delicate whites.

Arbin   Savoie r. ∗∗ Drink at 1–2 years
>   Deep-coloured lively red of Mondeuse grapes, like a good
>   LOIRE Cabernet.

Arbois   Jura r. p. or w. (dr. sp.) ∗∗ D.Y.A.
>   Various pleasant light wines; speciality VIN JAUNE.

l'Ardèche, Coteaux de   Central France r. (w.dr.) ∗ D.Y.A.
>   Light country reds, the best made of SYRAH. A change from
>   BEAUJOLAIS.

Armagnac
>   Region of s.w. France famous for its excellent brandy, a fiery
>   spirit of rustic character. The chief town is Condom.

Auxey-Duresses   B'y. r. or w. ∗∗ **71** 75w. **76** 77 78 **79 80** 82
>   Second-rank CÔTE DE BEAUNE village: has affinities with
>   VOLNAY and MEURSAULT. Best estates: Duc de Magenta,
>   Prunier, Roy, HOSPICES DE BEAUNE Cuvée Boillot.

Avize   Champ. ∗∗∗∗
>   One of the best white-grape villages of CHAMPAGNE.

Ay   Champ. ∗∗∗∗
>   One of the best black-grape villages of CHAMPAGNE.

Ayala   NV "Château d'Ay" and **71 73** 75
>   Once-famous Ay-based old-style champagne concern.

Bandol   Prov. r. p. or (w.) ∗∗ **74 76 78** 80 **81 82**
>   Little coastal region near Toulon with strong tasty reds from
>   the Mourvèdre grape.

Banyuls   Pyr. br. sw. ∗∗ NV
>   One of the best VIN DOUX NATURELS (fortified sweet red wines)
>   of the s. of France. Not unlike port.

Barsac   B'x. w. sw. ∗∗→ ∗∗∗ **70 71** 75 76 78 79 80 81
>   Neighbour of SAUTERNES with similar superb golden wines
>   often more racy and less rich. Top ch'x.: CLIMENS and COUTET.

Barton & Guestier
>   Important Bordeaux shipper dating from the 18th century,
>   now owned by Seagram's.

Bâtard-Montrachet   B'y. w. dr.   ★★★★   71 72 73 76 77 78 **79** 81 82
Neighbour and almost equal of MONTRACHET, the top white
burgundy. As rich in flavour as dry white wine can be.

Béarn   S.W. France r. p. or w. dr. ★
Minor appellation of growing local interest.

Beaujolais   B'y. r. (p. w.) ★ 81 82 D.Y.A.
The simple appellation of the big Beaujolais region: light
short-lived fruity red.

Beaujolais de l'année
The Beaujolais of the latest vintage, until the next.

Beaujolais Primeur (or Nouveau)
The same made in a hurry (often only 4–5 days fermenting)
for drinking 15 Nov. to the end of Feb. The best come from
light sandy soil and are as strong as 12.5% alcohol.

Beaujolais Supérieur   B'y. r. (w.) ★ D.Y.A.
Beaujolais 1° of natural alcohol stronger than the 9° minimum. Since sugar is almost always added this means little.

Beaujolais-Villages   B'y. r. ★★ 81 82
Wine from the better (northern) half of Beaujolais, stronger
and tastier than plain Beaujolais. The 9 (easily) best
"villages" are the "crus": FLEURIE, BROUILLY, etc. Of the 30
others the best lie around Beaujeu. The crus cannot be released "en primeur" before December 15th.

Beaumes de Venise   Rh. (r. p.) br. sw.   ★★★   NV
France's best dessert MUSCAT, from the s. Côtes-du-Rhône;
high-flavoured, subtle, lingering. The red and rosé from the
co-operative are also good.

Beaune   B'y. r. or (w. dr.) ★★★ 71 72 76 78 **79** 80 82
Middle-rank classic burgundy. Négociants' "CLOS" wines
(usually "Premier Cru") are often best. "Beaune du Château"
is a (good) brand of BOUCHARD PÈRE. V'yds incl.: Grevès,
Bressandes, Teurons, Marconnets, Fèves.

Bellet   Prov. p. r. w. dr. ★★
Highly fashionable, much above average, local wine from
near Nice. Tiny production. Very expensive.

Bergerac   Dordogne r. or w. sw. or dr.   ★★   81 82
Light-weight, often tasty, Bordeaux-style. Drink young, the
white very young.

Besserat de Bellêfon   NV, Crémant, Brut Intégral
Rising champagne house for fine light wines, owned by
Pernod-Ricard.

Beyer, Leon
Ancient ALSACE family wine business at Eguisheim making
forceful dry wines that age well.

Bichot, Maison Albert
BEAUNE-based grower and merchant. V'yds in CHAMBERTIN,
CLOS DE VOUGEOT, RICHEBOURG, etc., and Domaine Long-
Depaquit in CHABLIS. Said to be the biggest B'y. exporter.

Blagny   B'y. r. or w. dr.   ★★   71 72 73 76 78 **79** 81w. 82.
Hamlet between MEURSAULT and PULIGNY-MONTRACHET;
affinities with both and VOLNAY for reds. Ages well.

Blanc de Blancs
Any white wine made from (only) white grapes, esp.
champagne, which is usually made of black and white.

Blanc de Noirs   White wine made from black grapes.

Blanquette de Limoux   Midi w. dr. sp.   ★★   normally NV
Good cheap sparkler from near Carcassonne made by a
version of the MÉTHODE CHAMPENOISE. Very dry and clean.

Blaye   B'x. r. or w. dr. ★→★★ 75 76 78 79 81 82
Your average Bordeaux from e. of the Gironde. PREMIÈRES
CÔTES DE BLAYE are better.

Boisset   Expanding modern merchant at Nuits St Georges.

Bollinger   NV "Special Cuvée" and **66 69 70 73 75 76**
Top champagne house, at AY. Dry full-flavoured style. Luxury wines "Tradition R. D."; and "Vieilles Vignes Françaises" (**69 70 73** 75) from ungrafted vines.

Bommes
Village of SAUTERNES. Best ch'x.: LA TOUR-BLANCHE, LAFAURIE-PEYRAGUEY, etc.

Bonnes Mares   B'y. r.   ★★★★   **66 69 71 72 73 76 77** 78 79 80 82
37-acre Grand Cru between CHAMBOLLE-MUSIGNY and MOREY-SAINT-DENIS. Often better than CHAMBERTIN.

Bonnezeaux   Lo. w. sw.   ★★★   **70 71 73 75 76 78 79 80** 81 82
Unusual fruity/acidic wine from CHENIN BLANC grapes, the best of COTEAUX DU LAYON.

Bordeaux   B'x. r. or (p.) or w. ★ **75 78 79 81 82** (for ch'x. see p. 54)
Basic catch-all appellation for low-strength Bordeaux wine.

Bordeaux Supérieur
Ditto, with slightly more alcohol.

Bordeaux Côtes-de-Castillon   B'x. r.   ★   **75 76 78 79** 81 82
Fringe Bordeaux from east of ST-EMILION, and not far from some St-Emilions in quality.

Bordeaux Côtes-de-Francs   B'x. r. or w. dr.   ★   **75 76 78 79 81** 82
Fringe Bordeaux from east of ST-EMILION. Light wines.

Borie-Manoux
Bordeaux shippers and château-owners, owned by the Castéja family. Ch'x. incl. BATAILLEY, HAUT BAGES-MONPELOU, DOMAINE DE L'EGLISE, TROTTEVIEILLE,' BEAU-SITE, LYNCH-MOUSSAS.

Bouchard Aîné
Famous and long-established burgundy shipper and grower with 60 acres in Beaune, Mercurey, etc.

Bouchard Père et Fils
Important burgundy shipper (est. 1731) with 200 acres of excellent v'yds., mainly in the CÔTE DE BEAUNE, and cellars at the Château de Beaune.

Bourg   B'x. r. or (w. dr.) ★★ **75 78 79** 81 82
Meaty, un-fancy claret from e. of the Gironde. CÔTES DE BOURG are better.

Bourgogne   B'y. r. (p.) or w. dr. ★★ **78 79 80 82**
Catch-all appellation for burgundy, but with theoretically higher standards than basic BORDEAUX. Light but often good flavour. BEAUJOLAIS crus can be sold as Bourgogne.

Bourgogne Grand Ordinaire   B'y. r. or (w.) ★ D.Y.A.
The lowest burgundy appellation for Gamay wines. Rare.

Bourgogne Passe-tout-grains   B'y. r. or (p.)   ★   Age 1–2 years
Often enjoyable junior burgundy. ⅓ PINOT NOIR and ⅔ GAMAY grapes mixed in the vat. Not as "heady" as BEAUJOLAIS.

Bourgueil   Lo. r. ★★★ **71 75 76 78 79 80** 81 82
Delicate fruity CABERNET red from Touraine, the best from St. Nicolas de Bourgueil.

Bouvet-Ladubay
Major producer of sparkling SAUMUR, controlled by TAITTINGER.

Bouzy Rouge   Champ. r. ★★★ **70 71 73 75 76** 79
Still red wine from famous black-grape CHAMPAGNE village.

Brédif, Marc
One of the most important growers and traders of VOUVRAY.

Brouilly   B'y. r. ★★★ **81 82**
One of the 9 best CRUS of BEAUJOLAIS: fruity, round, refreshing. One year in bottle is enough.

Brut   Term for the driest wines of CHAMPAGNE until recently, when some completely unsugared wines have become available as "Brut Intégrale", "Brut non-dosé", "Brut zéro" etc.

Bugey   Savoie w. dr. or sp. ⋆ D.Y.A.
District with a variety of light sparkling, still or half-sparkling wines. The grape is the Roussette (or Roussanne).

Cabernet
See Grapes for red wine

Cabernet d'Anjou   Lo. p. ⋆⋆ D.Y.A.
Delicate, often slightly sweet, grapy rosé.

Cahors   S.W. France r. ⋆→ |⋆⋆| 70 75 76 78 79 80 81 82
Traditionally hard "black" wine, now made more like Bordeaux but can be full-bodied and increasingly distinct.

Cairanne   Rh. r. p. or w. dr. |⋆⋆| 76 78 79 80 81
Village of CÔTE-DU-RHÔNE-VILLAGES. Good solid wines.

Calvet   Great family wine business, originally on the Rhône, now important in Bordeaux and Burgundy.

Canard-Duchêne
NV, Vintage Charles VII and (sometimes) Coteaux Champenois. High quality champagne house owned (since 1978) by Veuve Clicquot.

Canon-Fronsac
See Côtes-Canon-Fronsac

Cantenac   B'x. r. ⋆⋆⋆
Village of the HAUT-MÉDOC entitled to the Appellation MARGAUX. Top ch'x. include PALMER, BRANE-CANTENAC, etc.

Caramany   Pyr. r. (w. dr.) |⋆| 80 81 82
New appellation for part of CÔTES DE ROUSSILLON.

Cassis   Prov. (r. p.) w. dr. ⋆⋆ D.Y.A.
Seaside village e. of Marseille known for its very dry white, above the usual standard of Provence. Not to be confused with cassis, a blackcurrant liqueur made in Dijon.

Cave   Cellar, or any wine establishment.

Cave co-opérative
Wine-growers' co-operative winery. Formerly viticultural dustbins, most are now well run, well equipped and making some of the best wine of their areas.

Cépage
Variety of vine, e.g. CHARDONNAY, MERLOT.

Cérons   B'x. w. dr. or sw. ⋆⋆ 71 75 76 78 79 80 81
Neighbour of SAUTERNES with some good sweet-wine ch'x.

Chablis   B'y. w. dr. ⋆⋆ 76 77 78 79
Distinctive full-flavoured greeny gold wine. APPELLATION CONTRÔLÉE essential.

Chablis Grand Cru   B'y. w. dr. |⋆⋆⋆⋆| 71 75 76 78 79 80 81 82
Strong, subtle and altogether splendid. One of the great white burgundies. There are seven v'yds: Blanchots, Bougros, Clos, Grenouilles, Preuses, Valmur, Vaudésir. See also MOUTONNE.

Chablis Premier Cru   B'y. w. dr. |⋆⋆⋆| 76 78 79 80 81 82
Second-rank but often excellent and more typical of Chablis than Grands Crus. Best v'yds incl.: Côte de Lechet, Fourchaume, Mont de Milieu, Montmains – 1,500 acres in all.

Chai   Building for storing and maturing wine, esp. in Bordeaux.

Chambertin   B'y. r. ⋆⋆⋆⋆ 66 69 71 72 73 76 77 78 79 80 82
32-acre Grand Cru giving the meatiest, most enduring and often the best red burgundy. 15 growers, incl. LATOUR, JABOULET-VERCHERRE, Rebourseau, ROUSSEAU, Trapet.

Chambertin-Clos-de-Bèze   B'y. r. ⋆⋆⋆⋆ 71 72 73 76 77 78 79 80 82
37-acre neighbour of CHAMBERTIN. Similarly splendid wine. Ten growers, incl. CLAIR-DAÜ, DROUHIN, Drouhin-Laroze.

Chambolle-Musigny   B'y. r. (w.) |⋆⋆⋆| 69 71 72 76 77 78 79 80 82
420-acre CÔTE DE NUITS village with fabulously fragrant, complex wine. Best v'yds.: MUSIGNY, part of BONNES-MARES, Les Amoureuses, Les Charmes. Best growers incl.: de Vogüé, DROUHIN, FAIVELEY, Roumier.

Champagne

> Sparkling wine from 55,000 acres 90 miles e. of Paris, made by the MÉTHODE CHAMPENOISE: wines from elsewhere, however good, cannot be Champagne. (See also name of brand.)

Champagne, Grande

> The appellation of the best area of COGNAC.

Champigny

> See Saumur

Chanson Père et Fils

> Growers (with 110 acres) and traders in fine wine at BEAUNE. Reds can be pale but generally last well.

Chante-Alouette

> A famous brand of white HERMITAGE.

Chantovent

> Major brand of VIN DE TABLE, largely from MINERVOIS.

Chanturgues   Central France r. * D.Y.A.

> Well-known Gamay local wine of Clermont-Ferrand.

Chapelle-Chambertin   B'y. r. *** **69 71 72** 76 **77** 78 79 80 82

> 13-acre neighbour of CHAMBERTIN. Wine not so meaty.

Chapoutier

> Long-established firm of growers and traders of Rhône wines.

Chardonnay

> See Grapes for white wine

Charmes-Chambertin   B'y. r. *** **71 72 76 77** 78 79 80 82

> 76-acre neighbour of CHAMBERTIN.

Chassagne-Montrachet   B'y. r. or w. dr. *** **69 71 72** r. **73 76** 78 **79** **80**w. 81w. 82.

> 750-acre CÔTE DE BEAUNE village with superlative rich dry whites and sterling hefty reds. Best v'yds.: MONTRACHET, BÂTARD-MONTRACHET, CRIOTS-BÂTARD-MONTRACHET, Ruchottes, Caillerets, Boudriottes (r., w.), Morgeot (r., w.), CLOS-ST-JEAN (r.). Growers incl. RAMONET-PRUDHON, Morey, Magenta, DELAGRANGE-BACHELET.

Château

> An estate, big or small, good or indifferent, particularly in Bordeaux. In Burgundy the term "domaine" is used. For all Bordeaux ch'x see pp. 54–70.

Château-Chalon   Jura w. dr. ***

> Unique strong dry yellow wine, almost like sherry. Ready to drink when bottled.

Château Corton-Grancey   B'y. r. *** **71 72 73** 76 **77** 78 79 82

> Famous estate at ALOXE-CORTON, the property of Louis LATOUR. Impressive wine.

Château de la Chaize   B'y. r. *** **78 79 81** 82

> The best-known estate of BROUILLY, with 200 acres.

Château de la Maltroye   B'y. r. w. dr.   ***

> First-class burgundy estate at CHASSAGNE-MONTRACHET.

Château de Meursault   B'y. r. w. ***

> 100-acre estate owned by PATRIARCHE with good v'yds in Meursault, VOLNAY, POMMARD, BEAUNE. Splendid cellars open to the public.

Château de Panisseau   Dordogne w. dr.   **   D.Y.A.

> Leading estate of BERGERAC: good dry SAUVIGNON BLANC.

Château de Selle   Prov. r. p. or w. dr. ** D.Y.A.

> Estate near Cotignac, Var. Well-known and typical wines.

Château des Fines Roches   Rh. r. *** **71 72 74 76** 78 79 80 81

> Large (114 acres) and distinguished estate in CHÂTEAUNEUF-DU-PAPE. Strong old-style wine.

Château du Nozet   Lo. w. dr. *** **81 82**

> Biggest and best-known estate of Pouilly (FUMÉ) sur Loire.

Château Fortia Rh. r. ★★★ **70 71 72 74 76** 78 **79** 80 81
First-class property in CHÂTEAUNEUF-DU-PAPE. Traditional methods. The owner's father, Baron Le Roy, also fathered the APPELLATION CONTROLÉE system.

Château-Grillet Rh. w. dr. ★★★★ **79 80 81**
3½-acre v'yd. with one of France's smallest appellations. Intense, fragrant, expensive. Drink fairly young.

Burgundy boasts one of the world's most famous and certainly its most beautiful hospital, the Hospices de Beaune, founded in 1443 by Nicolas Rolin, Chancellor to the Duke of Burgundy, and his wife Guigone de Salins. The hospital he built and endowed with vineyards for its income still operates in the same building and still thrives, tending the sick of Beaune without charge, on the sale of its wine. Many growers since have bequeathed their land to the Hospices. Today it owns 125 acres of prime land in Beaune, Pommard, Volnay, Meursault, Corton and Mazis-Chambertin. The wine is sold by auction every year on the third Sunday in November.

Château-Gris B'y. r. ★★★ **71 72** 76 78 **79** 82
Famous estate at NUITS-ST-GEORGES, linked with BICHOT.

Châteaumeillant Lo. r. p. or w. dr. ★ D.Y.A.
Small VDQS area near SANCERRE.

Châteauneuf-du-Pape Rh. r. (w. dr.) ★★★ **71 72 76** 78 **79** 80 81
7,500 acres near Avignon. Best estate ("domaine") wines are dark, strong, long-lived. Others may be light and/or disappointing. The white is heavy: at best rich, almost sweet.

Château Rayas Rh. r. (w. dr.) ★★★ **69 71 72 76 77** 78 79 80 81
Excellent old-style property in Ch'neuf-du-Pape.

Château Simone Prov. r. p. or w. dr. ★★ D.Y.A.
Well-known property in Palette; the only one in this appellation near Aix-en-Provence.

Château Vignelaure Prov. r. ★★★ **70 71 76 77** 78 79 80
Very good Provençal estate near Aix making expensive Bordeaux-style wine with CABERNET grapes.

Chatillon-en-Diois Rh. r. p. or w. dr. ★ D.Y.A.
Small VDQS e. of the Rhône near Die. Good GAMAY reds; white (some Aligoté) mostly made into CLAIRETTE DE DIE.

Chavignol
Village of SANCERRE with famous v'yd., Les Monts Damnés.

Chauvenet, F.
Merchant at NUITS-ST-GEORGES controlled by MARGNAT.

Chénas B'y. r. ★★★ **76 78** 81 82
Good Beaujolais cru, neighbour to MOULIN-À-VENT and JULIÉNAS. One of the weightier Beaujolais.

Chenin Blanc
See Grapes for white wine

Chevalier-Montrachet B'y. w. dr. ★★★★ **71 73 76 77** 78 **79 80** 81 82
17-acre neighbour of MONTRACHET with similar luxurious wine, perhaps a little less powerful. Includes Les Demoiselles. Growers incl. BOUCHARD PÈRE, LEFLAIVE.

Cheverny Lo. w. dr. ★ D.Y.A.
Light sharp Loire country wine from near Chambord.

Chignin Savoie w.dr. ★ D.Y.A.
Light soft white of Jacquère grapes.

Chinon Lo. r. ★★★ **71 75 76 78 79 80** 81 82
Delicate fruity CABERNET from TOURAINE. Drink cool when young. Good vintages age like Bordeaux.

Chiroubles B'y. r. ★★★ **81 82**
Good but tiny Beaujolais cru next to FLEURIE; freshly fruity silky wine for early drinking.

Chusclan   Rh. r. p. or w. dr.   ★   **78 80 81**
Village of CÔTE-DU-RHÔNE-VILLAGES. Good middle-weight wines from the co-operative.

Cissac
HAUT-MÉDOC village just w. of PAUILLAC.

Clair-Daü
First-class 100-acre burgundy estate of the northern CÔTE DE NUITS, with cellars at MARSANNAY-la-Côte.

Clairet
Very light red wine, almost rosé.

Clairette
Mediocre white grape of the s. of France. Gives neutral wine.

Clairette de Bellegarde   Midi w. dr. ★ D.Y.A.
Plain neutral white from near Nîmes.

Clairette de Die   Rh. w. dr. or s./sw. sp. ★★ NV
Popular dry or semi-sweet rather MUSCAT-flavoured sparkling wine from the e. Rhône, or straight dry CLAIRETTE white, surprisingly ageing well 3–4 years.

Clairette du Languedoc   Midi w. dr. ★ D.Y.A.
Plain neutral white from near Montpellier.

La Clape   Midi r. p. or w. dr.   ★ → ★★
Full-bodied VDQS wines from near Narbonne. The red gains character after 2–3 years, the white even longer.

Claret   Traditional English term for red BORDEAUX.

Climat
Burgundian word for individual named v'yd., e.g. Beaune Grèves, Chambolle-Musigny les Amoureuses.

Clos
A term carrying some prestige, reserved for distinct, usually walled, v'yds., often in one ownership. Frequent in Burgundy and Alsace.

Clos-de-Bèze
See Chambertin-Clos-de-Bèze

Clos de la Roche   B'y. r.   ★★★   **69 70 71 72** 76 77 78 79 80
38-acre Grand Cru at MOREY-ST-DENIS. Powerful complex wine like CHAMBERTIN. Producers incl. BOUCHARD PÈRE, Ponsot.

Clos des Lambrays   B'y. r. ★★★ **71 72 73** 76 78
15-acre Grand Cru v'yd. at MOREY-ST-DENIS. Changed hands in 1979 after a shaky period. Being replanted.

Clos des Mouches   B'y. r. or w. dr. ★★★
Splendid Premier Cru v'yd. of BEAUNE owned by DROUHIN.

Clos de Tart   B'y. r. ★★★ **71 72 76 77** 78 **79** 80 82
18-acre Grand Cru at MOREY-ST-DENIS owned by MOMMESSIN. Relatively delicate wines, recently much improved.

Clos de Vougeot   B'y. r. ★★★ **66 69 70 71 72 73 76** 78 **79 80** 82
124-acre CÔTE-DE-NUITS Grand Cru with many owners. Variable, sometimes sublime. Maturity depends on the grower's technique and his position on the hillside.

Clos du Chêne Marchand
Well-known v'yd. at Bué, SANCERRE.

Clos du Roi   B'y. r. ★★★
Part of the Grand Cru CORTON; also a Premier Cru of BEAUNE.

Clos St Denis   B'y. r. ★★★ **69 71 72 73 76 77** 78 79 80 82
16-acre Grand Cru at MOREY-ST-DENIS. Splendid sturdy wine.

Clos St Jacques   B'y. r.   ★★★   **69 71 72 73** 76 **77** 78 79 80 82
17-acre Premier Cru of GEVREY-CHAMBERTIN. Excellent powerful wine, often better (and dearer) than some of the CHAMBERTIN Grands Crus.

Clos St Jean   B'y. r.   ★★★   **69 71 72 73** 76 78 79 80 82
36-acre Premier Cru of CHASSAGNE-MONTRACHET. Very good red, more solid than subtle.

Cognac
Town and region of western France and its brandy.

Collioure Pyr. r. ⟦*⟧ **76 78** 79 **80 81** 82
Strong dry RANCIO red from BANYULS area. Small production.

Condrieu Rh. w. dr. ✳✳✳ D.Y.A.
Outstanding soft fragrant white of great character (and price) from the Viognier grape. CH.-GRILLET is similar.

Corbières Midi r. or (p.) or (w.) ⟦*⟧ **79 80 81** 82
Good vigorous cheap VDQS reds, steadily improving.

Corbières de Roussillon Midi r. (p.) or (w.) ⟦*⟧ **79 80 81** 82
The same from slightly farther s.

Cordier, Ets D.
Important Bordeaux shipper and château-owner, including Ch'x. GRUAUD-LAROSE, TALBOT, CANTEMERLE.

Cornas Rh. r. ⟦**⟧ **71 72 73 76** 78 **79** 80 81
Expanding 300-acre district s. of HERMITAGE. Typical sturdy Rhône wine of good quality from the SYRAH grape.

The Confrérie des Chevaliers du Tastevin is Burgundy's wine fraternity and the most famous of its kind in the world. It was founded in 1933 by a group of Burgundian patriots, headed by Camille Rodier and Georges Faiveley, to rescue their beloved Burgundy from a period of slump and despair by promoting its inimitable products. Today it regularly holds banquets with elaborate and sprightly ceremonial for 600 guests at its headquarters, the old château in the Clos de Vougeot. The Confrérie has branches in many countries and members among lovers of wine all over the world.

Corse The island of Corsica. Strong ordinary wines of all colours. Better appellations include PATRIMONIO, SARTÈNE, AJACCIO.

Corton B'y. r. ⟦****⟧ **69 70 71 72 73** 76 **77** 78 79 80 82
The only Grand Cru red of the CÔTE DE BEAUNE. 200 acres in ALOXE-CORTON incl. les Bressandes and le CLOS DU ROI. Rich powerful wines.

Corton-Charlemagne B'y. w. dr. ✳✳✳✳ **71 72 73 76 77** 78 **79 80** 81 82
The white section (one-third) of CORTON. Rich spicy lingering wine. Behaves like a red wine and ages magnificently.

Coste, Pierre
Influential wine-broker and maker of LANGON, B'x.

Costières du Gard Midi r. p. or w. dr. ✳ D.Y.A.
VDQS of moderate quality from the Rhône delta.

Coteaux Champenois Champ. r. (p.) or w. dr. ✳✳✳ Champagne vintages. The appellation for non-sparkling champagne.

Coteaux d'Aix-en-Provence Prov r. p. or w. dr. ⟦*⟧ NV
Agreeable country wines tending to improve. CH. VIGNELAURE is far above average.

Coteaux d'Ancenis r. p. w. dr. ✳ D.Y.A.
Light Cabernet and Gamay reds and pinks; sharpish whites from MUSCADET country.

Coteaux de la Loire Lo. w. dr. sw. ⟦***⟧ **71 75 76 78 79** 80 82
Forceful and fragrant CHENIN BLANC whites from Anjou. The best are in SAVENNIÈRES. Excellent as aperitif.

Coteaux de l'Aubance Lo. p. or w. dr./sw. ✳✳ D.Y.A.
Light and typical minor Anjou wines.

Coteaux de Pierrevert Rh. r. p. or w. dr. or sp. ⟦*⟧ D.Y.A.
Minor southern VDQS from nr. Manosque. Well-made co-op wine.

Coteaux de Saumur Lo. w. dr./sw. ⟦**⟧ D.Y.A.
Pleasant dry or sweetish fruity CHENIN BLANC.

Coteaux des Baux-en-Provence Prov. r. p. or w. dr. ★ NV
  A twin to COTEAUX D'AIX, sharing the same VDQS.

Coteaux du Giennois r. w. dr. ★
  Minor Loire area n. of SANCERRE.

Coteaux du Languedoc Midi r. p. or w. dr. ⬚★⬚ D.Y.A.
  Scattered better-than-ordinary Midi areas with VDQS status.
  The best (e.g. Faugères, St Saturnin) age for a year or two.

Coteaux du Layon Lo. w. s./sw. or sw. ⬚★★⬚ **71 75 76 78** 79 80
  District centred on Rochefort, s. of Angers, making sweet
  CHENIN BLANC wines above the general Anjou standard.

Coteaux du Loir Lo. r. p. or w. dr./sw. ★★ **64 69 71 73 76** 78 79 80
  Small region n. of Tours. Occasionally excellent wines. Best
  v'yd.: JASNIÈRES. The Loir is a tributary of the Loire.

Coteaux du Tricastin Rh. r. p. or w. dr. ★★ D.Y.A.
  Fringe CÔTES-DU-RHÔNE of increasing quality from s. of Val-
  ence. Pierre Labeye is the chief producer.

Coteaux du Vendomois Lo. r. p. or w. dr. ★ D.Y.A.
  Fringe Loire from n. of Blois.

Côte(s)
  Means hillside; generally a superior vineyard to those on the
  plain. Many appellations start with either Côtes or
  Coteaux, which means the same thing. In ST-EMILION it
  distinguishes the valley slopes from the higher plateau.

Côte Chalonnaise B'y. r. w. dr. sp. ⬚★★→★★★⬚
  Lesser-known v'yd. area between BEAUNE and MÂCON. See
  Mercurey, Givry, Rully, Montagny.

Côte de Beaune B'y. r. or w. dr. ★★→★★★★
  Used geographically: the s. half of the CÔTE D'OR. Applies as
  an appellation only to parts of BEAUNE.

Côte de Beaune-Villages B'y. r. or w. dr. ★★ **76 78 79 80** 82
  Regional appellation for secondary wines of the classic area.
  They cannot be labelled "Côte de Beaune" without either
  "Villages" or the village name.

Côte de Brouilly B'y. r. ★★★ **78 79 80** 81 82
  Fruity, rich, vigorous Beaujolais cru. One of the best. Leading
  estate: Ch. Thivin.

Côte de Nuits B'y. r. or (w. dr.) ★★→★★★★
  The northern half of the CÔTE D'OR.

Côte de Nuits-Villages B'y. r. (w.) ★★ **76 78 79 80** 82
  A junior appellation, rarely seen but worth investigating.

Côte d'Or
  Département name applied to the central and principal
  Burgundy v'yd. slopes, consisting of the CÔTE DE BEAUNE
  and CÔTE DE NUITS. The name is not used on labels.

Côte Rôtie Rh. r. ★★★ **69 70 71 72 73 76** 78 79 80 81 82
  The finest Rhône red, from just s. of Vienne; achieves complex
  delicacy with age. Very small production. Top growers include JABOULET, CHAPOUTIER, VIDAL-FLEURY, Jasmin, Guigal.

(Côtes) Canon-Fronsac B'x. r. ⬚★★⬚ **70 71 75 76** 78 79 80 81 82
  Attractive solid reds from small area w. of ST-EMILION. Ch'x.
  include Bodet, Canon, Canon de Brem, Junayme, Moulin-
  Pey-Labrie, Toumalin. The appellation should be simply
  "Canon-Fronsac". See also FRONSAC.

Côtes d'Auvergne Central France r. p. or (w. dr.) ★ D.Y.A.
  Flourishing small VDQS area near Clermont-Ferrand. Red (at
  best) like light Beaujolais.

Côtes de Blaye B'x. w. dr. ★ D.Y.A.
  Run-of-the-mill Bordeaux white from BLAYE.

Côtes de Bordeaux Saint-Macaire B'x. w. dr./sw. ★ D.Y.A.
  Run-of-the-mill Bordeaux white from e. of Sauternes.

Côtes de Bourg B'x. r. `* → **` 70 75 76 78 79 81 82
   Appellation used for many of the better reds of BOURG.
   Ch'x incl. de Barbe, La Barde, du Bousquet, La Croix
   de Millorit, de la Grave, Grand-Jour, Lalibarde, Lamothe,
   Mendoce, Mille-Secousses, Peychaud, de Thau.

Côtes de Buzet S.W. France r. or w. dr. `**` 76 78 79 81 82
   Good light wines from just s.e. of Bordeaux. Promising area
   with well-run co-operative. Best wine: Cuvée Napoléon.

Côtes de Castillon
   See Bordeaux—Côtes de Castillon.

Côtes de Duras Dordogne r. or w. dr. `*` 81 82
   Neighbour to BERGERAC. Similar light wines.

Côtes de Francs
   See Bordeaux—Côtes de Francs.

Côtes de Fronsac
   See FRONSAC.

Côtes de Jura Jura r. p. or w. dr. (sp.) `*` NV
   Various light tints and tastes. ARBOIS is better.

Côtes de Montravel Dordogne w. dr./sw. `*` NV
   Part of BERGERAC; trad. medium-sw. wine, now often dry.

Côtes de Provence Prov. r. p. or w. dr. `* → **` NV
   The wine of Provence; often more alcohol than character.
   Standards have recently been improving. A dozen properties
   have the right to say "Cru Classé".

Côtes de Roussillon Pyr. r. p. or w. dr. `* → **` 75 76 78 79 81
   Country wine of e. Pyrenees. The hefty dark reds are best.
   Some whites are sharp VINS VERTS.

Côtes de Toul E. France r. p. or w. dr. `*` D.Y.A.
   Very light wines from Lorraine; mainly VIN GRIS (rosé).

Côtes du Forez Central France r. or p. `*` D.Y.A.
   Light Beaujolais-style red, can be good in warm years.

Côtes du Fronton S.W. France r. or p. `* → **` D.Y.A.
   The local wine of Toulouse, locally admired. Ch. Bellevue-la-
   Forêt is outstanding.

Côtes du Haut-Roussillon S.W. France br. sw. `* → **` NV
   Sweet-wine area n. of Perpignan.

Côtes du Luberon Rh. r. p. or w. dr. sp. `*` D.Y.A.
   Improving country wines from northern Provence; especially
   the sparkling, and Château de Sannes.

Côtes du Marmandais Dordogne r. p. or w. dr. `*` D.Y.A.
   Undistinguished light wines from s.e. of Bordeaux.

Côtes-du-Rhône Rh. r. p. or w. dr. `*` 78 79 80 81 82
   The basic appellation of the Rhône valley. Best drunk young.
   Wide variations of quality due to grape ripeness, therefore
   rising with degree of alcohol. See CÔTES-DU-RHÔNE-VILLAGES.

Côtes-du-Rhône-Villages Rh. r. p. or w. dr. `** →` `**` 78 79 80 81
   The wine of the 14 best villages of the southern Rhône.
   Substantial and on the whole reliable.

Côtes du Ventoux Prov. r. (w. dr.) `**`
   Booming appellation for tasty reds between the Rhône and
   Provence.

Côtes du Vivarais Prov. r. p. or w. dr. `*` NV
   Pleasant country wines from s. Massif Centrale.

Côtes Frontonnais See Côtes du Fronton

Coulée de Serrant Lo. w. dr./sw. `***` 64 69 71 73 75 76 78 79 80
   81 82
   10-acre v'yd. on n. bank of Loire at Savennières, Anjou.
   Intense strong fruity/sharp wine, ages well.

La Cour Pavillon
   Reliable brand of red and white Bordeaux from Gilbey's.

Cour-Cheverny Lo. w. dr. `*` D.Y.A.
   Fragile, often sharp Touraine white.

Crémant
>In Champagne means "Creaming"—i.e. half-sparkling. Since 1975 an appellation for high-quality champagne-method sparkling wines from Alsace, the Loire and Bourgogne—often a notable bargain.

Crémant de Loire   w. dr./sp. ** NV
>High-quality semi-sparkling wine from ANJOU and TOURAINE.

Crépy   Savoie w. dr. ** D.Y.A.
>Light, Swiss-style white from s. shore of La. Geneva. "Crépit-ant" has been coined for its faint fizz.

Criots-Bâtard-Montrachet   B'y. w. *** 71 73 76 77 78 79 80 81 82
>7-acre neighbour to BÂTARD-MONTRACHET. Similar wine.

Crozes-Hermitage   Rh. r. or (w. dr.)   ⟦**⟧   76 78 79 80 81 82
>Larger and less distinguished neighbour to HERMITAGE. Robust and often excellent reds, but choose carefully.

Cru
>"Growth", as in "first-growth"—meaning vineyard.

Cru Bourgeois
>General term for Médoc châteaux below CRU CLASSÉ.

Cru Bourgeois Supérieur
>Official rank one better than the last. Aged in barrels.

Cru Classé
>Classed growth. One of the first five official quality classes of the Médoc, classified in 1855. Also any classed growth of another district (e.g. Graves, St Emilion, Sauternes).

Cru Exceptionnel
>Official rank above CRU BOURGEOIS SUPÉRIEUR, immediately below CRU CLASSÉ. Several fine châteaux are unofficially Exceptionnel.

Cruse et Fils Frères
>Long-established Bordeaux shipper famous for fine wine. Owner of CH. D'ISSAN.

Cubzac, St.-André-de   B'x. r. or w. dr.   ⟦*⟧   75 78 79 81 82
>Town 15 miles n.e. of Bordeaux, centre of the minor Cubzaguais region. Sound reds have the appellation Bordeaux. Estates include: Ch. du Bouilh, Ch. de Terrefort-Quancard, Ch. Timberlay, Domaine de Beychevelle.

Cussac
>Village just s. of ST. JULIEN. Appellation Haut-Médoc.

Cuve Close
>Short-cut way of making sparkling wine in a tank. The sparkle dies away in the glass much quicker than with MÉTHODE CHAMPENOISE wine.

Cuvée
>The quantity of wine produced in a "cuve" or vat. Also a word of many uses, incl. "blend". In Burgundy interchangeable with "Cru". Often just refers to a "lot" of wine.

d'Angerville, Marquis
>Famous burgundy grower with immaculate estate in VOLNAY.

Danglade, L. et Fils
>Shipper of St-Emilion and Pomerol, now owned by J-P MOUEIX of Libourne.

Degré alcoolique
>Degrees of alcohol, i.e. per cent by volume.

Delagrange-Bachelet
>One of the leading proprietors in CHASSAGNE-MONTRACHET.

Delas Frères
>Long-established firm of Rhône-wine specialists at Tournon, v'yds. at CÔTE RÔTIE, HERMITAGE, CORNAS etc.

Delorme, André
>Leading merchants and growers of the CÔTE CHALONNAISE. Specialists in sparkling wine and excellent RULLY.

De Luze, A. et Fils
>Bordeaux shipper and owners of Ch'x. CANTENAC-BROWN and PAVEIL-DE LUZE; owned by Rémy-Martin of Cognac.

Demi-Sec
>"Half-dry": in practice more than half-sweet.

Depagneux, Jacques et Cie
>Well-regarded merchants of BEAUJOLAIS.

Deutz & Geldermann NV, rosé **71 73 75**, Blanc de Blancs **73** and **66 69 70 71 73** 75 **76**
>One of the best of the smaller champagne houses. Luxury brand: Cuvée William Deutz.

Domaine
>Property, particularly in Burgundy.

Domaine de Belair
>A light-weight branded red Bordeaux of reliable quality.

Domaine de l'Eglantière
>Important CHABLIS estate. See DURUP.

Dom Pérignon **66 69 70 71 73** 75 76
>Luxury brand of MOËT ET CHANDON named after the legendary blind inventor of champagne. Also occasionally a rosé (**69 71**).

Dopff "au Moulin"
>Ancient family wine-house at Riquewihr, Alsace. Best wines: Riesling Schoenenbourg, Gewürztraminer Eichberg.

Dopff & Irion
>Another excellent Riquewihr (ALSACE) business. Best wines include Muscat les Amandiers, Riesling de Riquewihr.

Doudet-Naudin
>Burgundy merchant and grower at Savigny-lès-Beaune. V'yds. incl. BEAUNE CLOS DE ROI. Rather heavy wines.

Dourthe Frères
>Well-reputed Bordeaux merchant representing a wide range of ch'x., mainly good Crus Bourgeois, incl. Ch'x. MAUCAILLOU, TRONQUOY-LALANDE, BELGRAVE. "Beau-Mayne" is their reliable branded Bordeaux.

Doux Sweet.

Drouhin, J. et Cie
>Prestigious Burgundy grower and merchant. Offices in BEAUNE, v'yds. in MUSIGNY, CLOS DE VOUGEOT, etc.

Duboeuf, Georges
>Top-class BEAUJOLAIS merchant at Romanèche-Thorin.

Duclot, Ets
>Bordeaux merchant specializing in the top growths. Controlled by MOUEIX.

Dufouleur Frères
>Growers and merchants of toothsome burgundy at NUITS-ST-GEORGE and MERCUREY.

Dujac, Domaine
>Perfectionist burgundian grower at MOREY-ST-DENIS with v'yds in that village, ECHÉZEAUX, BONNES-MARES, GEVREY-CHAMBERTIN, etc.

Durup, Jean
>One of the biggest Chablis growers with 140 acres, including the DOMAINE DE L'EGLANTIÈRE.

Echézeaux B'y. r. |***| **71 72 73 76 77** 78 **79** 80 82
>74-acre Grand Cru between VOSNE-ROMANÉE and CLOS DE VOUGEOT. Superlative fragrant burgundy without great weight.

Edelzwicker Alsace w. |*| D.Y.A.
>Light white from mixture of grapes, often fruity and good.

Entre-Deux-Mers B'x. w. dr. |*| D.Y.A.
>Standard dry white Bordeaux from between the Garonne and Dordogne rivers. Often a good buy, esp. "La Gamage".

Les Epenots   B'y. r. ★★★
Famous Premier Cru v'yd. of POMMARD. Also spelt Epeneaux for the 12-acre Clos des Epeneaux owned by Comte Armand.

Eschenauer, Louis
Famous Bordeaux merchants, owners of Ch'x. RAUSAN-SÉGLA and SMITH-HAUT-LAFITTE, De Lamouroux and LA GARDE in GRAVES. Controlled by John Holt, part of the Lonrho group.

l'Etoile   Jura (r.) (p.) or w. dr./sw./sp. ★★
Sub-region of the Jura with typically various wines, incl. VIN JAUNE like CHÂTEAU-CHALON.

Faiveley, J.
Family-owned growers (with 250 acres) and merchants at NUITS-ST-GEORGES, with v'yds. in CHAMBERTIN-CLOS-DE-BÈZE, CHAMBOLLE-MUSIGNY, CORTON, NUITS and MERCUREY (150 acres).

Faugères   Midi r. (p. or w. dr.)   ⬚ ★   78 79 80 81 82
Isolated village of the COTEAUX DU LANGUEDOC making above-average wine. Became Appellation Controlée in 1982.

Fitou   Midi r. ★★ 75 76 78 79 80 81 82
Superior CORBIÈRES red; powerful and ages well.

Fixin   B'y. r.   ⬚ ★★   71 72 73 76 78 79 80 82
A worthy and under-valued neighbour to GEVREY-CHAMBERTIN. Often splendid reds. Best v'yds.: Clos du Chapitre Les Hervelets, Clos Napoléon.

Fleurie   B'y. r.   ⬚ ★★★   78 81 82
The epitome of a Beaujolais cru: fruity, scented, silky, racy.

Frais   Fresh or cool.

Frappé
Ice-cold.

Froid   Cold.

Fronsac   B'x. r.   ⬚ ★→★★   70 75 76 78 79 80 82
Pretty hilly area of good reds just w. of St-Emilion. Ch'x incl. La Dauphine, Mayne-Vieil, la Rivière, de Carles, Richelieu, Villars. See also (CÔTES) CANON-FRONSAC.

Frontignan   Midi br. sw.   ⬚ ★   NV
Strong sweet and liquorous muscat wine.

Gaillac   S.W. France r. p. or w. dr./sw. or sp.   ⬚ ★   NV
Generally dull but usually adequate everyday wine. Showing signs of improvement. Slightly fizzy "Perlé" is good value.

Gamay
See Grapes for red wine

Geisweiler et Fils
One of the bigger merchant-houses of Burgundy. Cellars and 50 acres of v'yds. at NUITS-ST-GEORGES. Also 150 acres at Bevy in the HAUTES CÔTES DE NUITS and 30 in the CÔTE CHALONNAISE.

Gevrey-Chambertin   B'y. r. ★★★ 71 72 73 76 78 79 80 82
The village containing the great CHAMBERTIN and many other noble v'yds. as well as some more commonplace.

Gewürztraminer
The speciality grape of ALSACE: perfumed and spicy, whether dry or sweet.

Gigondas   Rh. r. or p.   ⬚ ★★   76 78 79 80 81
Worthy neighbour to CHÂTEAUNEUF-DU-PAPE. Strong full-bodied, sometimes peppery wine.

Gilbey, S.A.
British firm long-established as Bordeaux merchants at Ch. LOUDENNE in the MÉDOC. Now owned by International Distillers and Vintners.

Ginestet
Third-generation Bordeaux merchants and former owners of CH. MARGAUX.

Gisselbrecht, Louis
> High-quality Alsace shippers at Dambach-la-ville.

Givry   B'y. r. or w. dr.   `**` **76 78 79** 81w. 82
> Underrated village of the CÔTE CHALONNAISE: light but tasty and typical burgundy.

Gosset
> Small, very old champagne house at Ay. Fine full wines. Now linked with Philiponnat.

Gouges, Henri
> Leading burgundy grower of NUITS-ST-GEORGES. Good reds and very rare white "La Perrière".

Goulet, Georges   NV, rosé **73 75 76**, Crémant Blanc de Blancs **74** 75, and **71 73 75 76**
> High-quality Reims champagne house. Abel Lepitre is label for cheaper range. Luxury brand: Cuvée du Centenaire **73** 74

Goût   Taste, e.g. "goût anglais"—as the English like it (i.e. dry).

Grand Cru
> One of the top Burgundy v'yds. with its own Appellation Contrôlée. Similar in Alsace but more vague elsewhere.

Grand Roussillon   Midi br. sw. `**` NV
> Broad appellation for muscat and other sweet fortified wines of eastern Pyrenees.

Grands-Echézeaux   B'y.r. `****` **69 71 72 73** 76 78 **79** 80 82
> Superlative 22-acre Grand Cru next to CLOS DE VOUGEOT.

Gratien, Alfred and Gratien & Meyer
> Good smaller champagne house (fine, very dry, long-lasting wine) and its counterpart at SAUMUR on the Loire.

Graves   B'x. r. or w. `*→****`
> Large region s. of Bordeaux city. Its best wines are red, but the name is used chiefly for its dry or medium whites.

Graves de Vayres   B'x r. or w. `*`
> Part of ENTRE-DEUX-MERS; of no special character.

Les Gravières   B'y. r. `***`
> Famous Premier Cru v'yd. of SANTENAY.

Griotte-Chambertin   B'y. r. `***` **69 71 72 73** 76 77 78 79 80 82
> 14-acre Grand Cru adjoining CHAMBERTIN. Similar wine, but less masculine and more "tender". Growers incl. DROUHIN.

Gros Plant du Pays Nantais   Lo. w.   `*`   D.Y.A.
> Junior cousin of MUSCADET, sharper and lighter; made of the COGNAC grape also known as Folle Blanche, Ugni Blanc etc.

Haut-Benauge   B'x. w. dr. `*` D.Y.A.
> Appellation for a limited area within ENTRE-DEUX-MERS.

Haut Comtat   Rh. r. or p. `**` **78 79** 80 81 82
> Small appellation n. of Avignon. Sound strong wines.

Hautes-Côtes de Beaune   B'y. r. or w. dr.   `**`   **76 78 79** 81w. 82
> Appellation for a dozen villages in the hills behind the CÔTE DE BEAUNE. Light wines, worth investigating.

Hautes-Côtes de Nuits   B'y. r. or w. dr.   `**`   **76** 78 **79** 80 82
> The same for the CÔTE DE NUITS. An area on the way up.

Haut-Médoc   B'x. r. `**→***` 66 70 71 73 75 **76 77 78 79 80** 81 82
> Big appellation including all the best areas of the Médoc. Most wines have château names: those without should still be above average.

Haut-Montravel   Dordogne w. sw. `*` **76 78 79 80** 81 82
> Medium-sweet BERGERAC.

Haut Poitou
> Up-and-coming VDQS area s. of ANJOU. Co-operative makes good whites, incl. CHARDONNAY and SAUVIGNON BLANC.

Heidsieck, Charles   NV and **66 69 70 71 73** 75 76
> Major champagne house of Reims, family-owned, now merged with Champagne Henriot. Luxury brand: Cuvée Royal Champagne.

Heidsieck, Dry Monopole   NV, rosé **71 73** and **71 73 75** 76 79
>   Important champagne merchant and grower of Reims. Luxury brand: Diamant Bleu (**71 73**)

Henriot   NV, Blanc de Blancs
>   Old family champagne house now linked with CHARLES HEID-SIECK. Very dry style. Luxury brand: Réserve Baron Philippe de Rothschild.

Hérault   Midi
>   The biggest v'yd. *département* in France with 400,000 hectares of vines. Chiefly vin ordinaire.

Hermitage   Rh. r. or w. dr.   ⟨★★★⟩   **66 69 70 71 72 73** 76 78 79 80 82
>   The "manliest" wine of France. Dark, powerful and profound. Needs long ageing. The white is heady, golden and long-lived.

Hospices de Beaune
>   Hospital in BEAUNE, with excellent v'yds. in MEURSAULT, POMMARD, VOLNAY, BEAUNE, CORTON, etc. See panel on page 31.

Hugel Père et Fils
>   The best-known ALSACE growers and merchants. Founded at Riquewihr in 1639 and still in the family. Best wines: Cuvées Exceptionnelles.

Imperiale
>   Bordeaux bottle holding 8½ normal bottles (5 litres).

Irancy   B'y. r. or (p.)   ⟨★★⟩   **76 78 79** 82
>   Good light red made near CHABLIS of Pinot Noir and 'César'. The best vintages are long-lived and mature well.

Irouléguy   S.W. France (r.) or w. dr. ★★ D.Y.A.
>   Agreeable local wine of the Basque country.

l'Isle de Beauté
>   Name given to VINS DU PAYS from CORSICA.

Jaboulet, Paul
>   Old family firm at Tain, leading growers of HERMITAGE (esp. 'La Chapelle') and merchants in other Rhône wines.

Jaboulet-Vercherre et Cie
>   Well-known Burgundy merchant-house with v'yds. (34 acres) in POMMARD, etc., and cellars in Beaune.

Jadot, Louis
>   Much-respected top-quality Burgundy merchant-house with v'yds (50 acres) in BEAUNE, CORTON, etc.

Jardin de la France
>   Name given to VINS DU PAYS of the LOIRE.

Jasnières   Lo. (r.) (p.) or w. dr. ★★★ **70 71 73 75 76** 78 79 80 82
>   Rare VOUVRAY-like wine of n. Touraine.

Jeroboam
>   In Bordeaux a 6-bottle bottle, or triple magnum; in Champagne a double magnum.

Juliénas   B'y. r. ★★★ **78 79 81** 82
>   Leading cru of Beaujolais: vigorous fruity wine.

Jura   See Côtes de Jura

Jurançon   S.W. France w. sw. or dr. ★★ **75 76 78 79** 81 82
>   Unusual high-flavoured and long-lived speciality of Pau in the Pyrenean foothills. Ages well for several years.

Kressman, E. S. & Cie
>   Family-owned Bordeaux merchants and owners of CH. LATOUR-MARTILLAC in GRAVES. "Monopole Rouge" is very good.

Kriter
>   Popular low-price sparkling wine processed in Burgundy by PATRIARCHE.

Krug   "Grande Cuvée" and **66 69 71 73** 76
>   Small but very prestigious champagne house known for full-bodied very dry wine of the highest quality.

Kuentz-Bas
> High-quality ALSACE grower and merchant at Husseren-les-Châteaux.

Labarde
> Village just s. of MARGAUX and included in that appellation. Best ch.: GISCOURS.

Lalande de Pomerol   B'x. r.   ★★   70 71 73 75 **76** 78 **79** 81 82
> Neighbour to POMEROL. Wines similar but considerably less fine. Ch. BEL-AIR is well known.

Langlois-Château
> Producer of sparkling SAUMUR, controlled by BOLLINGER.

Langon
> The principal town of the s. GRAVES/SAUTERNES district.

Lanson Père et Fils   NV rosé NV, and **69 71 75 76**
> Important growers and merchants of Champagne, cellars at Reims. Luxury brand: Red Label.

Laroche, Domaine
> Important (160 acres) grower of CHABLIS, incl. Dom. La Jouchère.

Latour, Louis
> Top Burgundy merchant and grower with v'yds. (120 acres) in CORTON, BEAUNE, etc. Among the best, esp. for whites.

Latour de France   r. (w. dr.) ★→★★ 78 79 80 81
> New appellation in CÔTES DE ROUSSILLON.

Latricières-Chambertin   B'y. r. ★★★ **69 70 71 72 73** 76 78 **79 80** 82
> 17-acre Grand Cru neighbour of CHAMBERTIN. Similar wine, but lighter and "prettier".

Laudun   Rh. r. p. or w. dr.   ★
> Village of CÔTES-DU-RHÔNE-VILLAGES. Attractive wines from the co-operative.

Laurent-Perrier   NV, rosé brut and **66 70 71 73** 75
> Well-known champagne house of Tours-sur-Marne. Luxury brand: Cuvée Grand Siécle. New in 1981: Ultra Brut.

Leflaive, Domaine
> Top-quality white burgundy grower at PULIGNY-MONTRACHET. Best v'yd.: Clavoillons.

Léognan   B'x.
> Leading village of the GRAVES. Best ch'x.: DOMAINE DE CHEVALIER, MALARTIC-LAGRAVIÈRE and HAUT-BAILLY.

Leroy   Important burgundy merchants at AUXEY-DURESSES, part-owners and distributors of the DOMAINE DE LA ROMANÉE-CONTI.

Lichine, Alexis et Cie
> Post-war Bordeaux merchants, proprietors of CH. LASCOMBES.

Lie, sur
> "On the leès." Muscadet is often so bottled, for maximum freshness.

Limoux   Pyr. r. or w. dr.   ★★   D.Y.A.
> The non-sparkling version of BLANQUETTE DE LIMOUX and a remarkable claret-like red: Anne des Joyeuses.

Lirac   Rh. r. p. or (w. dr.) ★★ **76 78 79** 80 **81**
> Neighbouring village to TAVEL. Similar wine; the red becoming more important than the rosé, esp. Ch. de Segriés.

Listel   Midi r. p. w. dr.   ★   D.Y.A.
> Estate in the Camargue owned by the giant Salins du Midi, making pleasant light "vins des sables". Domaine du Bosquet is a fruity red.

Listrac   B'x. r. ★★
> Village of HAUT-MÉDOC next to MOULIS. Best ch'x.: FOURCAS-HOSTEN and FOURCAS-DUPRÉ.

Loire
> The major river of n.w. France. See under wine and regional names.

Loron et Fils
Big-scale burgundy grower and merchant, specialist in BEAU-JOLAIS and sound *vins de table*.

Loupiac   B'x. w. sw.   **⋆⋆**   **67 70 71 75 76** 79 80 81
Neighbour to SAUTERNES with similar but less good wine.

Ludon
HAUT-MÉDOC village s. of MARGAUX. Best ch.: LA LAGUNE.

Lugny   ("Macon-Lugny") B'y. r. w. dr.   **⋆⋆**   **78 80 81** 82
Village next to VIRÉ with active and good co-operative. Wine of Les Genevrières v'yd. is sold by LOUIS LATOUR.

Lupé-Cholet et Cie
Merchants and growers at NUITS-ST-GEORGES controlled by BICHOT. Best estate wines: Château Gris and Clos de Lupé.

Lussac-Saint-Emilion   B'x. r.   **⋆⋆**   **75 78 79 81** 82
North-eastern neighbour to ST-EMILION. Often good value. Co-operative makes "Roc de Lussac".

Macau
HAUT-MÉDOC village s. of MARGAUX. Best ch.: CANTEMERLE.

macération carbonique
Traditional Beaujolais technique of fermentation with whole bunches of unbroken grapes in an atmosphere saturated with carbon dioxide. Fermentation inside each grape eventually bursts it, giving vivid and very fruity mild wine for quick consumption. Now much used in the Midi.

Burgundy: a grower's own label

MISE EN BOUTEILLES AU DOMAINE **NUITS ST GEORGES** **LES PRULIERS** APPELLATION CONTROLÉE DOMAINE HENRI GOUGES A NUITS ST GEORGES, CÔTE D'OR

Domaine is the burgundy equivalent of château.
The Appellation Controlée is Nuits St Georges.
The individual v'yd. in Nuits is called Les Pruliers.
The name and address of the grower/producer.
(The word propriétaire is often also used.)

A merchant's label

SANTENAY **LES GRAVIERES** APPELLATION CONTROLÉE PROSPER MAUFOUX NEGOCIANT A SANTENA

The village.
The vineyard.
The wine qualifies for the Appellation Santenay.
Prosper Maufoux is a Négociant, or merchant, who bought the wine from the grower to mature, bottle and sell.

Machard de Gramont
Family estate in Burgundy with cellars in NUITS and v'yds. in NUITS, SAVIGNY, BEAUNE, POMMARD. Extremely well-made reds.

Mâcon   B'y. r. (p.) or w. dr. ⋆⋆ 76 78 79 81 82
Southern district of sound, usually unremarkable, reds and tasty dry (CHARDONNAY) whites. Wine with a village name (e.g. Mâcon-Prissé) is better. POUILLY-FUISSÉ is best appellation of the region. See also Mâcon-Villages.

Mâcon-Lugny   see Lugny

Mâcon Supérieur
The same but slightly stronger from riper grapes.

Mâcon-Villages   B'y. w. dr.   **⋆⋆**   **75 76 78 79 81** 82
Increasingly well-made and typical white burgundies. Mâcon-Prissé, MÂCON-VIRÉ are examples.

Mâcon-Viré   See Mâcon-Villages and Viré

Madiran S.W. France r. `**` **70 71 73 75 76** 78 79 81 82
Dark vigorous fragrant red from ARMAGNAC. Needs ageing.
Magenta, Duc de
Burgundy estate (45 acres) based at CHASSAGNE-MONTRACHET.
Magnum A double bottle (1.5 litres).
Mähler-Besse
First-class Dutch wine-merchants in Bordeaux, with a majority share in Ch. PALMER and good brands, incl. Cheval Noir.
Maire, Henri
The biggest grower and merchant of JURA wines.
Marc Grape skins after pressing; also the strong-smelling brandy made from them.
Margaux B'x. r. `**→****` **66 70 71 73** 75 **76** 78 79 81 82
Village of the HAUT-MÉDOC making the most "elegant" red Bordeaux. The name includes CANTENAC and several other villages as well. Top ch'x. include MARGAUX, LASCOMBES, etc.
Margnat
Major producer of everyday VIN DE TABLE.
Marque déposée
Trade mark.
Marsannay B'y. (r.) or p. `***` **78 79 80** 82
Village near Dijon with excellent light red and delicate rosé, perhaps the best rosé in France.
Martillac
Village in the GRAVES appellation, Bordeaux.
Maufoux, Prosper
Family firm of burgundy merchants at SANTENAY. Solid, reliable wines with good keeping qualities.
Maury Pyr. r. sw. `*→**` NV
Red VIN DOUX NATUREL from ROUSSILLON.
Mazis-Chambertin B'y. r. `***` **70 71 72 73 76** 78 79 80 82
30-acre Grand Cru neighbour of CHAMBERTIN. Lighter wine.
Médoc B'x. r. `**` **70 75 76** 78 **79** 81 82
Appellation for reds of the less good (n.) part of Bordeaux's biggest and best district. HAUT-MÉDOC is better.
Ménétou-Salon Lo. r. p. or w. dr. `**` D.Y.A.
Attractive light wines from w. of SANCERRE. SAUVIGNON white; CABERNET red.
Mercier et Cie NV and **70 71 73 75 78**
One of the biggest champagne houses, at Epernay. Controlled by MOËT & CHANDON.
Mercurey B'y. r. or w. dr. `**` **71 76** 78 **79** 82
Leading red-wine village of the CÔTE CHALONNAISE. Good middle-rank burgundy.
méthode champenoise
The traditional laborious method of putting the bubbles in champagne by refermenting the wine in its bottle.
Meursault B'y. (r.) w. dr. `***` **69 71 73 76 77** 78 **79** 81 82
CÔTE DE BEAUNE village with some of the world's greatest whites: rich, smooth, savoury, dry but mellow. Best v'yds. incl. Perrières, Genevrières, Charmes.
Meursault-Blagny See Blagny
Midi General term for the south of France, where standards have risen consistently in recent years.
Minervois Midi r. or (p.) (w.) or br. sw. `*→**` **76 78 79 80 81** 82
Hilly VDQS area with some of the best wines of the Midi: lively and full of flavour. Also sweet MUSCAT de St. Jean de M.
mise en bouteilles au château, au domaine
Bottled at the château, at the property or estate. N.B. dans nos caves (in our cellars) or dans la région de production (in the area of production) mean little.

Moelleux
> Mellow. Used of the sweet wines of VOUVRAY, etc.

Moët & Chandon   NV, rosé 75 and **70 71 73 75 76 78**
> The biggest champagne merchant and grower, with cellars in Epernay and sparkling wine branches in Argentina, Brazil and California. Luxury brand: DOM PÉRIGNON **71 73** 76.

Moillard
> Big firm of growers and merchants in NUITS-ST-GEORGES.

Mommessin, J.
> Major Beaujolais merchant and owner of CLOS DE TART.

Monbazillac   Dordogne w. sw.   **★★**   **71 73 75 76 78** 79 80 81
> Golden SAUTERNES-style wine from BERGERAC. Ages well. Ch. Monbazillac is best known.

Mondeuse
> Red grape of SAVOIE. Good, deep-coloured wine.

Monopole
> Vineyard in single ownership.

Montagne-Saint-Emilion   B'x. r.   **★★**   **71 75 76** 78 79 81 82
> North-east neighbour of ST-EMILION with similar wines.

Montagny   B'y. w. dr.   **★★**   →**★★★** **76 78 79** 81 82
> CÔTE CHALONNAISE village between MÂCON and MEURSAULT, both geographically and gastronomically.

Montée de Tonnerre   B'y.
> Famous and excellent PREMIER CRU of CHABLIS.

Monthélie   B'y. r.   **★★★**   **71 76** 78 79 80 82
> Little-known neighbour and almost equal of VOLNAY. Excellent fragrant reds. Best estate: Château de Monthélie.

Montlouis   Lo. w. sw./dr. **★★ 64 69 71 73 74 75 76** 78 79 80 82
> Neighbour of VOUVRAY. Similar sweet or dry long-lived wine.

Montrachet   B'y. w. dr. **★★★★ 69 70 71 73 75 76 77** 78 79 80 81 82
> 19-acre Grand Cru v'yd. in both PULIGNY and CHASSAGNE-MONTRACHET. The greatest white burgundy: strong, perfumed, intense, dry yet luscious. (The "ts" are silent.)

Montravel
> See Côtes de Montravel

Mont-Redon, Domaine de   Rh. r. (w. dr.) **★★★ 70 71 76 77** 78 79 80 81
> Outstanding 215-acre estate in CHÂTEAUNEUF-DU-PAPE.

Moreau et Fils
> CHABLIS merchant and grower with 170 acres. Also major table-wine producer.

Morey-Saint-Denis   B'y. r.   **★★★**   **69 70 71 72 73** 76 77 78 79 80 82
> Small village with four Grands Crus between GEVREY-CHAMBERTIN and CHAMBOLLE-MUSIGNY. Glorious wine, often overlooked.

Morgon   B'y. r. **★★★ 76 78 79 80** 81 82
> The "firmest" cru of Beaujolais, needing time to develop its rich flavour.

Moueix, J-P et Cie
> The leading proprietor and merchant of St-Emilion and Pomerol. Ch'x. incl. MAGDELAINE, LAFLEUR-PETRUS, and part of PETRUS.

Moulin-à-Vent   B'y. r. **★★★ 76 78 79 80** 81 82
> The "biggest" and best wine of Beaujolais; powerful and long-lived when not unbalanced by too much added sugar.

Moulis   B'x. r. **★★→★★★**
> Village of the HAUT-MÉDOC with its own appellation and several good, not top-rank ch'x.: CHASSE-SPLEEN, POUJEAUX-THEIL, MAUCAILLOU, etc.

Mousseux
> Sparkling.

Mouton Cadet
> Best-selling brand of red Bordeaux.

Moutonne
CHABLIS GRAND CRU *honoris causa* owned by BICHOT.

Mumm, G. H. & Cie   NV "Cordon Rouge", rosé **73**, Crémant de
Cramant and **69 71** 73 75 76
Major champagne grower and merchant owned by Seagram's.
Luxury brand: Président René Lalou. The Cramant is superb.

Muscadet   Lo. w. dr.   ⟦**⟧ D.Y.A.
Popular, good-value, often delicious dry wine from round
Nantes in s. Brittany. Perfect with fish.

Muscadet de Sèvre-et-Maine
Wine from the central and usually best part of the area.

Muscat
Distinctively perfumed grape and its (usually sweet) wine.

Muscat de Beaumes de Venise
The best French muscat (see Beaumes de Venise).

Muscat de Frontignan   Midi br. sw. ** D.Y.A.
Sweet Midi muscat.

Muscat de Lunel   Midi br. sw. ** NV
Ditto. A small area but good.

Muscat de Mireval   Midi br. sw. ** NV
Ditto, from near Montpellier.

Muscat de Rivesaltes   Midi br. sw. * NV
Sweet muscat from a big zone near Perpignan.

Musigny   B'y. r. (w. dr.) **** **66 69 70 71 72 73** 76 **77** 78 79 80 82
25-acre Grand Cru in CHAMBOLLE-MUSIGNY. Often the best, if
not the most powerful, of all red burgundies (and a little
white). Best growers: DE VOGÜÉ, DROUHIN, Jacques Prieur.

Nature   Natural or unprocessed, esp. of still champagne.

Néac   B'x. r. **
Village n. of POMEROL. Wines sold as LALANDE-DE-POMEROL.

Négociant-élèveur
Merchant who "brings up" (i.e. matures) the wine.

Nicolas, Ets.
Paris-based wholesale and retail wine merchants; one of the
biggest in France and one of the best.

Nuits-St-Georges   r. **→ *** **66 69 70 71 72 73 76 77** 78 **79** 80 82
Important wine-town: wines of all qualities, typically sturdy
and full-flavoured. Name can be shortened to "Nuits". Best
v'yds. incl. Les St-Georges, Vaucrains, Les Pruliers, Clos des
Corvées, Les Cailles, etc.

Ordinaire
Commonplace, everyday: not necessarily pejorative.

Ott, Domaine
Important producer of high-quality PROVENCE wines.

Pacherenc-du-Vic-Bilh   S.W. France w. sw. * NV
Rare minor speciality of the ARMAGNAC region.

Palette   Prov. r. p. or w. dr. **
Near Aix-en-Provence. Aromatic reds and good rosés.

Pasquier-Desvignes
Very old firm of Beaujolais merchants at St Lager, BROUILLY.

Passe-tout-grains
See Bourgogne Passe-tout-grains.

Patriarche
One of the bigger firms of burgundy merchants. Cellars in
Beaune; also owns Ch. de Meursault (100 acres), KRITER, etc.

Pauillac   B'x. r. **→ **** **66 67 70 71 73** 75 76 78 79 81 82
The only village in Bordeaux (HAUT-MÉDOC) with three first-
growths (Ch'x. LAFITE, LATOUR, MOUTON-ROTHSCHILD) and
many other fine ones, famous for high flavour and a scent of
cedarwood.

Pécharmant   Dordogne r. ★★ **78 79 80 81** 82
> Slightly better-than-typical light BERGERAC red.

Pelure d'oignon
> "Onion skin"—tawny tint of certain rosés.

Perlant or Perlé
> Very slightly sparkling.

Pernand-Vergelesses   B'y. r. or (w. dr.) ★★★ **71 76** 78 **79 80** 81 82
> Village next to ALOXE-CORTON containing part of the great CORTON and CORTON-CHARLEMAGNE v'yds. and one other top v'yd.: Ile des Vergelesses.

Perrier, Joseph   NV and **66 69 71 73** 75 76
> Family-run champagne house with considerable v'yds. at Chalon-s-Marne. Consistent light and fruity style.

Perrier-Jouet   NV, **69 71 73** 75 76 and rosé brut **73** 75
> Excellent champagne-growers and makers at Epernay. Luxury brands: Belle Epoque and Blason de France.

Pétillant
> Slightly spagkling.

Petit Chablis   B'y. w. dr. ★★ **81 82**
> Wine from fourth-rank CHABLIS v'yds. Lacks great character but can be good value.

Piat Père et Fils
> Important growers and merchants of Beaujolais and Mâcon wines at MÂCON, now controlled by Grand Metropolitan Ltd. V'yds. in MOULIN-À-VENT, also CLOS DE VOUGEOT. BEAUJOLAÏS and MÂCON-VIRÉ in special Piat bottles are good value.

Pic, Albert
> Well-reputed CHABLIS grower.

Picpoul-de-Pinet   Midi w. dr. ★ NV
> Rather dull very dry southern white.

Pineau de Charente
> Strong sweet apéritif made of white grape juice and Cognac.

Pinot   See Grapes for white wine

Piper-Heidsieck   NV, rosé **75** and **71 73 75** 76
> Champagne-makers of old repute at Reims. Luxury brand: Florens Louis. Also (NV) "Brut Sauvage".

Pol Roger   NV, rosé **71 73**, Blanc de Blancs **71 73** and **71 73 75** 76
> Excellent champagne house at Epernay. Particularly good non-vintage White Foil. Luxury cuvée: "P.R."

Pomerol   B'x. r. ★★→★★★★ **66 70 71 73** 75 **76 78 79** 81 82
> The next village to ST-EMILION: similar but more "fleshy" wines, maturing sooner, on the whole reliable and delicious. Top ch.: PETRUS.

Pommard   B'y. r. ★★★ **66 69 70 71 72 73 76** 78 79 80 82
> The biggest and best-known village ın Burgundy. No superlative wines, but many warmly appealing ones. Best v'yds.: Rugiens, EPENOTS and HOSPICES DE BEAUNE cuvées.

Pommery & Greno   NV, NV rosé and **69 71 73** 75 76
> Very big growers and merchants of champagne at Reims, recently revitalized by new owners.

Ponnelle, Pierre
> Well-established family wine-merchants of BEAUNE.

Pouilly-Fuissé   B'y. w. dr. ★★→★★★ **76 78 79 80 81** 82
> The best white of the MÂCON area. At its best (e.g. Ch. Fuissé) excellent, but often over-priced. Buy it domaine-bottled.

Pouilly-Fumé   Lo. w. dr. ★★→★★★ **81 82**
> Smoky-fragrant, fruity, often sharp pale white from the upper Loire, next to SANCERRE. Grapes must be SAUVIGNON BLANC. Good vintages improve for 2–3 yrs.

Pouilly-Loché   B'y. w. dr. ★★
> Neighbour of POUILLY-FUISSÉ. Similar wine but little of it.

Pouilly-Sur-Loire Lo. w. dr. ★ D.Y.A.
>   Inferior wine from the same v'yds. as POUILLY-FUMÉ, but different grapes (CHASSELAS).

Pouilly-Vinzelles B'y. w. dr. [★★]
>   Neighbour of POUILLY-FUISSÉ. Similar wine.

Pradel
>   Well-known brand of Provençal wines, esp. a dry rosé.

Preiss Zimmer, Jean
>   Old-established Alsace wine-merchants at Riquewihr.

Premières Côtes de Blaye B'x. r. w. dr. ★→★★ 75 78 79 81 82
>   Restricted appellation for better reds of BLAYE. Ch'x. include Barbé, Charron, Bourdieu, Perenne, Segonzac, Le Menaudat.

Premier Cru
>   First-growth in Bordeaux (see page 54), but the second rank of v'yds. (after Grand Cru) in Burgundy.

Premières Côtes de Bordeaux B'x. r. (p.) or w. dr. or sw. [★→★★]
>   Large area east of GRAVES: a good bet for quality and value, though never brilliant. Ch'x incl. Laffitte (sic).

"Noble rot" (in French pourriture noble, in German Edelfäule, in Latin Botrytis cinerea) is a form of mould that attacks the skins of ripe grapes in certain vineyards in warm and misty autumn weather.

Its effect, instead of rotting the grapes, is to wither them. The skin grows soft and flaccid, the juice evaporates through it, and what is left is a super-sweet concentration of everything in the grape except its water content.

The world's best sweet table wines are all made of nobly rotten grapes. They occur in good vintages in Sauternes, the Rhine, the Mosel (where wine made from them is called Trockenbeerenauslese), in Tokaji in Hungary, in Burgenland in Austria, and occasionally elsewhere—California included. The danger is rain on the pulpy grapes when they are already far gone in noble rot. All too often, particularly in Sauternes, the grower's hopes are dashed by a break in the weather.

Primeur
>   Early wine, like early vegetables; esp. of BEAUJOLAIS.

Prissé See Mâcon-Villages

Propriétaire-récoltant
>   Owner–manager.

Provence
>   See Côtes de Provence

Puisseguin-Saint-Emilion B'x. r. [★★]   75 78 79 81 82
>   Eastern neighbour of ST-EMILION; wines similar—not so fine but often good value. No famous ch'x. but a good co-operative.

Puligny-Montrachet B'y. w. dr. ★★★ 69 71 73 76 78 79 80 81 82
>   Bigger neighbour of CHASSAGNE-MONTRACHET with equally glorious rich dry whites. Best v'yds.: MONTRACHET, CHEVALIER-MONTRACHET, BÂTARD-MONTRACHET, Bienvenue-Bâtard-Montrachet, Les Combettes, Clavoillon, Pucelles, Champ-Canet, etc.

Quarts de Chaume Lo. w. sw. ★★★ 70 71 73 75 76 78 79 80 82
>   Famous 120-acre plot in COTEAUX DU LAYON, Anjou. CHENIN BLANC grapes. Long-lasting, intense, rich golden wine.

Quatourze Midi r. (p.) or w. dr. ★ 81 82
>   Minor VDQS area near Narbonne.

Quincy Lo. w. dr. ★★ 81 82
>   Small area making very dry SANCERRE-style wine of SAUVIGNON BLANC.

Ramonet-Prudhon

One of the leading proprietors in CHASSAGNE-MONTRACHET with 34 acres. Excellent whites, and red Clos St-Jean.

Rancio

Term for the tang of wood-aged fortified wine, esp. BANYULS and other VINS DOUX NATURELS. A fault in table wines.

Rasteau   Rh. (r. p. w. dr.) or br. sw. ★★ NV

Village of s. Rhône valley. Good strong sweet dessert wine is the local speciality.

Ratafia de Champagne

Sweet apéritif made in Champagne of ⅔ grape juice and ⅓ brandy.

Récolte   Crop or vintage.

Reine Pédauque, La

Burgundy growers and merchants at ALOXE-CORTON.

Remoissenet Père et Fils

Fine merchants with a tiny estate at BEAUNE.

Rémy Pannier

Important Loire-wine merchants at Saumur.

Reuilly   Lo. (r.p.) w. dr. ★★ 79 81 82

Neighbour of QUINCY with similar wine; also good PINOT GRIS.

Richebourg   B'y. r. ★★★★ 66 69 70 71 73 76 77 78 79 80 82

19-acre Grand Cru in VOSNE-ROMANÉE. Powerful, perfumed, fabulously expensive wine, among Burgundy's best.

Riesling

See Grapes for white wine

Rivesaltes   Midi r.w. dr. br. sw. ★★ NV

Fortified sweet wine, some muscat-flavoured, from e. Pyrenees. An ancient tradition still very much alive.

La Roche-aux-Moines   Lo. w. dr./sw. ★★★ 69 71 73 75 76 78 79 80 81 82

60-acre v'yd. in Savennières, Anjou. Intense strong fruity/sharp wine ages well.

Roederer, Louis   NV, rosé 75 and 69 70 71 73 74 75 77

One of the best champagne-growers and merchants at Reims. Excellent non-vintage wine. Luxury brand: Cristal Brut (in white glass bottles).

La Romanée   B'y. r. ★★★★ 66 69 70 71 72 73 76 77 78 79 80 82

2-acre Grand Cru in VOSNE-ROMANÉE just uphill from ROMANÉE-CONTI, owned by Bichot of BEAUNE.

Romanée-Conti   B'y. r. ★★★★ 66 71 72 73 76 77 78 79 80

4½-acre Grand Cru in VOSNE-ROMANÉE. The most celebrated and expensive red wine in the world, though seldom the best.

Romanée-Conti, Domaine de la

The grandest estate of Burgundy, owning the whole of ROMANÉE-CONTI and LA TÂCHE and major parts of RICHE-BOURG, GRANDS ECHÉZEAUX, ECHÉZEAUX and ROMANÉE-ST-VIVANT (under Marey-Monge label). Also a small part of Le MONTRACHET.

Romanée-St-Vivant   B'y. r. ★★★★ 71 72 73 76 77 78 79 80 82

23-acre Grand Cru in VOSNE-ROMANÉE. Similar to ROMANÉE-CONTI but usually lighter.

Ropiteau

Burgundy wine-growers and merchants at MEURSAULT controlled by CHANTOVENT. Specialists in Meursault and CÔTE DE BEAUNE wines.

Rosé d'Anjou   Lo. p. ★ D.Y.A.

Pale, slightly sweet, rosé. Cabernet d'Anjou is better.

Rosé de Loire   Lo. p. dr. ★→★★ D.Y.A.

Appellation for dry Loire rosé (Anjou is sweet).

Rosette   Dordogne w. s./sw./dr. ★★ D.Y.A.

Mild BERGERAC white.

Roty, Joseph
> Small grower of classic GEVREY-CHAMBERTIN.
Rousseau, Domaine A.
> Major burgundy grower famous for CHAMBERTIN, etc.
Roussette de Savoie   Savoie w. dr. ⭐⭐ D.Y.A.
> Pleasant light fresh white from s. of Geneva.
Roussillon
> See Côtes du Roussillon. "Grands Roussillon" are VINS DOUX
> NATURELS.
Ruchottes-Chambertin   B'y. r. ⭐⭐⭐ **69 70 71 72 73** 76 **77** 78 79 80 82
> 7½-acre Grand Cru neighbour of CHAMBERTIN. Similar splen-
> did long-lasting wine.
Ruinart Père et Fils   NV, rosé 71 and **71 73 75** 76
> The oldest champagne house, now belonging to Moët-
> Hennessy. Luxury brand: Dom Ruinart, Blanc de Blancs.
Rully   B'y. r. or w. dr. or (sp.) ⭐⭐ **78 79 80 81** 82(w.)
> Village of the CÔTE CHALONNAISE famous for sparkling bur-
> gundy. Still reds and white light but tasty and good value.
Sablant   Lo. w. dr. sp. ⭐⭐ NV
> Brand name for high-quality CRÉMANT DE LOIRE.
Saint-Amour   B'y. r. ⭐⭐ **81 82**
> Northernmost cru of BEAUJOLAIS: light, fruity, irresistible.
Saint-Aubin   B'y. (r.) or w. dr. ⭐⭐ **76 78 79 80 81** 82
> Little-known neighbour of CHASSAGNE-MONTRACHET, up a
> side-valley. Not top-rank, but typical and good value. Also
> sold as CÔTE-DE-BEAUNE-VILLAGES.
Saint Bris   B'y. w. dr. ⭐ D.Y.A.
> Village w. of CHABLIS known for its fruity ALIGOTÉ, making
> good sparkling burgundy, and hillside cherry orchards. See
> also Sauvignon-de-St-Bris.
Saint Chinian   Midi r. ⭐→⭐⭐ **76 78 79 80** 81 82
> Hilly area of growing reputation. Appellation Controlée since
> 1982. Tasty reds.
Sainte Croix-du-Mont   B'x. w. sw. ⭐⭐ **67 70 71 75 76 79 80** 81
> Neighbour to SAUTERNES with similar golden wine. No super-
> latives but well worth trying. Very reasonably priced.
Sainte-Foy-Bordeaux   B'x.
> Part of ENTRE-DEUX-MERS, more akin to BERGERAC.
Saint-Emilion   B'x. r. ⭐⭐→⭐⭐⭐⭐ **66 67 70 71 73 75 76 78 79** 81 82
> The biggest (13,000 acres) top-quality Bordeaux district;
> solid, rich, tasty wines from scores of ch'x., incl. CHEVAL-
> BLANC, AUSONE, CANON, MAGDELAINE, FIGEAC, etc.
Saint-Estèphe   B'x. r. ⭐⭐ →⭐⭐⭐⭐ **70 71 73** 75 **76 77** 78 79 80 81 82
> Northern village of HAUT-MÉDOC. Solid, satisfying, occasion-
> ally superlative wines. Top ch'x.: CALON-SÉGUR, COS D'ESTOUR-
> NEL, MONTROSE, etc., and many good CRUS BOURGEOIS.
St-Gall
> Brand-name used by the very good champagne-growers' Co-
> operative at AVIZE.
Saint-Georges-Saint-Emilion
> Part of MONTAGNE-ST-EMILION. Best ch.: ST-GEORGES.
Saint-Joseph   Rh. r. (p. or w. dr.) ⭐⭐ **71 72 73 76** 78 **79** 80
> Northern Rhône appellation of second rank but reason-
> able price. Substantial wine often better than CROZES-
> HERMITAGE.
Saint-Julien   B'x. r. ⭐⭐⭐→⭐⭐⭐⭐ **66 70 71 73 75 76** 78 **79 80** 81 82
> Mid-Médoc village with a dozen of Bordeaux's best ch'x., incl.
> three LÉOVILLES, BEYCHEVELLE, DUCRU-BEAUCAILLOU, GRUAUD-
> LAROSE, etc. The epitome of well-balanced red wine.
Saint-Laurent
> Village next to SAINT-JULIEN. Appellation Haut-Médoc.

Saint-Nicolas-de-Bourgueil   Lo. r. ** **71 76 78 79 80** 81 82
>   The next village to BOURGUEIL: the same light but lively and
>   fruity CABERNET red.

Saint-Péray   Rh. w. dr. or sp. ** NV
>   Rather heavy white from the n. Rhône, much of it made
>   sparkling. A curiosity.

Saint Pourçain   Central France r. p. or w. dr ⌞*⌝ D.Y.A.
>   The agreeable local wine of Vichy, becoming fashionable in
>   Paris. Made from GAMAY and/or PINOT NOIR, the white from
>   CHARDONNAY or SAUVIGNON BLANC.

Saint-Sauveur
>   HAUT-MÉDOC village just w. of PAUILLAC.

Saint-Seurin-de-Cadourne
>   HAUT-MÉDOC village just n. of SAINT-ESTÈPHE.

Saint-Véran   B'y. w. dr. ⌞**⌝ **78 79 80 81** 82
>   Next-door appellation to POUILLY-FUISSÉ. Similar but better
>   value: dry white of real character from the best slopes of
>   MÂCON-VILLAGES.

Salon   **61 64 66 69 71** 73
>   The original Blanc de Blancs champagne, from Le Mesnil.
>   Fine very dry wine with great keeping qualities.

Sancerre   Lo. (r. p.) or w. dr. *** **81 82**
>   Very fragrant and fresh SAUVIGNON white almost indistin-
>   guishable from POUILLY-FUMÉ, its neighbour over the Loire.
>   Drink young. Also light PINOT NOIR red and a little rosé, best
>   drunk very young.

Santenay   B'y. r. or (w. dr.) *** **66 69 70 71 72 73 76** 78 **79** 82
>   Very worthy, rarely rapturous, sturdy reds from the s. of the
>   CÔTE DE BEAUNE. Best v'yds.: Les Gravières, Clos de Tavan-
>   nes, La Comme.

Saumur   Lo. r. p. or w. dr. and sp. *→⌞**⌝
>   Big versatile district in ANJOU, with fresh fruity whites,
>   good-value champagne-method sparklers, pale rosés and in-
>   creasingly good CABERNET reds, the best from Saumur-
>   Champigny, esp. Ch. de Chaintres.

Sauternes   B'x. w. sw. ⌞**⌝ →**** **67 70 71** 75 **76 78 79** 80 81
>   District of 5 villages (incl. BARSAC) making France's best
>   sweet wine: strong (14%+ alcohol) luscious and golden, im-
>   proving with age. Top ch'x.: D'YQUEM, SUDUIRAUT, COUTET,
>   CLIMENS, GUIRAUD, etc. Also a few heavy dry wines which
>   cannot be sold as Sauternes.

Sauvignon Blanc
>   See Grapes for white wine

Sauvignon-de-St-Bris   B'y. w. dr. ⌞**⌝ D.Y.A.
>   A baby VDQS cousin of SANCERRE from near CHABLIS.

Sauzet, Etienne
>   Excellent white burgundy estate at PULIGNY-MONTRACHET.

Savennières   Lo. w. dr./sw. *** **69 70 71 73 75 76** 78 79 80 81 82
>   Small ANJOU district of pungent, traditionally long-lived
>   whites, incl. COULÉE DE SERRANT, LA ROCHE AUX MOINES, Clos
>   du Papillon. Recent wines show less character.

Savigny-lès-Beaune   B'y. r. or (w. dr.) ⌞***⌝ **71 76 77** 78 **79 80** 82
>   Important village next to BEAUNE, with similar well-balanced
>   middle-weight wines, often deliciously delicate and fruity.
>   Best   v'yds.:   Marconnets,   Dominode,   Serpentières,
>   Vergelesses, les Guettes.

Savoie   E. France r. or w. dr. or sp. ** D.Y.A.
>   Alpine area with light dry wines like some Swiss wine or
>   minor Loires. CRÉPY and SEYSSEL are best known whites. Also
>   MONDEUSE red.

Schlumberger et Cie
>   Excellent Alsace growers and merchants at Guebwiller.

Schröder & Schyler
>
> Old family firm of Bordeaux merchants, owners of CH. KIRWAN.

Sec Literally means dry, though champagne so-called is medium-sweet.

Selection de Grains Nobles
>
> Description coined by HUGEL for Alsace equivalent to German BEERENAUSLESE. "Grains nobles" are individual grapes with "noble rot" (see page 47).

Sèvre-et-Maine
>
> The *département* containing the central and best v'yds. of MUSCADET.

Seyssel Savoie w. dr. or sp. ⬚ ** NV
>
> Delicate pale dry white making admirable sparkling wine.

Sichel & Co.
>
> Famous Bordeaux (and Burgundy and Germany) merchants, owners of CH. D'ANGLUDET and part-owners of CH. PALMER.

Soussans
>
> Village just n. of MARGAUX, sharing its appellation.

Sylvaner
>
> See Grapes for white wine

Syrah See Grapes for red wine

La Tâche B'y. r. **** **62 69 70 71 72 73 74** 76 **77** 78 79 80
>
> 15-acre Grand Cru of VOSNE-ROMANÉE and one of the best v'yds. on earth: dark, perfumed and luxurious wine. Owned by the DOMAINE DE LA ROMANÉE-CONTI.

Taittinger NV and **69 70 71 73 76**
>
> Fashionable champagne growers and merchants of Reims. Luxury brand: Comtes de Champagne **75** (also rosé **75**).

Tastevin, Confrèrie du
>
> Burgundy's colourful and successful promotion society. Wine carrying their Tastevinage label has been approved by them and will usually be good. A tastevin is the traditional shallow silver wine-tasting cup of Burgundy. See panel, page 33.

Tavel Rh. p. *** D.Y.A.
>
> France's most famous rosé, strong and dry, starting vivid pink and fading to orange. Avoid orange bottles.

Tête de Cuvée
>
> Term vaguely used of the best wines of an appellation.

Thevenet, Jean
>
> A master maker of white Mâcon-Clessé at Quintaine-Clessé, near LUGNY.

Thévenin, Roland
>
> Burgundy shipper and owner of the Ch. de PULIGNY-MONTRACHET.

Thorin, J.
>
> Fine grower and major merchant of BEAUJOLAIS, at Pontanevaux, owner of the Château des Jacques, Moulin à Vent.

Tokay d'Alsace
>
> See Pinot Gris under Grapes for white wine

Tollot-Beaut
>
> Excellent burgundy grower with some 50 acres in the CÔTE DE BEAUNE, incl. CORTON, BEAUNE, Grèves, SAVIGNY (Les Champs Chevrey) and at Chorey-lès-Beaune where he is based.

Touraine Lo. r. p. w. dr./sw./sp. ⬚ *→ ***
>
> Big mid-Loire province with immense range of wines, incl. dry white SAUVIGNON, dry and sweet CHENIN BLANC (e.g. Vouvray), red CHINON and BOURGUEIL, light red CABERNETS, GAMAYS and rosés. Cabernets, Sauvignons and Gamays of good years are bargains.

Trimbach, F. E.
Distinguished ALSACE grower and merchant at Ribeauvillé. Best wines incl. Riesling Clos Ste. Hune mature magnificently.

Vacqueyras   Rh. r.   ⟦ ** ⟧   76 78 79 80 81
Up-and-coming village of s. CÔTES-DU-RHÔNE, neighbour to GIGONDAS; comparable with CHÂTEAUNEUF-DU-PAPE but less heavy and more "elegant".

Valençay   Lo. w. dr. ⋆ D.Y.A.
Neighbour of CHEVERNY: similar pleasant sharpish wine.

Varichon & Clerc
Principal makers and shippers of SAVOIE sparkling wines.

Varoilles, Domaine des
Excellent burgundy estate of 25 acres, principally in GEVREY-CHAMBERTIN.

Vaudésir   B'y. w. dr.   ⟦ **** ⟧   71 75 76 77 78 79 80 81 82
Arguably the best of the 7 Grands Crus of CHABLIS (but then so are the others).

VDQS   Vin Délimité de Qualité Supérieure (see p. 23).

Vendange
Vintage.

Vendange tardive
Late vintage. In ALSACE equivalent to German AUSLESE.

Veuve Clicquot   NV and 69 70 73 75 76 78
Historic champagne house of the highest standing. Cellars at Reims. Luxury brand: La Grande Dame.

Vidal-Fleury, J.
Long-established shippers and growers of top Rhône wines.

Vieilles Vignes
"Old vines" – therefore the best wine. Used for such wine by BOLLINGER and DE VOGÜÉ.

Viénot, Charles
Grower and merchant of good burgundy, at NUITS-ST-GEORGES. 70 acres in Nuits, CORTON, RICHEBOURG, etc., recently bought by BOISSET.

Vignoble
Area of vineyards.

Vin de garde
Wine that will improve with keeping.

Vin de l'année
This year's wine. See Beaujolais.

Vin de paille
Wine from grapes dried on straw mats, consequently very sweet, like Italian passito. Especially in the JURA.

Vin de Pays
The junior rank of country wines (see Introduction).

Vin de Table
Standard everyday table wine, not subject to particular regulations about grapes and origin.

Vin Doux Naturel ("VDN")
Sweet wine fortified with alcohol, so scarcely "natural". Common in ROUSSILLON. A vin doux liquoreux is several degrees stronger.

Vin Gris
"Grey" wine is very pale pink, made of red grapes pressed before fermentation begins, unlike rosé, which ferments briefly before pressing.

Vin Jaune   Jura w. dr. ⋆⋆⋆
Speciality of ARBOIS: odd yellow wine like fino sherry. Ready when bottled.

Vin nouveau
See Beaujolais Nouveau

Vin vert
>A very light, acidic, refreshing white wine, a speciality of ROUSSILLON.

Vinsobres   Rh. r. (p. or w. dr.)   ★★   **76 78 79** 80 **81**
>Contradictory name of good s. Rhône village. Strong substantial reds which mature well.

Viré   B'y. w. dr.   ★★   **78 79 80 81** 82
>One of the best white-wine villages of Mâcon. Good co-op and excellent Ch. de Viré.

Visan   Rh. r. p. or w. dr. ★★ **76 78 79** 80 **81**
>One of the better s. Rhône villages. Reds better than white.

Viticulteur
>Wine-grower.

Vogüé, Comte Georges de
>First-class 30-acre burgundy domaine at CHAMBOLLE-MUSIGNY. The ultimate MUSIGNY and BONNES MARES.

As a simple rule of thumb one vine gives one bottle of top-class table wine. A Bordeaux vineyard is normally planted with 5,269 vines per hectare (2,133 per acre) and produces 4,000 litres (5,333 bottles). 10 per cent of the wine is lost in ageing, so the final figure is 4,800 or 400 dozen. The equivalent in tons of grapes per acre is about 2¼ tons, yielding about 1,942 (162 dozen) finished bottles.

In bulk-wine areas and in Germany, where productivity is often very high, the yield may reach over 10,000 litres (100 hectolitres) per hectare, or six tons per acre. On the other hand, Château Yquem, which uses only grapes dehydrated by noble rot (p47), produces only about 900 litres per hectare, or 486 bottles per acre.

Volnay   B'y. r. ★★★ **66 69 71 72 76** 78 **79 80** 82
>Village between POMMARD and MEURSAULT: the best reds of the CÔTE DE BEAUNE, not strong or heavy but fragrant and silky. Best v'yds.: Caillerets, Clos des Ducs, Champans, Clos des Chênes, etc.

Volnay-Santenots   B'y. r. ★★★
>Excellent red wine from MEURSAULT is sold under this name. Indistinguishable from VOLNAY.

Vosne-Romanée   B'y. r. ★★★→★★★★ **69 70 71 72 73** 76 **77** 78 **79** 80 82
>The village containing Burgundy's grandest Crus (ROMANÉE-CONTI, LA TÂCHE, etc.). There are (or rather should be) no common wines in Vosne.

Vougeot
>See Clos de Vougeot

Vouvray   Lo. w. dr./sw./sp. ★★→★★★★ **69 70 71 73 75 76** 78 **79 80** 82
>Small district of TOURAINE with very variable wines, at their best intensely sweet and almost immortal. Good dry sparkling.

"Y" (Pronounced ygrec)
>Brand name of powerful dry wine of great character, occasionally made at CH. D'YQUEM.

Ziltener, André
>Swiss-owned merchants at GEVREY-CHAMBERTIN.

Châteaux of Bordeaux

Some 300 of the best-known châteaux of Bordeaux are listed below in alphabetical order.

The vintage information for each château was entirely revised for the 1982 edition in consultation with the château-proprietors as well as the many friends who have contributed their notes, as in previous editions, to supplement my own.

The vintages marked with an accent "'" are those by which the owner would wish his château to be judged. Whether they are mature yet or will improve with keeping is indicated, as elsewhere in the book, by the style of type.

As in previous editions, but to a much lesser extent, the information is necessarily incomplete, and, since no one person has ever tasted all these wines, it cannot be taken as guaranteed. It does, however, go very much further in guiding you through the complexities of Bordeaux than any previous publication.

Information on the wines of 1980 was incomplete at the time of going to press; only those châteaux already known to have made an outstanding wine in a generally pleasant but not remarkable vintage have been noted. This does *not* mean that others are not worth buying with reasonable expectations. Details of the '80s and the very good 1981 vintage will be published in the next edition. General information on the style of each vintage will be found on the vintage charts on pages 24 and 25. Further details about each village or appellation will be found among the general French entries.

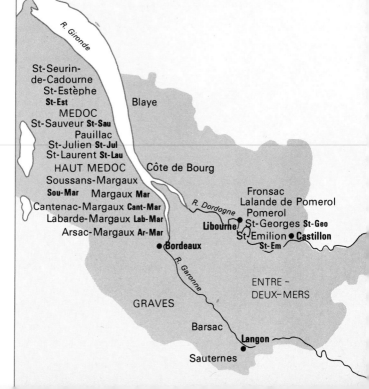

d'Agassac   Ludon, Haut-Médoc r.   ⟦ ** ⟧   75′ 76 78 79 80 81
14th-century moated fort with 86 acres. Same owners as Ch'x
CALON-SÉGUR and DU TERTRE and a growing reputation.

L'Angélus   St-Em. r. ** **66 70′ 75′ 76 78** 79′ 80 81
Well-situated classed-growth of 60 acres on the St-Emilion
Côtes w. of the town. Recent vintages have not been exciting.

d'Angludet   Cant-Mar. r.   ⟦ ** ⟧   **66** 70′ **73 74 76**′ 78′ 79 80 81
72-acre British-owned Cru Exceptionnel of classed-growth
quality.

D'Arche   Sauternes w. sw. ** **69 70 71 73** 78 79
Substantial second-rank classed-growth of 88 acres. Ch.
d'Arche-Lafaurie is its lesser wine.

Ausone   St-Em. r. **** **67 70 71**′ 75′ 76′ 78 79 80 81′
Celebrated first-growth with 17 acres in a commanding position on the Côtes and famous rock-hewn cellars under the
v'yd. Off form in the sixties but first class since 1970.

Bahans-Haut-Brion   Gr. r. *** N.V.
The second-quality wine of Ch. HAUT-BRION.

Balestard-la-Tonnelle   St-Em. r. ** **66 67 70**′ **71** 75′ **76**′ 78 79 81
Historic 21-acre classed-growth on the plateau near the
town. Mentioned by the 15c poet Villon and still in the
same family (which also owns Ch. Cap-de Mourlin).

de Barbe   Côtes de Bourg r. (w.)   ⟦ ** ⟧   **70**′ **71 73** 75′ **76** 78 79′ 81
The biggest (148 acres) and best-known ch. of the right bank
of the Gironde. Good full-bodied largely Merlot red.

Baret   Graves r. and w. dr. ** **75 76 77**w. 78 81w.
Little estate of good quality, better known for its white wine.

Batailley   Pauillac r. *** **61 64 66 70 71 73** 75′ **76 77** 78′ 79′ 80 81
The bigger of the famous pair of fifth-growths (with HAUT-
BATAILLEY) on the borders of Pauillac and St-Julien. 110
acres. Firm strong-flavoured wine. Sold by Borie-Manoux.

Beaumont   Cussac, Haut-Médoc r. ** 75 **76** 78′ 79 80 81
Considerable Cru Bourgeois, well-known in France for full-
bodied, consistent wines. In new hands since '79. Second label:
Ch. Moulin d'Arvigny.

Beauregard   Pomerol r.   ⟦ *** ⟧   **70 71** 75′ **76 77** 78′ 79 80 81
32-acre v'yd. with pretty 17th-century ch. near LA
CONSEILLANTE. Well-made delicate "round" wines.

Beau Séjour-Bécot   St-Em. r. *** **70 71 73** 75′ 76′ **78** 79 **80** 81
Half of the famous old Beau Séjour estate on the w. slope of
the Côtes. 16 acres. Dynamic management welcomes visitors.
The Bécots also own CH. GRAND PONTET.

Beauséjour-Duffau-Lagarosse   St-Em. r. *** **70 71** 75 76 78 79 80
81
The other half of the above, in old family hands and making
traditional wine for long maturing.

Beau Site   St-Est. r. ** **70**′ **71** 75′ **76** 78′ **79** 80 81
55-acre Cru Bourgeois in same hands as Ch'x BATAILLEY,
TROTTEVILLE, etc. Regular quality.

Belair   St-Em. r.   ⟦ *** ⟧   **70 71** 75′ 76′ **78** 79′ 80 81
Sister-ch. and neighbour of AUSONE with 28 acres on the
Côtes. Steady improvement in recent vintages.

de Bel-Air   Lalande de Pomerol r.   ⟦ ** ⟧   **70 71**′ **73 75**′ **76**′ **78** 79 80 81
The best-known estate of this village just n. of Pomerol, with
very similar wine. 25 acres.

Bel-Air-Marquis d'Aligre   Sou-Mar. r. ** **70**′ **71** 75′ 76 78′ 79 81
Reliable Cru Exceptionnel with 42 acres of old vines.

Belgrave   St-Lau. r. **
Obscure fifth-growth in St-Julien's back-country. 107 acres.
Recently acquired by DOURTHE. To watch.

Bellevue   St-Em. r. **
Well-known little classed-growth on the w. Côtes.

Bel-Orme-Tronquoy-de-Lalande St-Seurin-de-Cadourne (Haut-Médoc) r. ****** **70′ 71** 75′ 76 78′ 79′
    Reputable 60-acre Cru Bourgeois n. of St-Estèphe. Old v'yd. producing tannic wines. Same owner as Ch. RAUZAN-GASSIES.

Beychevelle St-Jul. r. ***** 61 66 70′ 71 74** 75′ **76 79** 80 81
    170-acre fourth-growth with the Médoc's finest mansion. Wine of more elegance than power, recently disappointing.

Le Bourdieu Vertheuil (Haut-Médoc) r. **** 70 71** 75′ **76** 78′ 79 80 81
    Cru Bourgeois with sister ch. Victoria (134 acres in all) known for St-Estèphe-style wines.

Bourgneuf-Vayron Pomerol r. ****** 75′ **76** 78 79 **80** 81
    21-acre v'yd. on clay soil making good rather heavy wines.

Bouscaut Graves r. w. dr. ******* 70′ **73 74** 75′ **76** 78′ 79
    Neglected classed-growth at Cadaujac brought back to life by American enthusiasts since 1969. Bought in 1980 by Lucien Lurton, owner of Ch. BRANE-CANTENAC, etc. 75 acres red (largely Merlot); 15 acres white (D.Y.A.).

du Bousquet Côte de Bourg r. ******   **75′ 76 78 79** 81
    Reliable estate with 148 acres making attractive solid wine.

Boyd-Cantenac Margaux r. ***** 66 70′ 71 74** 75′ **76′** 78 79 80 81
    44-acre third-growth regularly producing attractive wine; tending to improve. See also Ch. POUGET.

Branaire-Ducru St-Jul. r. *******   **66 70′ 71 74** 75′ **76** 78 79′ 80 81
    Fourth-growth of 118 acres producing notably spicy and flavoury wine: attractive and reliable.

Brane-Cantenac Cant-Mar. r. *******   **66 71** 75′ 76′ 78′ 79 80 81
    Big (211 acres) well-run second-growth. Round, smooth and (at their best) delightful wines. Same owners as Chx. DURFORT-VIVENS, VILLEGEORGE, CLIMENS, BOUSCAUT, etc.

du Breuil Cissac, Haut-Médoc r. **** 70′ 71′ 73** 75′ **76 77** 78′ 79 81
    57-acre v'yd. with a 10th-century castle producing full-bodied stylish wine, generally ageing well. Also nuts and melons.

Brillette Moulis, Haut-Médoc r. ****** 75 76 78 79 80 81′
    70-acre v'yd. whose pebbly soil is said to "shine" – hence the name. Reliable rather country-style wine, improving.

A Bordeaux label

CHATEAU GISCOURS
GRAND CRU CLASSE

APPELLATION MARGAUX
CONTROLEE

MIS EN BOUTEILLES AU
CHATEAU

1 A château is an estate, not necessarily with a mansion or a big expanse of v'yd.
2 Reference to the local classification. It varies from one part of Bordeaux to another.
3 The Appellation Controlée: look up Margaux in the France A–Z.
4 "Bottled at the château" — becoming the normal practice with classed-growth wines.

La Cabanne Pomerol r. *******   **70′ 71 73** 75′ **76** 78 79 81
    Highly-regarded 22-acre property near the great Ch. TROTANOY.

Cadet Piola St-Em. r. ******   **70′ 71 73** 75′ **76** 78 79 80 81
    Reliable little property (17 acres) on the plateau just n. of the town of St-Emilion. Ch. Faurie de Souchard has the same enthusiastic owner; slightly less fine wine.

Calon-Ségur St-Est. r. *******   **61 66 70 71 73** 75 76 **77** 78′ 79 80 81
    Big (123-acre) third-growth of great reputation. Often the best St-Estèphe but has had off-moments. Recent vintages confirm a return to top form.

Camensac   St-Lau. r.   ★★   **66 70**′ **71 74 75**′ **76** 78′ 79 80 81
Re-emerging 149-acre fifth-growth, replanted in the '60s
with new equipment and the same expert direction as LAROSE-
TRINTAUDON. Fine vigorous full-bodied wines.

Canon   St-Em. r.   ★★★   **66 70 71** 75′ **76** 78′ 79′ 80 81
Famous first-classed-growth with 44+ acres on the plateau
w. of the town. Conservative methods; impressive wine.

Canon-la-Gaffelière   St-Em. r.   ★★   **70 71 75 76 77** 78 79 81
45-acre classed-growth on the lower slopes of the Côtes.

Cantemerle   Macau r. ★★★ **61 64 66** 70′ **71 73 74** 75′ **76** 78′ 79 81
Superb estate at the extreme s. of the Médoc, with a romantic
ch. in a wood and 50 acres of vines. Officially fifth-growth: in
practice nearer second-growth. Traditional methods make
longlasting, richly subtle wine. Bought by CORDIER in 1981.

Cantenac-Brown   Cant-Mar. r. ★★★ **61 66 70 71 73** 75 76 78 79 81
Formerly old-fashioned 77-acre third-growth but not among
the exciting Margaux. Big wines.

Capbern-Gasqueton   St-Est. r. ★★
85-acre Cru Bourgeois; same owner as Ch. CALON-SÉGUR.

Cap de Mourlin   St-Em. r. ★★★ **70**′ **71** 75′ **78 79**′
Well-known 63-acre property shared in 2 parts by the Cap de
Mourlin family, owners of CH. BALESTARD.

Carbonnieux   Graves r. and w. dr. ★★★ **70** 75′ **76** 78′ 79 **80**w. 81
Historic estate at Léognan making good fairly light wines by
modern methods. The white is much the better, drunk young.

La Cardonne   Blaignan (Médoc) r. ★★ 78 **79** 80 81
Large (156 acres) Cru Bourgeois in the n. Médoc recently
bought by the Rothschilds of Ch. LAFITE.

Les Carmes-Haut-Brion   Graves r.   ★★   **75 76** 78 79 81
Small neighbour of HAUT-BRION with good bourgeois standards, distributed by Chantecaille.

Caronne-Ste-Gemme   St-Lau. (Haut-Médoc) r. ★★ **70** 75′ **76 77** 78
79 80 81
Substantial Cru Bourgeois of 100 acres. Steady quality.

du Castéra   Médoc r.   ★★   **70 75 76** 78 79 81
Beautiful property at St-Germain in the n. Médoc. Sturdy,
longlasting wine.

Certan de May   Pomerol r.   ★★   **70 71 73** 75′ **76** 78 79 81
Neighbour of VIEUX-CHÂTEAU-CERTAN. Tiny property with
full-bodied tannic wine, needing time to mature.

Certan-Giraud   Pomerol r. ★★★ **71 73** 75 **76 78** 79 81
Small (17-acre) property next to the great Ch. PETRUS.

Chasse-Spleen   Moulis r.   ★★★   **70**′ **71 74** 75′ **76 77** 78′ **79** 80 81
127-acre Cru Exceptionnel of classed-growth quality. Con-
sistently good, sometimes outstanding, long-maturing wine.

Cheval Blanc   St-Em. r. ★★★★ **61 66 70**′ **71**′ **74** 75′ **76** 78 79 80 81
By reputation the best wine of St-Em. rich, full-blooded, from
an old family estate of 86 acres on the border of Pomerol.

Cissac   Cissac r.   ★★   **66 70**′ **71** 72 74 75′ **76 77** 78′ 79 80 81
A pillar of the bourgeoisie. 80-acre Grand Bourgeois Exceptionnel with a steady record for splendid wine.

Citran   Avensan, Haut-Médoc r. ★★ **70**′ **75 76** 78′ **79** 81
Grand Bourgeois Exceptionnel of 178 acres. Rich, tasty wine.

Clarke Listrac, Haut-Médoc r.   ★★   78 79 80 81
Big (185-acre) Cru Bourgeois replanted by a (LAFITE)
Rothschild. Ch'x. Malmaison and Peyrelebade are second
labels.

Clerc-Milon   Pauillac r. ★★★ **70**′ **71 73 74** 75′ **76** 78′ 79 80 81
Forgotten little fifth-growth bought by Baron Philippe de
Rothschild in 1970. Now 68 acres make first-rate wine.

Climens   Sauternes w. sw.   `***`   67 70 71′ 73 75′ 76′ 78′ 79 80 81
Famous 74-acre classed-growth at Barsac making some of the best and richest sweet wine in the world. Same owner as Ch. BRANE-CANTENAC, etc.

Clinet   Pomerol r. `**` 70 71 75′ 76 78 79 80 81
15-acre property in central Pomerol making tannic "Pauillac-style" wine.

Clos l'Eglise   Pomerol r.   `***`   71 73 75 76 78 79 80 81
14-acre v'yd in one of the best sites in Pomerol. Excellent wine. The same family owns CH. PLINCE.

Clos Fourtet   St-Em. r.   `***`   67 70 73 75 76 78 79 80 81
Well-known 42-acre first-growth on the plateau with cellars almost in the town. Back on form after a middling patch. Same owner as CLIMENS, etc.

Clos des Jacobins   St-Em. r. `**` 75′ 76 78 79 80 81
Well-known and well-run little (18-acre) classed-growth owned by the shipper CORDIER. Matures rather quickly.

Clos René   Pomerol r.   `***`   61 66 67 70 71′ 73 75 78 79 80 81
Leading ch. on the w. of Pomerol. 38 acres making powerful wine; eventually delicate. Also sold as ch. Moulinet-Lasserre.

La Clotte   St-Em. r.   `**`   66 70 71′ 75′ 76′ 78 79 81
Côtes classed-growth with attractive "supple" wine.

La Conseillante   Pomerol r. `***` 70′ 71′ 75′ 76 78 79 80 81
29-acre classed-growth on the plateau between PETRUS and CHEVAL BLANC. Some of the most fragrant Pomerol, worthy of its superb position.

Corbin   St-Em. r. `**`
28-acre classed-growth in n. St-Emilion where a cluster of Corbins occupy the edge of the plateau.

Corbin-Michotte   St-Em. r.   `**`   66 70 71 73 75 76 78 79 81
Well-run small property making attractive and reliable wine.

Cos-d'Estournel   St-Est. r.   `***`   61 64 66 70 71 73 74 75′ 76′ 78′ 79 80 81
140-acre second-growth with eccentric chinoiserie building overlooking Ch. LAFITE. Usually full-flavoured, often magnificent, wine. Now regularly one of the best in the Médoc.

Cos Labory   St-Est. r. `**` 70′ 75′ 76 78′ 79′ 80 81′
Little-known fifth-growth neighbour of COS D'ESTOURNEL with 37 acres. Blunt fruity wines mature early.

Coufran   St-Seurin-de-Cadourne (Haut-Médoc) r.   `**`   70′ 73 74 76′ 78′ 79 80 81
Coufran and Ch. Verdignan, on the northern-most hillock of the Haut-Médoc, are under the same ownership. Coufran has mainly Merlot vines; rich soft wine. 148 acres.

Couhins   Graves (r.) w. dr.   `**`   78 79 80 81
17-acre v'yd. at Villenave-d'Ornon run by the State. Fine white for drinking young.

La Couronne   Pauillac r.   `**`   67 70 73 75 76 78 79
Excellent small Cru Exceptionnel made at Ch. HAUT-BATAILLEY.

Coutet   Sauternes w. sw.   `***`   62 67 70′ 71′ 73 75′ 76 78 79 80 81
Rival to Ch. CLIMENS; 91 acres in Barsac. Said to be slightly less rich but certainly equally fine. "Cuvée Madame" is a selection of the very best (71 75 76).

Couvent des Jacobins   St-Em. r. `**`
Well-known vineyard of 17 acres adjacent to the town of St-Emilion on the east.

Le Crock   St-Est. r. `**`
Well-situated Cru Bourgeois of 74 acres in the same family as Ch. LÉOVILLE-POYFERRÉ.

La Croix   Pomerol r. ★★ **70′ 71′ 73** 75′ **76** 78 79 81
> Well-reputed little property of 32 acres. Old-fashioned tough wine; matures well.

La Croix de Gay   Pomerol r. ★★★ **70′ 71′** 75′ **76** 78 79 80 81
> 28 acres in the best part of the commune. Recently on fine form.

Croizet-Bages   Pauillac r. ★★   **61 66 70′ 71 73** 75′ **76** 78′ **79′** 80 81
> 52-acre fifth-growth (lacking a ch.) with the same owners as Ch. RAUZAN-GASSIES. Sound sturdy wines with growing finesse.

Croque-Michotte   St-Em. r.★★ **66 70 75 76 78** 79 81
> 30-acre Pomerol-style classed-growth on the Pomerol border.

Curé-Bon-la-Madeleine   St-Em. r. ★★★ **66 70′ 71′** 75 76′ **78** 79 80 81
> Small (11-acre) property among the best of the Côtes; between AUSONE and CANON. Managed by MOUEIX.

Dauzac   Lab-Mar. r. ★★ **66 70 73** 75 **76** 78 79
> Substantial but somewhat neglected fifth-growth near the river s. of Margaux. In new hands since '79. 75+ acres.

Desmirail   Mar. r. ★★
> Third-growth now 27 acres recently revived by the owner of BRANE-CANTENAC.

Why do the Châteaux of Bordeaux have such a large section of this book devoted to them? The reason is simple: collectively they form by far the largest supply of high-quality wine on earth.

A single typical Médoc château with 150 acres (some have far more) makes approximately 26,000 dozen bottles of identifiable wine a year — the production of two or three Californian "boutique" wineries. The tendency over the last two decades has been for the better-known châteaux to buy more land. Many classed-growths have expanded by as much as 10 times since they were classified in 1855.

Dillon   Haut-Médoc r. ★★   **70 73** 75′ **77** 78′ **79′** 81
> Often very well-made wine. Run by local wine college of Blanquefort, just n. of Bordeaux. 73 acres.

Doisy-Daëne   Barsac w. sw. and dr. ★★★   **71′ 75 76′** 78 79 80 81
> Forward-looking 34-acre estate making crisp dry white (incl. Riesling grapes) as well as traditional sweet Barsac.

Doisy-Dubroca   Barsac w. sw. ★★   **71′ 73** 75′ **76** 78′ 79 80 81
> Tiny (8½-acre) Barsac classed-growth allied to Ch. CLIMENS.

Doisy-Védrines   Sauternes w. sw. ★★★   **70′ 71** 75′ **76′** 78 79 80 81
> 50-acre classed-growth at Barsac, near CLIMENS and COUTET and generally in the same high class.

Domaine de Chevalier   Graves r. and w. dr. ★★★★ **61 64 66 67 70′ 71 72 73** 74 75′ **76** 77 78′ **79′** 80 81′
> Superb small estate of 36 acres at Léognan. The red is stern at first, richly subtle with age. The white is delicate but matures to rich flavours. (w. **70 71** 75 **76** 78 79 81)

Domaine de l'Eglise   Pomerol r. ★★ **66 67 70 71** 75′ **76** 78 79′ 81
> Small property: good wine distributed by BORIE-MANOUX.

La Dominique   St-Em. r. ★★★   **70 71 73** 75 **76 78** 79 81
> Fine 40-acre classed-growth next door to Ch. CHEVAL BLANC.

Ducru-Beaucaillou   St-Jul. r. ★★★   **61 62 64 66 67 70′ 71 74** 75′ **76 77** 78′ **79** 80 81
> Outstanding second-growth; 110 acres overlooking the river. The owner, M. Borie, makes classical "cedar-pencil" claret.

Duhart-Milon-Rothschild   Pauillac r. ★★★ **66 70′ 71 73 75′ 76′** 77 78 79′ 80 81
> Fourth-growth neighbour of LAFITE under the same management. Maturing young wines show fine quality. 100 acres.

Durfort-Vivens Margaux r. ⎡★★★⎤ **66 70 71 73** 75' **76** 78' 79' 80 81
Relatively small (49-acre) second-growth owned by M. Lurton of BRANE-CANTENAC. Fine if rather harder wine.

Dutruch-Grand-Poujeaux Moulis r. ⎡★★⎤ **70 71 73**' 75 76 78' 79
Rising star of Moulis, making typically hard tannic wines.

L'Eglise-Clinet Pomerol r. ★★★ **66 70 71 74** 75 **76** 78 79
Highly ranked; full, fleshy wine. Changed hands in '82.

L'Enclos Pomerol r. ⎡★★★⎤ **64 67 70 71 73 74** 75 **76** 78 79 80 81
Respected little property on the w. side of Pomerol, near CLOS-RENÉ. Big, well-made, long-flavoured wine.

L'Evangile Pomerol r. ⎡★★★⎤ **66 67 70**' **71**' **73 74** 75' **76** 78 79 80 81
33 acres between PETRUS and CHEVAL BLANC. Impressive wines. In the same area and class as LA CONSEILLANTE.

Fargues Sauternes w. sw. ⎡★★⎤ **70**' **71**' **73** 75' **76**' **77** 78 79 80 81
25-acre v'yd. in same ownership as Ch. YQUEM. Fruity and good but much lighter wines.

Ferrière Margaux r. ★★ **66 70** 75 78 79 81
Little-known third-growth of only 10+ acres. The wine is made at Ch. LASCOMBES and sold to a chain of French hotels.

Feytit-Clinet Pomerol r. ★★ **64 70**' **71**' 75' 76 **78** 79 80 81
Little property next to LATOUR-POMEROL. Has made some fine big strong wines. Managed by J-P MOUEIX.

Fieuzal Graves r. and (w. dr.) ⎡★★★⎤ **64 66 70**' **73** 75' 76 78' 79 80 81
42-acre classed-growth at Léognan. Changed hands in peak condition in 1973; now making some of the best GRAVES.

Figeac St-Em. r. ⎡★★★⎤ **61 70**' **71 73 74** 75' **76** 78 79 80 81
Famous first-growth neighbour of CHEVAL BLANC. Superb 85-acre v'yd. gives one of Bordeaux's most attractive full-bodied wines maturing fairly quickly.

Filhot Sauternes w. sw. and dr. ⎡★★★⎤ **67 70 71**' 75 **76**' 78 79' 80 81
Second-rank classed-growth with splendid ch., 148-acre v'yd. Very good sweet wines, a little dry and red.

La Fleur St-Em. r. ★★ **70 73** 75 76 78 79 80 81
Very small but well-regarded Côtes estate.

La Fleur-Petrus Pomerol r. ⎡★★★⎤ **66 67 70 71**' **73** 75' **76**' 78 79 80 81
18-acre v'yd. flanking PETRUS and under the same MOUEIX management. Very fine rich plummy wines.

Fombrauge St-Em. r. ⎡★★⎤ **70**' **71** 75' **76 77 78**' 79 80 81
Major property of St-Christophe-des-Bardes, e. of St-Emilion with 103 acres. Reliable St-Emilion making great efforts.

Fonbadet Pauillac r. ★★ **70** 75 78 79 81
Well-known Cru Bourgeois with 38 acres next door to Ch. PONTET-CANET. The Peyronies own several small Pauillac crus.

Fonpiqueyre See Ch. Liversan.

Fonplégade St-Em. r. ★★ **71 73** 75 **76 78** 79 80 81
42-acre v'yd. on the Côtes w. of St. Emilion in another branch of the MOUEIX family.

Fonréaud Listrac r. ★★ **70**' **71** 75' **76 77** 78' 79 80 81
One of the bigger (96 acres) and better Crus Bourgeois of its area, selling mainly in France and at the door.

Fonroque St-Em. r. ★★★ **66 67 70 71**' **73** 75' **76**' **78** 79 80 81
42 acres on the plateau n. of St-Emilion, MOUEIX property. Big dark wine.

Les Forts de Latour Pauillac r. ★★★ **66 67 70 71 72 73** 74 75
The second wine of Ch. Latour; well worthy of its big brother. Unique in being bottle-aged at least three years before release. Fetches the price of a second-growth Château.

Fourcas-Dupré Listrac r. ★★ **70**' **71** 75 76 78' 79 80 81
A top-class 100-acre Cru Bourgeois making consistent and elegant wine. To follow.

Fourcas-Hosten Listrac r. ** 66 70 71 73' 75 76 77 78' 79 80 81
Reliable 96-acre Cru Bourgeois of the central Médoc.
Changed hands in '79. Rather hard wine is typical of Listrac.

Franc-Mayne St-Em. r. ** 70 71 73 75 76 78 79 80
Small well-regarded v'yd. on the Côtes w. of St-Emilion.

La Gaffelière St-Em. r. *** 61 66 67 70 71 75' 76 78 79 81
Excellent though not always reliable 40-acre first-growth at
the foot of the Côtes below Ch. BEL-AIR.

La Garde Graves r. (w. dr.) ** 70' 71 74 75' 76' 78 79 80 81
Substantial ESCHENAUER property making reliably sound red.

Le Gay Pomerol r. *** 70 71 74 75' 76' 78 79 81
Well-known 14-acre v'yd. on the northern edge of Pomerol.
Same owners as Ch. LAFLEUR

Gazin Pomerol r. *** 66 67 70' 71' 75' 76 78 79 81
Large property (for Pomerol) with 56 acres. Not quite as
splendid as its position next to PETRUS.

Giscours Lab-Mar. r. *** 66 67 70 71 73 74 75' 76 78' 79' 80 81
Splendid 182-acre third-growth s. of CANTENAC. Dynamically
run and making excellent wine for long maturing.

du Glana St-Jul. r. ** 66 70' 75' 78 79
Big Cru Bourgeois in centre of St-Julien. Variable quality.

Gloria St-Jul. r. *** 66 67 70' 71 73 75' 76 78' 79' 80 81
Outstanding Cru Bourgeois making wine of vigour and
finesse, among good classed-growths in quality. 110
acres. The owner, Henri Martin, bought Ch. ST-PIERRE in 1982.

Grand-Barrail-Lamarzelle-Figeac St-Em. r. ** 66 67 70 71 72
73 75 76 78 79 81
Substantial property near FIGEAC. Well-reputed and popular.

Grand-Corbin-Despagne St-Em. r. ** 70 71 75 78 79 81
One of the better classed-growths on the CORBIN plateau.

Grand-Pontet St-Em. r. **
Widely distributed 35-acre neighbour of Ch. BEAU SÉJOUR-
BÉCOT, now in the same hands. "Supple", smooth wine.

Grand-Puy-Ducasse Pauillac r. *** 66 70 75 76 77 78 79 80 81
Well-known little fifth-growth bought in '71, renovated and
enlarged to 80 acres under expert management.

Grand-Puy-Lacoste Pauillac r. *** 66 70' 71 73 75 76 78' 79'
80 81
Leading fifth-growth famous for fine full-bodied vigorous
Pauillac. 86 acres among the "Bages" ch'x. s. of the town,
recently bought by M. Borie of DUCRU-BEAUCAILLOU.

La Grave Trigant de Boisset Pom. r. ** 70 75' 76' 78 79 80 81
Verdant ch. with small but first-class v'yd. owned by a
MOUEIX. One of the lighter Pomerols.

Gressier Grand Poujeaux Moulis r. ** 66 70 71 73 75' 76 78'
79 80 81
Good Cru Bourgeois. Fine firm wine.

Greysac Médoc r. ** 70' 71 75' 76 78 79' 80 81'
Elegant 140-acre property well-known in the U.S.A.

Gruaud-Larose St-Jul. r. *** 66 70' 71 73 75' 76 77 78' 79 80 81
One of the biggest and best-known second-growths. 189 acres
making smooth rich stylish claret. Owned by CORDIER. The
excellent second wine is called Sarget de Gruard-Larose.

Guiraud Sauternes (r.) w. sw. (dr.) *** 67 70' 71 76 78' 79 80 81'
Newly restored classed-growth of top quality. 170 acres.
Excellent sweet wine and a small amount of red and dry white.

La Gurgue Margaux r. **
Small well-placed property with fine typical Margaux recently bought by owners of Ch. CHASSE-SPLEEN. To watch.

Hanteillan Cissac r. ** 73 75' 76 79' 80 81
Large v'yd. renovated and enlarged since 1973. Ch. Tour du
Vatican is second quality. See also LARRIVAUX-HANTEILLAN.

Haut-Bages-Libéral Pauillac r. ★★ 75 **76** 78 79 80 81
> Lesser-known fifth-growth of 54 acres recently bought by the CRUSE family. There are encouraging signs.

Haut-Bages-Monpelou Pauillac r. ★★ **70 71'** 75' 76 78 79 80 81
> 25-acre Cru Bourgeois stable-mate of CH. BATAILLEY on former DUHART-MILON land.

Haut-Bailly Graves r. ⌗★★★⌗ **64 66 70'** 71 75 **77** 78' 79 80 81
> 60-acre estate at Léognan. Potentially one of the best red Graves. New regime (since '79) will justify its reputation.

Haut-Batailley Pauillac r. ⌗★★★⌗ **70' 71 73** 75' **76 77** 78' 79 80 81
> The smaller but currently better section of the fifth-growth Batailley estate: 49 acres owned by M. Borie of Ch. DUCRU-BEAUCAILLOU. One of the most reliable Pauillacs.

Haut-Brion Pessac, Graves r. (w.) ★★★★ **59 61 62 64 66 67** 70' **71 73** 75' 76 77 78' 79 80 81'
> The oldest great ch. of Bordeaux and the only non-Médoc first-growth of 1855. 108 acres. Splendid firm reds, particularly good since 1975. A little full dry white in **70 71 75 76 77** 78 79 81. See also BAHANS-HAUT-BRION.

Haut-Marbuzet St-Estèphe r. ★★ **70' 71** 75' 76 **77** 78' 79 80 81
> One of the best of many St-Estèphe Crus Bourgeois. 100 acres.

Haut-Pontet St-Em. r. ★★ **70 71 73** 75 78 79
> Well-regarded 12-acre v'yd. of the Côtes.

Houissant St-Estèphe r. ⌗★★⌗
> Typical robust well-balanced St-Estèphe Cru Bourgeois Exceptionnel, also called Ch. Leyssac; well known in Denmark.

d'Issan Cant-Mar. r. ⌗★★★⌗ **66 70 71 73**' 75' **76**' 78 79' 80 81
> Beautifully restored moated ch. with 75-acre third-growth v'yd. well known for round and gentle wine.

Kirwan Cant-Mar. r. ⌗★★⌗ **70' 71** 75' **76** 78 79' 80 81
> Well-run 86-acre third-growth owned by SCHRÖDER & SCHYLER. Recently much replanted: worth watching.

Labégorce Margaux r. ★★ **70' 73** 75' 76 78' 79 81
> Substantial 69-acre property north of Margaux with rather old-fashioned long-lived wines.

Labégorce-Zédé Margaux r. ⌗★★⌗ **70' 71' 73** 75' **76 78 79** 81
> Reputable little Cru Bourgeois on the road n. from Margaux. 43 acres. Typical delicate fragrant Margaux. The same family as VIEUX-CHÂTEAU-CERTAN.

Lafaurie-Peyraguey Sauternes w. sw. ⌗★★★⌗ **67 70 71' 75' 76' 77** 78 79 80 81
> Fine classed-growth of only 49 acres at Bommes, belonging to CORDIER. Excellent wines, though not the richest.

Lafite-Rothschild Pauillac r. ⌗★★★★⌗ **61 66** 70' 75' 76' 78 79' 80 81'
> First-growth of fabulous style and perfume in its great vintages, which keep for decades. Off-form for several years but resplendent since '76. 225 acres.

Lafleur Pomerol r. ★★★ **66 67 70' 71' 73** 75' **76** 78 79 80 81
> Property of 33 acres just n. of PETRUS. Excellent wine of the finer, less "fleshy" kind. Same owner as LE GAY.

Lafleur-Gazin Pomerol r. ⌗★★⌗ **70 71' 73** 75' 76' **78** 79 81
> Distinguished small MOUEIX estate on the n.e. border of Pomerol.

Lafon-Rochet St-Est. r. ★★★ **61 64 66 67** 70' **71** 75' 76 78
> Fourth-growth neighbour of Ch. COS D'ESTOURNEL, restored to prominence in the '60s. 110 acres. Typical dark full-bodied St-Estèphe. Same owner as Ch. PONTET-CANET.

Lagrange Pomerol r. ★★ **66 67 70' 71'** 75' **76** 78 79 80 81
> 20-acre v'yd. in the centre of Pomerol run by the ubiquitous house of MOUEIX. Fairly low-key by their high standards.

Lagrange   St-Jul. r. ★★★ **66 70′ 71** 75′ 76 78 79′
Rather run-down third-growth remote from most of St-Julien. Changed hands in '82. 123 acres.

La Lagune   Ludon r.   ★★★   **66 70′ 71 73′ 74** 75′ 76′ **77** 78′ 79 80 81
Well-run ultra-modern 137-acre third-growth in the extreme s. of the Médoc. Attractively rich and fleshy wines.

Lamarque   Lamarque (Haut-Médoc) r. ★★ **70′ 75′ 76** 78 79 **80** 81′
Splendid medieval fortress of the central Médoc with 113 acres giving admirable light wine.

"BREATHING IS FOR PEOPLE"
Fierce arguments take place between wine-lovers over whether it is a good thing or a bad to decant wine from its bottle into a carafe. The argument in favour is that it allows the wine to "breathe" and its bouquet to expand: against, that its precious breath is dissipated — or at the least that it makes no difference.

Two additional practical reasons in favour concern old wine which has deposited dregs, which can be left in the bottle by careful decanting, and young wine being consumed before it is fully developed: thorough aeration helps to create the illusion of maturity. An aesthetic one is that decanters are handsome on the table.

Decanting is done by pouring the wine into another container very steadily until any sediment reaches the shoulder of the bottle. To see the sediment clearly hold the bottle's neck over a light-bulb or a candle.

Lanessan   Cussac (Haut-Médoc) r.   ★★   **70′ 71** 75′ **76 77** 78′ 79 81
Well-known 108-acre Cru Bourgeois Exceptionnel just s. of St-Julien. Same owner as PICHON-LONGUEVILLE-BARON.

Langoa-Barton   St-Jul. r.   ★★★   **66 70′ 71 73 74** 75′ 76 78′ 79 80 81
Fine 18th-century ch. housing the wine of third-growth Langoa (49 acres) as well as second-growth LÉOVILLE-BARTON. The wines are similar: Langoa slightly less fine.

Larcis-Ducasse   St-Em. r. ★★★ **66 70′ 71′ 73** 75′ **76** 78 79 80 81
The top property of St-Laurent, eastern neighbour of St-Emilion, on the Côtes next to Ch. PAVIE. 24 acres. Rather heavy wine from largely Merlot v'yd.

Laroque   St-Em. r. ★★ **70′ 71** 75′ 76′ **78** 79 80 81
Important 108-acre v'yd. with an impressive mansion on the St-Emilion côtes. MOUEIX property.

Larose-Trintaudon   St-Lau. (Haut-Médoc) r.   ★★   **70 75′ 76** 78 79 80 81
The biggest v'yd. in the Médoc: 388 acres. Modern methods and reliable full-flavoured Cru Bourgeois wine.

Laroze   St-Em. r. ★★★ **70 71′** 75′ **76** 78′ 79 80 81
Big v'yd. (70 acres) on the w. Côtes. Relatively light wines from sandy soil. Sometimes excellent.

Larrivaux-Hanteillan   Cissac (Haut-Médoc) r. ★★ 81
Ch. Larrivaux was bought and added to HANTEILLAN in 1979. The name is used for lighter wines from younger vines.

Larrivet-Haut-Brion   Graves r. (w.)   ★★   **70′ 71** 75′ **76** 79′ 80 81
Little property at Léognan with perfectionist standards.

Lascombes   Margaux r. (p.) ★★★ 61 66 **70′ 71′ 73** 75′ 76 78 79 80 81
240-acre second-growth owned by the British brewers Bass-Charrington and recently lavishly restored. Good vintages are rich for a Margaux. Also a pleasant rosé.

Latour   Pauillac r.   ★★★★   **61 62 64 66 67 69** 70′ **71 73** 74 75′ 76′ **77** 78′ 79 80 81
First-growth. The most consistent great wine in Bordeaux, in France and probably the world: rich, intense and almost immortal in great years, almost always classical and pleasing even in bad ones. British-owned. 123 acres. Second wine LES FORTS DE LATOUR.

Latour à Pomerol Pomerol r. ★★★ **66 70′ 71′** 75′ 76′ 78 79 80 81
Top growth of 19 acres under MOUEIX management. Rich, fruity but firm wine for long maturing.

Laujac Médoc r. ★★ **70′ 71 73 75′ 76** 78 81
Cru Bourgeois in the n. Médoc owned by the CRUSE family. Well known but scarcely outstanding. 62 acres.

Des Laurets St-Em. r. ★★ **70′ 71′** 75′ **76** 78 79 81
Major property of Puisseguin and Montagne-St-Emilion (to the e.) with 66 acres on the Côtes.

Laville-Haut-Brion Graves w. dr. ★★★ **71 73 75 76 77** 78 **79 80** 81
A small production of one of the very best white Graves made at Ch. LA MISSION-HAUT-BRION.

Léoville-Barton St-Jul. r. ★★★ **61 64 66 67 70′ 71 74** 75′ 76 78′ 79 80 81
80-acre portion of the great second-growth Léoville v'yd. in the Anglo-Irish hands of the Barton family for over 150 years. Glorious classical claret, made by traditional methods at the Bartons' third-growth Ch. LANGOA.

Léoville-Las Cases St-Jul. r. ★★★★ **61 64 66 67 70′ 71 73 74** 75′ 76 77 78′ 79 80 81
The largest portion of the old Léoville estate, 198 acres, with one of the highest reputations in Bordeaux. Elegant, never heavy wines. Second label Clos du Marquis.

Léoville-Poyferré St-Jul. r. ★★★ **66 67 70′ 73** 75′ **76** 78′ 79 80 81
At present the least outstanding of the Léovilles, though with famous old vintages to its credit and some recent ones promising well. 131 acres. Second label Ch. Moulin-Riche.

Lestage Listrac r. ★★ **75′ 76** 78′ 79 80 81
130-acre Cru Bourgeois in same hands as Ch. FONRÉAUD. Light, stylish wine.

Liot Barsac w. sw. ★★ **70′ 71 72** 75′ **76** 78
Consistent fairly light golden wines from 94 acres.

Liversan St-Sau. (Haut-Médoc) r. ★★ **70′ 71** 75′ **76** 78 79 80 81
100-acre Cru Bourgeois inland from Pauillac. Recently much improved by its new German proprietor. Ch. Fonpiqueyre is the same wine in certain markets.

Livran Médoc r. ★★ **75 76′ 77 78′ 79** 81
Big Cru Bourgeois at St-Germain in the n. Médoc. Consistent round wines (half Merlot).

Loudenne St-Yzans (Médoc) r. ★★★ **70′** 75′ **76 78′** 79 80 81
Beautiful riverside ch. owned by Gilbeys since 1875. Well-made Cru Bourgeois red and a little excellent "modern-style" dry white from 96 acres.

La Louvière Graves r. and w. dr. ★★ **75 76 78 79** 80 81
Noble estate at Léognan. Good modern-style white and agreeable red.

de Lussac St-Em. r. ★★ **73 74** 75′ **76** 78′ **79** 81
One of the best estates in Lussac-St-Emilion (to the n.e.).

Lynch-Bages Pauillac r. ★★★ **61 66 70′ 71** 75′ **76 77** 78′ 79 80 81
One of the biggest and most popular fifth-growths. 170 acres making old-style rich robust wine: delicious, if seldom great.

Lynch-Moussas Pauillac r. ★★ **71′** 75′ **76** 78 79 80 81
Neglected little fifth-growth bought by the director of Ch. BATAILLEY in 1969. Now 54+ acres and new equipment are making serious wine.

Magdelaine St-Em. r. ★★★ **66 67 70′ 71′ 73** 75′ 76 78 79 80 81
Leading first-growth of the Côtes, 21 acres next to AUSONE owned by J-P MOUEIX. Full-bodied wine. On top form.

Magence Graves r. w. dr. ★★ (r.) **71′** 75′ **78 79′** 81 (w.) DYA
Go-ahead 38-acre property at St Pierre de Mons, in the s. of the Graves, well known for distinctly SAUVIGNON-flavoured very dry white and fruity red for early drinking.

Malartic-Lagravière   Graves r. and (w. dr.)   ★★★   (r.) **64 66 70′ 71 73** 75′ 76′ 78 79 **80** 81 (w.) **71′ 75 76 79** 80 81′
Well-known Léognan classed-growth of 34 acres making excellent solid red for long maturing and a very little excellent fruity SAUVIGNON white.

Malescasse   Lamarque (Haut-Médoc) r. ★★ **75 76 78** 79′ 80 81
Renovated Cru Bourgeois with 70 acres in a good situation recently bought by M. Tesseron of Ch. LAFON-ROCHET.

Malescot St-Exupéry   Margaux r.   ★★★   **61 64 66 70′ 71** 75′ **76 77** 78′ 79′ 80 81
Third-growth of 74 acres allied until 1979 with Ch. MARQUIS-D'ALESME. Rather hard, long maturing, eventually classically fragrant and stylish Margaux.

de Malle   Sauternes r. w. sw./dr. ★★★ **70 71 75 76 78** 79 80 81′
Famous and beautiful ch. at Preignac. 55 acres. Good sweet and dry whites and red (Graves) Ch. de Cardaillan.

---

*Remember that vintage years generally ready for drinking in 1984 are printed in **bold type**. Those in light type will benefit from being kept. For an indication of how long they will improve consult the vintage charts on pages 24 and 25.*

---

de Marbuzet   St-Est. r.   ★★   **73** 75 76 78 79 81
The second label of Ch. COS D'ESTOURNEL. (The actual ch. overlooks the river from the hill n. of Cos.)

Margaux   Margaux r. (w. dr.) ★★★★ **61 66′ 70′ 71** 75′ **76** 78′ 79 80 81
First-growth, the most delicate and finely perfumed of all in its best vintages. Changed hands in 1977 and much improved since. Noble ch. and estate with 209 acres of vines. "Pavillon Blanc" is the best white wine of the Médoc, for 5 years ageing.

Marquis-d'Alesme   Margaux r. ★★ **70′ 71′ 72** 75′ 78 79 80 81
Tiny (17-acre) third-growth, formerly made with Ch. MALESCOT; independent since '79.

Marquis-de-Terme   Margaux r. ★★★ **66 70′** 75′ 76 77 78′ 79 80 81
Old-style fourth-growth making fine typical Margaux, tannic and harsh when young. 84 acres. Sells principally in France.

Martinens   Margaux r.   ★★   75 **76** 78′ 79′ 80 81
55-acre Cru Bourgeois at Cantenac, recently much improved.

Maucaillou   Moulis r.   ★★   **70′ 71 73** 75′ **76′** 78 79 80 81
100-acre Cru Bourgeois with high standards, property of DOURTHE FRÈRES. Full, fruity. "Franc Caillou" is second wine.

Meyney   St-Est. r.   ★★   **70′ 71 74** 75′ **76** 78′ 79 80 81
Big (125-acre) riverside property next door to Ch. MONTROSE, one of the best of many good Crus Bourgeois in St-Estèphe. Owned by CORDIER.

La Mission-Haut-Brion   Graves r.   ★★★★   **59 61 64 66 71′** 75′ 76 77 78 79 80 81
Neighbour and rival to Ch. HAUT-BRION. Serious and grand old-style claret for long maturing. 30 acres. Ch. Latour-H-B is its second-quality wine.

Monbousquet   St-Em. r.   ★★   **70′ 71 74 75 76 78′ 79′ 80** 81
Fine 70-acre estate in the Dordogne valley below St-Emilion. Attractive early-maturing wine from deep gravel soil.

Montrose   St-Est. r.   ★★★   **61 64 66** 70′ 71 **73** 75′ 76 77 78′ 79 80 81
158-acre family-run second-growth well known for deeply coloured, forceful, old-style claret. Needs long ageing.

Moulin-à-Vent   Moulis r. ★★ **70′ 71** 75′ **76** 78′ 79 80 81
55-acre property making successful efforts to improve its rather hard, typically Moulis wine.

Moulin des Carruades
The second-quality wine of Ch. LAFITE.

Moulin du Cadet   St-Em. r.   ★★   70 71' 73 75' 76' 78 79 80 81
  First-class little v'yd. on the Côtes managed by J. P. MOUEIX.

Moulinet   Pomerol r. ★★★ 70 71 73 75 76 78 79 81
  One of Pomerol's bigger estates; 43 acres on lightish soil.

Mouton-Baronne-Philippe   Pauillac r. ★★★ 66 70' 71 75' 76 78' 79
80 81
  Substantial fifth-growth with the enormous advantage of
  belonging to Baron Philippe de Rothschild, 125 acres making
  gentler, less rich and tannic wine than Mouton.

Mouton-Rothschild   Pauillac r. ★★★★ 61 66 67 70' 71 73 75' 76 78'
79 80 81
  Officially a first-growth since 1973, though for 20 years
  worthy of the title. 175 acres (87% CABERNET SAUVIGNON)
  making wine of majestic richness. Also the world's greatest
  museum of works of art relating to wine.

Nairac   Sauternes w. sw.   ★★   73 75 76 78 79 80 81
  Newly restored Barsac classed-growth. Fine wines to lay
  down.

Nenin   Pomerol r. ★★★ 66 67 70' 71' 75' 76 78 79 81
  Well-known 60-acre estate: good but not outstanding quality.

Olivier   Graves r. and r. dr. ★★★ (r.) 75' 76 78 79' 80 81 (w.) D.Y.A.
  80-acre classed-growth, run by the shipper ESCHENAUER, sur-
  rounding a moated castle. Well-known, if not exciting, white;
  less-known but serious red (37 acres).

Les Ormes-de-Pez   St-Est. r.   ★★   66 70' 73 75' 76 77 78' 79 80 81
  Popular 72-acre Cru Bourgeois managed by Ch. LYNCH-
  BAGES. Reliable full-flavoured St-Estèphe.

Palmer   Cant-Mar. r.   ★★★★   61 66 70 71' 73 74 75' 76 78' 79 80 81
  The star ch. of CANTENAC; a third-growth often on a level just
  below the first-growths. Wine of power and delicacy. 86 acres
  with Dutch, British and French owners.

Pape-Clément   Graves r. and w. dr.   ★★★   64 66 67 70 71 73 74 75'
76 78' 79' 80 81
  Ancient v'yd. at Pessac, now 65 acres in fine condition making
  one of the most attractive red Graves.

Patache d'Aux   Bégadan (Médoc) r. ★★ 70 71 75' 76' 78 79' 80 81
  90-acre Cru Bourgeois of the n. Médoc. Well-made wine.

Pauillac, La Rose   Pauillac r. ★★
  The wine of Pauillac's growers' co-op. Membership is dwindling as small growers sell out to big. Generally good value.

Paveil-de Luze   Margaux r.   ★★   70 71' 75' 76' 78 79 80 81
  Old family estate at Soussans. Small but highly regarded.

Pavie   St-Em. r.   ★★★   64' 66 67 70 71' 73 75' 76 78 79' 80 81
  Splendidly sited first-growth of 87 acres on the slope of the
  Côtes. Typically rich and tasty St-Em. consistently well
  made. The same family owns the smaller Ch. Pavie-Decesse.

Pavie-Macquin   St-Em. r.   ★★   73 74 75 76 78 79 81
  Reliable small Côtes v'yd. e. of St-Emilion.

Pedesclaux   Pauillac r. ★★ 70' 71 75' 76 78 79 80 81
  50-acre fifth-growth on the level of a good Cru Bourgeois.
  Solid strong wines loved by Belgians. Grand-Duroc-Milon
  and Bellerose are second labels.

Petit-Village   Pomerol r. ★★★ 66 67 70 71' 75' 76' 78 79 80 81
  One of the best-known little properties: 26 acres next to
  VIEUX-CH.-CERTAN, same owner as Ch. COS D'ESTOURNEL.
  Powerful long-lasting wine.

Petrus   Pomerol r. ★★★★ 61 62 66 67 70' 71' 73 75' 76' 78 79' 80 81
  The great name of Pomerol. 28 acres of gravelly clay giving
  the world's most massively rich and concentrated wine. 95%
  Merlot wines. '71 is considered the best of the decade.

Peyrabon   St. Sauveur r.   ★★   75 76 77 78 79 80 81
  Serious 82-acre Cru Bourgeois popular in the Low Countries.

de Pez   St-Est. r.   ★★★   **66 67 70′ 71′ 73** 75′ 76 78′ 79 80 81
  Outstanding Cru Bourgeois of 60 acres. As reliable as any of
  the classed growths of the village. Needs long storage.

Phélan-Ségur   St-Est. r.   ★★   **66 70′ 71** 75′ 76′ 78 79 80 81
  Big and important Cru Bourgeois (125 acres) with the same
  director as Ch. LÉOVILLE-POYFERRÉ.

Pichon-Longueville-Baron   Pauillac r. ★★★ **66 70′ 71 73** 75 76 78′
  79′ 80 81
  77-acre second-growth usually making fine sturdy Pauillac.

Pichon-Longueville, Comtesse de Lalande   Pauillac r.   ★★★★
  61 64 66 70′ 71 73 75′ 76 77 78′ 79′ 80 81′
  Second-growth neighbour to Ch. LATOUR. 148 acres. Recently
  among the very top performers; classic long-lived wine.

Pindefleurs   St-Em. r. ★★ **75 76** 78 79
  Up and coming 20-acre v'yd. on the St-Emilion plateau.

de Pitray   Castillon r. ★★ **75 76′ 78 79** 80 81
  Substantial (62 acre) v'yd. on the Côtes de Castillon e. of
  St-Emilion. Good lightish wines.

THE COLOUR OF AGE

*One very easy way of gauging the maturity of a red wine without
opening the bottle is simply to hold the neck of the bottle up to a bright
light. If the colour of the wine in the neck is deep red the wine is almost
certainly still young and vigorous. If it appears a light orange colour,
the wine is fully mature and should be drunk. If possible, compare a
very fine Bordeaux and a simple one at, say, ten years old to see the
difference: the better wine will look much darker.*

Plince   Pomerol r. ★★ **75 76** 78 **79** 80 81
  Reputable 20-acre property on the outskirts of Libourne.
  Lightish wine from sandy soil.

La Pointe   Pomerol r. ★★★ **66 70′ 71′** 75′ **76** 78 79 80 81
  Prominent 53-acre estate for typically fat fruity Pomerol. Ch.
  LA SERRE is in the same hands.

Pontet-Canet   Pauillac r. ★★★ **61 66 67 70 71** 75′ **76** 78′ 79′ 80 81
  One of the biggest classed-growths with about 182 acres,
  neighbour to MOUTON and potentially far better than its
  official rank of fifth-growth. Belonged to the CRUSE family for
  many years, now to M. Tesseron of Ch. LAFON-ROCHET.

Potensac   Potensac (Médoc) r.   ★★   **70 71 73 75′ 76 77** 78′ 79 80 81
  The best-known Cru Bourgeois of Ordonnac-et-Potensac in
  the n. Médoc. The neighbouring Ch'x. Lassalle and Gallais-
  Bellevue belong to the same family, the Delons, owners of Ch.
  LÉOVILLE–LASCASES.

Pouget   Margaux   ★★   **70′ 71** 75 **76** 78 80 81
  19-acre v'yd. attached to Ch. BOYD-CANTENAC. In 1983 separate chais were built. Similar, rather lighter, wines.

Poujeaux-Theil   Moulis r. ★★ **70′ 71** 75′ **76** 78 79′ 80 81
  Family-run Cru Exceptionnel of 108 acres selling its rather
  hard wine direct to an appreciative French public.

Prieuré-Lichine   Cant-Mar. r.   ★★★   **66 67 70 71 73 74** 75 **76** 78′
  79′ 80 81
  143-acre fourth-growth brought to the fore by Alexis Lichine
  since 1952. Excellent finely fragrant Margaux.

Puy Blanquet   St-Em. r ★★ **71′ 73** 75′ **76** 78 79 81
  The major property of St-Etienne-de-Lisse, e. of St-Emilion,
  with over 50 acres. Typical full St-Em., if below the top class.

Puy-Razac   St-Em. r.   ★★   **75 76** 78 79 80 81′
  Small property at the foot of the Côtes near Ch. PAVIE,
  connected with the well-known Ch. MONBOUSQUET.

Rabaud-Promis   Sauternes w. sw. ★★ **67 70 71 75 76** 78
 Classed-growth of 74 acres at Bommes. Good, not brilliant.

Rahoul   Graves r. and w. dr.   ★★   **75 76** 78′ 79 80 81 (w.) 81 82
 37-acre v'yd. at Portets making particularly good wine from
 maturing vines; 80% red.

Ramage-la-Batisse   Haut-Médoc r.   ★★   **70′ 71′** 75′ **76** 78 79 80 81
 Outstanding Cru Bourgeois of 118 acres at St-Sauveur, west
 of Pauillac. To watch.

Rausan-Ségla   Margaux r. ★★★ **61 66 70′ 71′** 75′ 76 77 78 79 81
 94-acre second-growth; famous for its fragrance; a great
 Médoc name, but recently below par. Owned by ESCHENAUER.

Rauzan-Gassies   Margaux r. ★★★ **61 66** 75′ 76 78′ 79′ 80 81
 74-acre second-growth neighbour of the last with a poor
 record in the '60s. Looking up recently.

Raymond-Lafon   Sauternes w. sw. ★★ **75 76** 78 79 81
 Serious Sauternes estate run by the manager of Ch. YQUEM.

de Rayne-Vigneau   Sauternes w. sw. ★★★ **67 70 71′ 73** 75′ 76′ 78
 164-acre classed-growth at Bommes with rich golden wine
 and a little dry. Brand new equipment in 1980.

Respide   Graves (r.) w. dr. ★★ **76 78 79** 81
 One of the better white-wine ch'x. of s. Graves, at St Pierre de
 Mons. Full-flavoured wines.

Reynon   1eres Côtes de Bordeaux w. dr.   ★★
 Tiny property producing extraordinary dry white from very
 old Sauvignon vines.

Reysson   Vertheuil   Haut-Médoc r. ★★
 Recently replanted, up-and-coming Cru Bourgeois with the
 same owners as Ch. CHASSE-SPLEEN.

Rieussec   Sauternes w. sw.   ★★★   **66 67 70 71′** 75′ **76′** 78 79 80 81′
 Worthy neighbour of Ch. D'YQUEM with 136 acres in Fargues.
 Not the sweetest; can be exquisitely fine. Also a dry wine: "R".

Ripeau   St-Em. r. ★★ **75** 78
 Above-average classed-growth in the centre of the plateau.

de Rochemorin   Graves r. (w. dr.)
 An important restoration at Martillac by the owner of ch. LA
 LOUVIÈRE. 113 acres of new vines.

Rouget   Pomerol r. ★★ **67 70 71 74** 75′ 76′ 78 79
 Attractive old estate with rising standards on the n. edge of
 Pomerol. Slow-maturing wine.

Royal St-Emilion
 Brand name of the important growers' co-operative.

St-André Corbin   St-Emilion r. ★★ **64 66 71** 75′ **76′ 78 79′** 81
 Considerable 54-acre property in Montagne-St-Emilion with
 a long record of above-average wines.

St-Estèphe, Marquis de   St-Est. r.   ★   **70 71 73** 75 76 78 79 81
 The growers' co-operative; over 200 members. Good value.

St-Georges   St-Geo., St-Em. r. ★★ **70 75 76** 78 **79** 80 81
 Noble 18th-century ch. overlooking the St-Emilion plateau
 from the hill to the n. 125 acres; wine sold direct to the public.

St-Pierre-Sevaistre   St-Jul. r.   ★★★   **70′ 71 73** 75′ **76** 78′ 79 **80** 81′
 Small (44-acre) fourth-growth many years in Belgian owner-
 ship; bought in 1982 by Henri Martin of Ch. GLORIA. Always
 attractively ripe and fruity wines.

St-Pierre   Graves (r.) w. dr.   ★★   78 79 81
 Estate at St Pierre de Mons making old-style Graves of
 notable character and flavour.

de Sales   Pomerol r. ★★★ **66 67 70′ 71 75′ 76′** 78′ 79 80 81
 The biggest v'yd. of Pomerol (116 acres), attached to the
 grandest ch. Not poetry but excellent prose. Second label: Ch.
 Chantalouette.

Ségur   Medoc r.   ★★
 Well-situated 80-acre Cru Bourgeois at Parempuyre.

Sénéjac   Haut-Médoc r. ★★ **70' 74'** 75 76' 78 79 80 81
    43-acre Cru Bourgeois in S. Médoc.

La Serre   St-Em. r. ★★ **70 75' 78 79**
    Well-run small property with same owner as LA POINTE.

Sigalas-Rabaud   Sauternes w. sw.   ★★   **71' 72 73** 75' **76'** 78 79 81
    The lesser part of the former Rabaud estate: 34 acres in
    Bommes, making first-class sweet wine.

Siran   Lab-Mar. r.   ★★★   **61 66 70 71'** 75' **78'** 79 80 81
    74-acre Cru Bourgeois of distinguished quality. Elegant,
    long-lived wines (and Bordeaux's first anti-nuclear cellar).

Smith-Haut-Lafitte   Graves r. and (w. dr.) ★★★ **70' 71' 74** 75' 76 78
    79 80 81
    Run-down old classed-growth at Martillac restored by
    ESCHENAUER in the '60s. Now 111 acres (14 of white). The
    white wine is light and fruity; the red dry and interesting.

Soutard   St-Em. r.   ★★   **66 70' 71 74** 75' **76** 78' 79 80 81
    Reliable 48-acre classed-growth n. of the town. Wine out-
    standingly "generous" rather than "fine".

Suduiraut   Sauternes w. sw.   ★★★   **67 70 71 75** 76' 78 79 80 81
    One of the best Sauternes: of glorious creamy richness. Over
    173 acres of the top class, under promising new management.

Taillefer   Pomerol r. ★★ **67 70 73** 75 **76** 78 79 81
    24-acre property on the edge of Pomerol owned by another
    branch of the MOUEIX family.

Talbot   St-Jul. r. (w.) ★★★ **66 70' 71 73** 75' **76 77** 78' 79 80 81
    Important 210-acre fourth-growth, sister-ch. to GRUAUD-
    LAROSE, with similarly attractive rich and satisfying wine.
    Second label: Connétable Talbot. A little white is called
    "Caillou Blanc".

du Tertre   Ar-Mar. r.   ★★★   **66 70'** 71 72 73 75 76 78 79' 80 81
    Fifth-growth, isolated s. of Margaux; restored to excellence by
    the owner of CALON-SEGUR. Fragrant and long-lived.

Tertre-Daugay   St-Em. r. ★★ 78 79 81
    Small classed-growth in a spectacular situation on the brow
    of the Côtes. Same owner as LA GAFFELIÈRE.

Timberlay   Bordeaux r. (w. dr.) ★
    The biggest and best-known property of Cubzac, with 185
    acres. Pleasant light wines.

La Tour-Blanche   Sauternes w. sw. (r.) ★★★ **70 71** 75' **76** 78' 79' 81
    Top-rank 57-acre estate at Bommes with a state wine-
    growing school. Not among the leaders recently.

La Tour-Carnet   St-Lau. r.   ★★   **66 70'** 75' **76** 78 79 80 81
    Fourth-growth reborn from total neglect in the '60s. Medieval
    tower with 79 acres just w. of St-Julien. Lightish, pretty wine.

La Tour de By   Bégadan (Médoc) r.   ★★   **70** 75' **76 77** 78' 79' **80** 81
    Very well-run 144-acre Cru Bourgeois in the n. Médoc in-
    creasing its reputation for sturdy, impressive wine.

La Tour-de-Mons   Sou-Mar. r. ★★★ **66 70' 71' 73 74** 75' 78 81
    Distinguished Cru Bourgeois of 46 acres, three centuries in
    the same family. Sometimes excellent claret with a long life.

La Tour-du-Pin-Figeac   St-Em. r. ★★
    24-acre classed-growth, once part of LA TOUR-FIGEAC. Off form.

La Tour-du-Pin-Figeac-Moueix   St-Em. r. ★★ **66 70 74** 75 **76** 78 79
    81
    Another 20-acre section of the same old property, owned by
    one of the famous MOUEIX family. Not better than steady.

La Tour-Figeac   St-Em. r.   ★★   **70** 75 78 79 81
    34-acre classed-growth between Ch. FIGEAC and Pomerol.
    Well run by a German proprietor.

La Tour-Haut-Brion   Graves r. ★★★ **66 70 74** 75 **76 77** 78 **79** 80 81
    The second label of Ch. LA MISSION-HAUT-BRION. A plainer,
    smaller-scale wine with the same fine pedigree.

La Tour-Martillac   Graves r. and w. dr.   ☐ ★★   **70' 71 74** 75' 77 78 79'

Small but serious property at Martillac. 10 acres of white grapes; 37 of black. Quantity is sacrificed for quality. The owner, Jean Kressmann, is resurrecting the neighbouring Ch. Lespault

La Tour St-Bonnet   Médoc r.   ☐ ★★   **70' 71 73** 75' **76** 78' **79** 80 81

Consistently well-made and typical n. Médoc from St-Christoly. 100 acres.

La Tour du Haut Moulin   Cussac (Haut-Médoc) r.   ☐ ★★   **70** 75' **76' 78** 79

Little-known 70-acre property; respectable firm wines.

Tournefeuille   Lalande de Pomerol r.   ☐ ★★   **67 70 71' 74** 75' **76'** 78 79 81'

The star of Néac, overlooking Pomerol from the n. A small property (43 acres), but excellent long-lived wine.

des Tours   Montagne-St-Em. r. ★★ **70 71'** 75' **76 78 79** 81

Spectacular ch. with modern 170-acre v'yd. Sound wine.

Tronquoy-Lalande   St-Est. r.   ☐ ★★   **70 71 73** 75 76 78 79 80 81

40-acre Cru Bourgeois making typical high-coloured St-Estèphe. Distributed by DOURTHE.

Troplong-Mondot   St-Em. r.   ☐ ★★   **66 70' 71' 75' 76** 78 79 81

One of the bigger classed-growths of St-Emilion. 70+ acres well sited on the Côtes above Ch. PAVIE.

Trotanoy   Pomerol r.   ☐ ★★★   **61 67 70 71' 73** 75' **76'** 78 79 80 81

One of the top Pomerols. Only 27 acres but a splendid fleshy perfumed wine (the '71 is famous). Managed by J-P MOUEIX.

Trottevieille   St-Em. r. ★★★ **66 67 70 71 75' 76** 78 79 80 81

Small but highly reputed first-growth of 18 acres on the Côtes e. of the town. Attractive full wines sold by BORIE-MANOUX.

Le Tuquet   Graves r. and w. dr. ★★ **76** 78 79 81

Substantial estate at Beautiran making light fruity wines; the white better.

Verdignan   Médoc r.   ☐ ★★   **75 76** 78 79 80 81

Substantial Grand Bourgeois sister property to ch. COUFRAN. More tannic wine.

Vieux-Château-Certan   Pomerol r. ☐ ★★★ **61 66 67 70' 71' 74** 75' 76 78 79 80 81

Perhaps the second ch. of Pomerol, just s. of PETRUS, the first, but totally different in style. 34 acres, Belgian owned.

Vieux-Château-St-André   St-Emilion r.   ☐ ★★   **71** 75' **76' 78** 79' 81

Small v'yd. in Montagne-St-Emilion owned by the leading wine-maker of Libourne. To watch.

Villegeorge   Avensan r.   ☐ ★★   **73'** 75' **76** 78' 79 80 81

24-acre Cru Exceptionnel to the n. of Margaux with the same owner as Ch. BRANE-CANTENAC. Excellent full-bodied wine.

Villemaurine   St-Em. r.   ☐ ★★   **70' 71** 75' **76 77** 78 79' 80 81

Good classed-growth well sited on the Côtes by the town. Firm wine with a high proportion of Cabernet.

Vraye-Croix-de-Gay   Pomerol ★★★ **70' 71' 73 74** 75' **76** 78 79 81

Very small ideally situated v'yd. in the best part of Pomerol.

d'Yquem   Sauternes w. sw. (dr.) ★★★★ **59 62 66 67' 69 70' 71' 73** 75' 76' 77 78 79

The world's most famous sweet-wine estate. 250 acres making only 500 bottles per acre of very strong, intense, luscious wine. Good vintages need a decade of maturity.

More Bordeaux châteaux are listed under Côtes Canon-Fronsac, Côtes de Bourg, Cubzac, Côtes de Fronsac.

Switzerland

Switzerland has some of the world's most efficient and productive vineyards. Costs are high and nothing less is viable. All the most important are lined along the south-facing slopes of the upper Rhône valley and Lake Geneva, respectively the Valais and the Vaud. Wines are known both by place-names, grape-names, and legally controlled type-names. All three, with those of leading growers and merchants, appear in the following list. On the whole, D.Y.A.

Aigle Vaud w. dr. ★★
> Principal town of CHABLAIS, between La. Geneva and the VALAIS. Dry whites of appropriately transitional style: at best strong and well balanced.

Amigne
> Traditional white grape of the VALAIS. Heavy but tasty wine, usually made dry.

Arvine Another old VALAIS white grape, similar to the last; perhaps better. Makes good dessert wine. Petite Arvine is similar.

Auvernier Neuchâtel r. p. w. dr. (sp.) ★★
> Village s. of NEUCHÂTEL known for PINOT NOIR, CHASSELAS and OEIL DE PERDRIX.

Blauburgunder
> One of the names given to the form of PINOT NOIR grown in German Switzerland.

Bonvin Old-established growers and merchants at SION.

Chablais Vaud (r.) w. dr. ★★
> The district between Montreux on La. Geneva and Martigny where the Rhône leaves the VALAIS. Good DORIN wines. Best villages: AIGLE, YVORNE, Bex.

Chasselas
> The principal white grape of Switzerland, neutral in flavour but taking local character. Known as FENDANT in VALAIS, DORIN in VAUD and PERLAN round Geneva.

Clevner (or Klevner)
> Another name for BLAUBURGUNDER.

Completer
> Rare Grisons grape giving liquorous wine.

Cortaillod Neuchâtel r. (p. w.) ★★
> Village near NEUCHÂTEL specializing in light PINOT NOIR reds.

Côte, La
> The n. shore of La. Geneva from Geneva to Lausanne. Pleasant DORIN and SALVAGNIN. Best villages incl. Féchy and Rolle.

Dézaley   Vaud w. dr. ★★★

Best-known village of LAVAUX, between Lausanne and Montreux. Steep s. slopes to the lake make fine fruity DORIN. Dézaley-Marsens is equally good.

Dôle   Valais r. ★★

Term for red VALAIS wine of PINOT NOIR or GAMAY or both grapes, reaching a statutory level of strength and quality.

Domaine Château Lichten

Property making first-class VALAIS wines at Loèche Ville.

Dorin   Vaud w. dr. ★→★★

The name for CHASSELAS wine in the VAUD, the equivalent of FENDANT from the VALAIS.

Epesses   Vaud w. dr. ★★

Well-known lakeside village of LAVAUX. Good dry DORIN.

Ermitage

VALAIS name for white wine from MARSANNE grapes. Rich, concentrated and heavy; usually dry.

Fendant   Valais w. dr. ★→★★★

The name for CHASSELAS wine in the VALAIS, where it reaches its ripest and strongest. SION is the centre.

Flétri   Withered grapes for making sweet wine, often MALVOISIE.

Glacier, Vin du

Almost legendary long-matured white stored at high altitudes. Virtually extinct today.

Goron   Valais r. ★

Red VALAIS wine that fails to reach the DÔLE standard.

Hammel

Major merchant and grower of La Côte at Rolle.

Herrschaft   Grisons r. (w. sw.) ★→★★★

District near the border of Austria and Liechtenstein. Small amount of light PINOT NOIR reds and a few sweet whites.

Humagne

Old VALAIS grape. Some red Humagne is sold: decent country wine. The strong white is a local speciality.

Johannisberg

The Valais name for SYLVANER, which makes pleasant soft dry wine here.

Lavaux   Vaud r. w. dr. ★→★★★

The n. shore of La. Geneva between Lausanne and Montreux. The e. half of the VAUD. Best villages incl. DÉZALEY, EPESSES, Villette, Lutry, ST-SAPHORIN.

Légèrement doux

Most Swiss wines are dry. Any with measurable sugar must be labelled thus or as "avec sucre résiduel".

Malvoisie

VALAIS name for PINOT GRIS.

Mandement   Geneva r. (p.) w. dr. ★

Wine district just w. of Geneva, (see Vin-Union-Genève). Very light reds, chiefly GAMAY, and whites (PERLAN).

Marsanne

The white grape of Hermitage on the French Rhône, used in the VALAIS to make ERMITAGE.

Merlot   Bordeaux red grape (see Grapes for red wine) used to make the better wine of Italian Switzerland (TICINO). See also Viti.

Mont d'Or, Domaine du   Valais w. dr. sw. ★★★★

The best wine estate of Switzerland: 60 acres of steep hillside near SION. Good FENDANT, JOHANNISBERG, AMIGNE, etc., and real Riesling. Very rich concentrated wines.

Neuchâtel   Neuchâtel r. p. w. dr. sp. ★→★★★

City of n.w. Switzerland and the wine from the n. shore of its lake. Pleasant light PINOT NOIR and attractive sometimes sparkling CHASSELAS.

Nostrano

Word meaning "ours" applied to the lesser red wine of the TICINO, made from a mixture of native and Italian grapes, in contrast to MERLOT from Bordeaux.

Oeil de Perdrix

Pale rosé of PINOT NOIR.

Orsat   Important and popular wine firm at Martigny, VALAIS.

Perlan   Geneva w. dr. *

The MANDEMENT name for the ubiquitous CHASSELAS, here at its palest, driest and least impressive.

Premier Cru

Any wine from the maker's own estate can call itself this.

Provins

The excellent central co-operative of the VALAIS.

Rèze   The grape, now rare, used for VIN DU GLACIER.

Rivaz   Vaud r. w. dr. **

Well-known village of LAVAUX.

St-Saphorin   Vaud w. dr. **

One of the principal villages of LAVAUX: wines drier and more austere than DÉZALEY or EPESSES.

Salvagnin   Vaud r. * → **

Red VAUD wine of tested quality: the equivalent of DÔLE.

Savagnin

Swiss name for the TRAMINER, called Païen in the VALAIS.

Schafiser   Bern (r.) w. dr. * → **

The n. shore of La. Bienne (Bielersee) is well known for light CHASSELAS sold as either Schafiser or Twanner.

Schenk, S.A.

The biggest Swiss wine firm, based at Rolle in the VAUD, with 570 acres as well as other world-wide interests.

Sion   Valais w. dr. * → ***

Centre of the VALAIS wine region, famous for its FENDANT.

Spätburgunder

PINOT NOIR: by far the commonest grape of German Switzerland, making very light wines.

Testuz, V. and P.

Well-known growers and merchants at Dézaley, LAVAUX.

Ticino

Italian-speaking s. Switzerland. See Merlot, Viti, Nostrano.

Twanner

See Schafiser

Valais

The Rhône valley between Brig and Martigny. Its n. side is an admirable dry sunny and sheltered v'yd., planted mainly, alas, to the second-rate CHASSELAS grape, which here makes its best wine.

Vaud   The region of La. Geneva. Its n. shore is Switzerland's biggest v'yd. and in places as good as any. DORIN and SALVAGNIN are the main wines.

Vétroz   Valais (r.) w. dr. **

Village near SION in the best part of the VALAIS.

Vevey

Town near Montreux with a famous wine festival once every 30-odd years. The last was in 1977.

Vin-Union-Genève

Big growers' co-operative at Satigny in the MANDEMENT. Light reds and white PERLAN are Geneva's local wine.

Viti   Ticino r. **

Legal designation of better-quality TICINO red, made of MERLOT and with at least 12% alcohol.

Yvorne

Village near AIGLE with some of the best CHABLAIS v'yds.

Germany

Germany has the most complicated labelling system in the world—a fact that has put most people off tackling it seriously and driven them to settle for pleasantly innocuous blended wines: Liebfraumilch and the like.

Yet those who funk its complications will never experience the real beauty of the style of wine which is Germany's unique contribution.

The secret of the style is the balance of sweetness against fruity acidity. A great vintage in Germany is one in which the autumn weather allows the late-ripening Riesling—the grape which makes virtually all the great German wines—to develop a high sugar content. What is so special about the Riesling is that as it ripens it also develops a concentration of fragrant acids and essences to balance the increasing sweetness. The resulting wine is tense and thrilling with this sugar/acid balance.

It smells and tastes extraordinarily flowery, lively and refreshing while it is young. But because of its internal equilibrium it also has the ability to live and mature for a remarkable length of time. As good Riesling matures all sorts of subtle scents and flavours emerge. Straight sweetness gives way to oily richness. Suggestions of countless flowers and fruits, herbs and spices develop.

These are the rewards for anyone who can be bothered to master the small print. They lead into realms of sensation where Liebfraumilch (with all the respect due to a perfectly decent drink) can never follow. The great German growers make wine for wine's sake. Food is irrelevant, except in so far as it gets in the way.

The Labels and the Law

German wine law is based on the ripeness of the grapes at harvest time. Recent vintages have been exceptionally kind to growers, but as a general rule most German wine needs sugar added to make up for the missing warmth and sunshine of one of the world's northernmost vineyards.

The exceptional wine, from grapes ripe enough not to need sugar, is kept apart as Qualitätswein mit Prädikat or QmP. Within this top category its natural sugar-content is expressed by traditional terms—in ascending order of ripeness: Kabinett, Spätlese, Auslese, Beerenauslese, Trockenbeerenauslese.

But reasonably good wine is also made in good vineyards from grapes that fail to reach the natural sugar-content required for a QmP label. The authorities allow this, within fairly strict controls, to be called Qualitätswein as well, but with the different qualification of bestimmter Anbaugebiete (i.e. QbA) instead of mit Prädikat. mP is therefore a vitally important ingredient of a fine-wine label.

Both levels are officially checked, tested and tasted at every bottling. Each batch is given an identifying test ("prüfungs") number. No other country has quality control approaching this. It can't make dull wine exciting, but it can and does make all "quality" wine a safe bet.

The third level, Tafelwein, has no pretensions to quality and is not allowed to give itself airs beyond the name of the village or the general region it comes from. (But see LAND-WEIN).

Though there is very much more detail in the laws this is the gist of the quality grading. Where it differs completely from the French system is in ignoring geographical difference. There are no Grands Crus, no VDQS. In theory all any German vineyard has to do to make the best wine is to grow the ripest grapes.

The law distinguishes only between degrees of geographical exactness. In labelling quality wine the grower or merchant is given a choice. He can (and always will) label the relatively small quantities of his best wine with the name of the precise vineyard or Einzellage where it was grown. Germany has about 3,000 Einzellage names. Obviously only particularly good ones are famous enough to help sell the wine. Therefore the law has created a second class of vineyard name: the Grosslage. A Grosslage is a group of neighbouring Einzellages of supposedly similar character and standing. Because there are fewer Grosslage names, and far more wine from each, Grosslages have a better chance of building reputations, brand-name fashion.*

Thirdly the grower or merchant (more likely the latter) may choose to sell his wine under a regional name: the word is Bereich. To cope with the vast demand for "Bernkasteler" or "Niersteiner" or "Johannisberger" these world-famous names have been made legal for considerable districts. "Bereich Johannisberg" is the whole of the Rheingau; "Bereich Bernkastel" the whole of the Mittel-Mosel.

As with all wine names, in fact, the better the wine the more precise the labelling. The trick with German labels is to be able to recognize which is the most precise. Finally, though, and above all, it is to recognize the grower and his vineyard.

The basic German label

The order of wording on German quality wine labels follows a standard pattern.

TRIERER
ABSTBERG
RIESLING AUSLESE

QmP
A.P. NR. 12345678
ERZEUGERABFÜLLUNG
WINZERVEREIN TRIER

The first name is the town or parish, with the suffix -er. The second is the vineyard (either Einzellage or Grosslage — see introduction). The third (optional) is the grape variety. The fourth is the quality in terms of ripeness. For QmP see page 86.
For A.P. Nr. see page 78.
Erzeugerabfüllung means bottled by the grower, in this case the grower's co-operative of Trier. For other words appearing on German labels see the Germany A–Z.

*Where the law is less than candid, however, is in pretending to believe that the general public will know a Grosslage name from an Einzellage name, when the two are indistinguishably similar (see any entry on the following pages). It is actually against the law to indicate on the label whether the name in question is that of a particular plot or a wider grouping. The names of all relevant Grosslages are given in this book. Note that Grosslage wines are only rarely of the stature of Einzellage wines.

N.B. on vintage notes opposite

Vintage notes after entries in the German section are given in a different form from those elsewhere, to show the style of the vintage as well as its quality.
Three styles are indicated:
The classic, super-ripe vintage with a high proportion of natural (QmP) wines, including Spätleses and Ausleses. Three of the six vintages shown, an unprecedented proportion, come into this category.
Example: **76**
The "normal" successful vintage with plenty of good wine but no great preponderance of sweeter wines. Example: 79
The cool vintage with generally poor ripeness but a fair proportion of reasonably successful wines, tending to be over-acid. Such wines sometimes mature better than expected. Example: *80*
Where no mention is made the vintage is generally not recommended, or most of its wines have passed maturity.

Recent Vintages

Mosel/Saar/Ruwer

Mosels (including Saar and Ruwer wines) are so attractive young that their keeping qualities are not often enough explored, and wines older than seven years or so are unusual. But well-made wines of Kabinett class gain from two or three years in bottle, Spätleses by a little longer, and Ausleses and Beerenausleses by anything from 10 to 20 years, depending on the vintage.

As a rule, in poor years the Saar and Ruwer fare worse than the Middle Mosel and make sharp, thin wines, but in the best years they can surpass the whole of Germany for elegance and "breed".

1982	A huge ripe vintage marred by rain. Most is plain QbA but good sites made ⅓ Kabinett, ⅛ Spätlese and a little Auslese.
1981	A wet vintage but very good middle Mosels up to Spätleses. Also Eiswein.
1980	A terrible summer. Some pleasant wines but little more.
1979	A patchy vintage after bad winter damage. But several excellent Kabinetts and better. Light but well-balanced wines now giving great pleasure.
1978	A similar vintage to '77, though very late and rather small. Very few sweet wines but many with good balance. Drink up.
1977	Big vintage of serviceable quality, mostly QbA. Drink up.
1976	Very good small vintage, with some superlative sweet wines and almost no dry. Most wines now ready; the best will keep 5 years.
1975	Very good; many Spätleses and Ausleses. Most now ready.
1974	Most wine needed sugaring; few Kabinetts, but some well-balanced wines which have kept well. Drink now.
1973	Very large, attractive, but low acid and extract have meant a short life. Good eiswein. Drink now.
1972	Large; medium to poor; few late-picked wines, many with unripe flavour. Should be drunk by now.
1971	Superb, with perfect balance. Some top wines will still improve.

Older fine vintages: '69, '67, '64, '59, '53, '49, '45.

Rhine/Nahe/Palatinate

Even the best wines can be drunk with pleasure after two or three years, but Kabinett, Spätlese and Auslese wines of good vintages gain enormously in character and complexity by keeping for longer. Rheingau wines tend to be longest-lived, often improving for 10 years or more, but wines from the Nahe and the Palatinate can last nearly as long. Rheinhessen wines usually mature sooner, and dry Franconian wines are best young.

The Riesling, predominant in the Rheingau, benefits most from hot summers; Palatinate wines can taste almost overripe.

1982	A colossal vintage gathered in torrential rain. Spätleses and even Kabinett are rare, but QbA wines will be good for early drinking.
1981	Poor conditions in the Rheingau but better in Nahe and Rheinhessen and very good in Palatinate.
1980	Bad weather from spring to autumn. Only passable wines.
1979	Uneven and reduced in size. Few great wines but many typical and good. For current drinking.
1978	Satisfactory vintage saved by late autumn. 25% QmP, but very few Spätleses. Some excellent wines in the south. Drink soon.
1977	Big and useful; few Kabinett wines or better. Not to keep. Rheinpfalz best.
1976	The richest vintage since 1921 in places. Very few dry wines. Balance less consistent than 1975. Maturing well.
1975	A splendid Riesling year, a high percentage of Kabinetts and Spätleses. Should be drunk fairly soon.
1974	Variable; the best fruity and good; many Kabinetts. Drink now.
1973	Very large, consistent and attractive, but not for keeping.
1972	Excess acidity was the problem; no exciting wines, but some presentable. Should be drunk now.
1971	A superlative vintage with perfect balance. The finest are still improving.

Older fine vintages: '69, '67, '66, '64, '59, '57, '53, '49, '45.

Achkarren Bad. (r.) w. ★→★★
Well-known wine village of the KAISERSTUHL.

Adelmann, Graf
Famous grower with 125 acres at Kleinbottwar, WÜRTTEM-
BERG. Uses the name Brussele. Light reds; good RIESLINGS.

Ahr Ahr r. ★→★★★ 71 75 76 79 *80 81* 82
Germany's best-known red-wine area, s. of Bonn. Very light
pale SPÄTBURGUNDERS.

Amtliche Prüfungsnummer
See Prüfungsnummer

Anbaugebiet
Wine-region. See QbA.

Anheuser
Name of two distinguished growers of the NAHE.

Annaberg Rhpf. w. ★★★ 71 75 76 77 78 79 *80* 81 82
Twelve-acre estate at DÜRKHEIM famous for sweet and
pungent wines, esp. SCHEUREBE, with prodigous keeping qualities.

A.P.Nr.
Abbreviation of AMTLICHE PRÜFUNGSNUMMER.

Assmannshausen Rhg. r. ★→★★★ 71 75 76 *78* 79 *80* 81 82
RHEINGAU village known for its pale, often sweet, reds. Top
v'yd.: Höllenberg. Grosslages: Steil and Burgweg.

---

*The German Wine Academy runs regular courses of wine-instruction
at all levels for both amateurs and professionals, in German and
English. The Academy is based at the glorious 12th-century Cistercian
monastery of Kloster Eberbach in the Rheingau. The course normally
includes tasting-tours of Germany's wine regions. Particulars can be
obtained from the Academy, P. O. Box 1705, D-6500 Mainz, West
Germany.*

Auslese
Late-gathered wine with high natural sugar content.

Avelsbach M-S-R (Ruwer) w. ★★★ 71 75 76 *78* 79 *80 81* 82
Village near TRIER. Supremely delicate wines. Growers:
Staatliche Weinbaudomäne (see Staatsweingut), BISCHÖF-
LICHE WEINGÜTER. Grosslage: Trierer Römerlay.

Ayl M-S-R (Saar) w. ★★★ 71 75 76 *78* 79 *80 81* 82
One of the best villages of the SAAR. Top v'yds.: Kupp, Herren-
berger. Grosslage: Scharzberg.

Bacchus
Modern highly perfumed grape variety.

Bacharach (Bereich)
District name for the s. Mittelrhein v'yds. downstream from
the RHEINGAU. No great or famous wines; some pleasant.

Baden
Huge area of scattered wine-growing. Few classic wines: most
are heavy or soft. Best areas are KAISERSTUHL and ORTENAU.

Badische Bergstrasse/Kraichgau (Bereich)
Principal district name of n. BADEN.

Bad Dürkheim See Dürkheim

Badisches Frankenland (Bereich)
Minor district name of n. BADEN.

Bad Kreuznach Na. w. ★★→★★★ 71 75 76 77 78 79 *80* 81 82
Main town of the NAHE with some of its best wines. Many fine
v'yds., incl. Brückes, Kahlenberg, Steinweg, Krötenpfuhl.
Grosslage: Kronenberg.

Balbach Erben
One of the best NIERSTEIN growers. 44 acres, 80% Riesling.

Basserman-Jordan
> 100-acre MITTEL-HAARDT family estate with many of the best v'yds. in DEIDESHEIM, FORST, RUPPERTSBERG, etc.

Beerenauslese
> Extremely sweet and luscious wine from very late-gathered individual bunches.

Bereich
> District within a Gebiet (region). See under Bereich names, e.g. Bernkastel (Bereich).

Bergzabern, Bad Rhpf. (r.) w. ★→★★ 75 76 77 78 79 *80* 81 82
> Town of SÜDLICHE-WEINSTRASSE. Pleasant sweetish wines. Grosslage: Liebfrauenberg.

Bernkastel M-M w. ★★→★★★★ 71 75 76 77 78 79 *80* 81 82
> Top wine-town of the Mosel; the epitome of RIESLING. Best v'yds.: Doktor, Bratenhöfchen, etc. Grosslages: Badstube (★★★) and Kurfürstlay (★★).

Bernkastel (Bereich)
> Wide area of mixed quality but decided flowery character. Includes all the Mittel-Mosel.

Bingen Rhh. w. ★★→★★★ 71 75 76 77 78 79 *80* 81 82
> Town on Rhine and Nahe with fine v'yds., incl. Scharlachberg. Grosslage: Sankt Rochuskapelle.

Bingen (Bereich)
> District name for w. Rheinhessen.

Bischöfliche Weingüter
> Outstanding M-S-R estate at TRIER, a union of the Cathedral properties with two famous charities. 230 acres of top v'yds. in AVELSBACH, WILTINGEN, SCHARZHOFBERG, AYL, KASEL, EITELSBACH, PIESPORT, TRITTENHEIM, ÜRZIG, etc.

Blue Nun
> The best-selling brand of LIEBFRAUMILCH, from SICHEL.

Bodensee (Bereich)
> Minor district of s. BADEN, on Lake Constance.

Boxbeutel
> Flask-shaped bottle used for FRANKEN wines.

Brauneberg M-M w. ★★★ 71 75 76 77 78 79 *80* 81 82
> Village near BERNKASTEL with 100 acres. Excellent full-flavoured wine. Best v'yd.: Juffer. Grosslage: Kurfürstlay.

Breisgau (Bereich)
> Minor district of BADEN, just n. of KAISERSTUHL.

Brentano, von
> 20-acre old family estate in WINKEL, Rheingau.

Bühl, von
> Great RHEINPFALZ family estate. 200+ acres in DEIDESHEIM, FORST, RUPPERTSBERG, etc. In the very top class.

Bullay M-S-R ★→ ★★ 76 77 78 79 *80* 81 82
> Lower Mosel village. Good light wine to drink young.

Bundesweinprämierung
> The top German Wine Award: a gold, silver or bronze medal on bottles of remarkable wines.

Burgerspital zum Heiligen Geist
> Ancient charitable estate at WÜRZBURG. 185 acres in WÜRZBURG, RANDERSACKER, etc., make rich dry wines.

Bürklin-Wolf
> Great RHEINPFALZ family estate. 222 acres in WACHENHEIM, FORST, DEIDESHEIM and RUPPERTSBERG, with rarely a dull, let alone poor, wine.

Castell'sches, Fürstlich Domäne
> 110-acre princely estate in STEIGERWALD. Good typical FRANKEN wines: Sylvaner, Müller-Thürgau. Also SEKT.

Crown of Crowns
> Popular brand of LIEBFRAUMILCH from LANGENBACH & CO.

Deidesheim   Rhpf. w. (r.)   [**]   →**** **71 75 76** 77 78 79 *80* 81 82
Biggest top-quality wine-village of RHEINPFALZ with 1,000
acres. Rich, high-flavoured, lively wines. V'yds. incl. Hohen-
morgen, Kieselberg, Grainhübel, Leinhöhle, Herrgottsacker,
etc. Grosslages: Hofstück (**), Mariengarten (***).

Deinhard
Famous old Koblenz merchants and growers in Rheingau (see
Wegeler), Mittel-Mosel (68 acres in Bernkastel, incl. part of
Doktor v'yd., Graach, etc.) and Rheinpfalz.

Deutscher Tafelwein
TAFELWEIN from Germany (only).

Deutsches Weinsiegel
A quality "seal" (i.e. neck label) for wines which have passed a
stiff tasting test.

DLG (Deutsche Landwirtshaft Gesellschaft)
The German Agricultural Society. The body that awards
national medals for quality.

Dhron
See Neumagen-Dhron

Diabetiker Wein
Wine with minimal residual sugar (less than 4gms/litre).
Suitable for diabetics — or those who like very dry wine.

Dienheim   Rhh. w. **→*** 78 79 *80* 81 82
Southern neighbour of OPPENHEIM. Mainly run-of-the-mill
wines. Top v'yds.: Kreuz, Herrenberg, Schloss. Grosslages:
Guldenmorgen, Krötenbrunnen.

Dom   German for Cathedral. Wines from the famous TRIER
Cathedral properties have "Dom" before the v'yd. name.

Domäne
German for "domain" or "estate". Sometimes used alone to
mean the "State domain" (Staatliche Weinbaudomäne).

Durbach   Baden w. (r.) *→*** **75 76** 77 78 79 *80* 81 82
150 acres of the best v'yds. of BADEN. Top growers: Schloss
Staufenberg, Wolf-Metternich, von Neveu. Choose their
RIESLINGS. and KLEVNERS, esp. D. Kochberg.

Dürkheim, Bad   Rhpf. w. or (r.)   [**]   →*** **75 76** 78 79 80 81 82
Main town of the MITTEL-HAARDT. Top v'yds.: Hochbenn,
Michelsberg. Grosslages: Feuerberg, Schenkenböhl.

Edel   Means "noble". Edelfäule means "noble rot": the condition
which gives the greatest sweet wines (see p. 47).

Edenkoben   Rhpf. w.(r.) *→   [**]   **75 76** 79 *80* 81 82
Important village of n. SÜDLICHE WEINSTRASSE Grosslage:
Ludwigshöhe.

Egon Müller-Scharzhof
Top Saar estate of 32 acres at WILTINGEN. His SCHARZHOF-
BERGER Rieslings are supreme in top years.

Eiswein
Wine made from frozen grapes with the ice (e.g. water content) rejected, thus very concentrated in flavour and sugar, of
Beerenauslese ripeness or more. Rare and expensive. Sometimes produced as late as the January or February following
the vintage.

Eitelsbach   Ruwer w. **→**** **71 75 76** 77 78 79 *80 81* 82
RUWER village now part of TRIER, incl. superb Karthäuserhof-
berg estate. Grosslage: Trierer Römerlay.

Elbling
Inferior grape widely grown on upper Mosel.

Eltville   Rhg. w.   [**]   →*** **71 75 76** 78 79 *80 81* 82
Major wine-town with cellars of the Rheingau State domain,
SCHLOSS ELTZ and VON SIMMERN estates. Excellent wines. Top
v'yds.: Sonnenberg, Taubenberg. Grosslage: Heiligenstock.

Eltz, Schloss
> Former Rheingau estate now divided. The name and a small portion are connected with PIEROTH.

Enkirch M-M w. ★★→ ⬚★★★⬚ 71 75 76 79 81 82
> Minor middle-Mosel village, often overlooked but with lovely light tasty wine. Grosslage: Schwarzlay.

Erbach Rhg. w. ★★★→★★★★ 71 75 76 79 *81* 82
> One of the best parts of the Rheingau with powerful, perfumed wines, incl. the great MARCOBRUNN; other top v'yds.: Schlossberg, Siegelsberg, Hönigberg, Michelmark. Grosslage: Mehrhölzchen. Major estates: SCHLOSS REINHARTSHAUSEN, von SCHÖNBORN.

Erden M-M w. ★★→★★★ 71 75 76 78 79 81 82
> Village between Urzig and Kröv with full-flavoured vigorous wine. Top v'yds.: Prälat, Treppchen. Leading grower: Beeres. Grosslage: Schwarzlay.

Erzeugerabfüllung
> Bottled by the grower.

Escherndorf Franc. w. ★★→★★★ 71 75 76 78 79 81 82
> Important wine-town near WÜRZBURG. Similar tasty dry wine. Top v'yds.: Lump, Berg. Grosslage: Kirchberg.

Remember that vintage information about German wines is given in a different form from the ready/not ready distinction applying to other countries. Read the explanation on page 76.

Feine, feinste, hochfeinste
> Terms formerly used to distinguish a good grower's best barrels. Now, unfortunately, illegal.

Forst Rhpf. w. ★★→★★★★ 71 75 76 78 79 *80* 81 82
> MITTEL-HAARDT village with 500 acres of Germany's best v'yds. Ripe, richly fragrant but subtle wines. Top v'yds.: Kirchenstück, Jesuitengarten, Ungeheuer, etc. Grosslages: Mariengarten, Schnepfenflüg.

Franken
> Franconia: region of excellent distinctive dry wines. The centre is WÜRZBURG. BEREICH names: MAINVIERECK, MAINDREIECK, STEIGERWALD.

Freiburg Baden w. (r.) ★→★★ D.Y.A.
> Centre of MARKGRÄFLERLAND. Good GUTEDEL.

Friedrich Wilhelm Gymnasium
> Superb 104-acre charitable estate with v'yds. in BERNKASTEL, ZELTINGEN, GRAACH, TRITTENHEIM, OCKFEN, etc., all M-S-R.

Geisenheim Rhg. w. ★★→★★★ 71 75 76 78 79 *81* 82
> Village famous for Germany's leading wine-school. Best v'yds. incl. Rothenberg, Kläuserweg. Grosslage: Burgweg.

Gemeinde
> A commune or parish.

Gewürztraminer
> Spicy grape of Alsace, used a little in s. Germany, esp. Rheinpfalz.

Gimmeldingen Rhpf. w. ★→ ⬚★★⬚ 75 76 78 79 81 82
> Village just s. of MITTEL-HAARDT. Similar wines. Grosslage: Meerspinne.

Goldener Oktober
> Popular Rhine-wine and Mosel blend from ST. URSULA.

Graach M-M w. ★★→ ⬚★★★⬚ 71 75 76 78 79 81 82
> Small village between BERNKASTEL and WEHLEN. Top v'yds.: Himmelreich, Domprobst, Abstberg, Josephshöfer. Grosslage: Münzlay.

Grosslage
> See Introduction, p. 76

Guntersblum   Rhh. w. *→** 75 76 78 79 81 82
 Big wine-town s. of OPPENHEIM. Grosslages: Krötenbrunnen, Vogelsgarten.

Guntrum, Louis
 Fine 130-acre family estate in NIERSTEIN, OPPENHEIM, etc.

Gutedel
 German for the Chasselas grape, used in s. BADEN.

Halbtrocken
 "Half-dry". Containing less than 18 grams per litre unfermented sugar. A rather vague category of wine intended for meal-times, often better-balanced than "TROCKEN".

Hallgarten   Rhg. w. **→*** 71 75 76 78 79 81 82
 Important little wine-town behind HATTENHEIM. Robust full-bodied wines. Top v'yds. incl. Schönhell, Jungfer. Grosslage: Mehrhölzchen.

Hallgarten, House of
 Well-known London-based wine-merchant.

Hanns Christof
 Top brand of LIEBFRAUMILCH from DEINHARD'S.

Hattenheim   Rhg. w. **→**** 71 75 76 78 79 81 82
 Superlative 500-acre wine-town. V'yds. incl. STEINBERG, MARCOBRUNN, Nüssbrunnen, Mannberg, etc. Grosslage: Deutelsberg.

Heilbronn   Württ. w. r. *→** 76 78 79 81 82
 Wine-town with many small growers and a big co-op. Seat of DLG competition.

Hessische Bergstrasse   Rhh. w. **→*** 75 76 78 79 81 82
 Minor (700-acre) region s. of Frankfurt. Pleasant Riesling from State domain v'yds. in Heppenheim and Bensheim.

Hessische Forschungsanstalt für Wein- Obst- & Gartenbau
 Germany's top wine-school and research establishment, at GEISENHEIM, Rheingau.

Heyl zu Herrnsheim
 Fine 72-acre estate at NIERSTEIN, 55% Riesling.

Hochfeinste
 "Very finest." Traditional label-term, now illegal.

Hochheim   Rhg. w. **→*** 71 75 76 78 79 81 82
 600-acre wine-town 15 miles e. of RHEINGAU. Similar fine wines. Top v'yds.: Domdechaney, Kirchenstück, Hölle, Königin Viktoria Berg. Grosslage: Daubhaus.

Hock   English term for Rhine-wine, derived from HOCHHEIM.

Huxelrebe
 Modern very fruity grape variety.

Ihringen   Bad. (r.) w. *→** 75 76 78 79 81 82
 One of the best villages of the KAISERSTUHL, BADEN. Heavy dryish wines.

Ilbesheim   Rhpf. w. *→ ** 76 79 81 82
 Base of important growers' co-operative of SÜDLICHE WEIN-STRASSE. See also Schweigen.

Ingelheim   Rhh. r. or w. * 76 79 81 82
 Town opposite the Rheingau historically known for red wine.

Iphofen   Franc. w. **→ ⟨***⟩ 71 75 76 79 81 82
 Village e. of WÜRZBURG. Superb top v'yd.: Julius-Echter-Berg. Grosslage: Burgweg.

Jesuitengarten
 15-acre vineyard in FORST. One of Germany's best.

Johannisberg   Rhg. w. **→**** 71 75 76 78 79 81 82
 260-acre village with superlative subtle wine. Top v'yds. incl. SCHLOSS JOHANNISBERG, Hölle, Klaus, etc. Grosslage: Erntebringer.

Johannisberg (Bereich)
 District name of the entire RHEINGAU.

Josephshöfer
>Fine v'yd. at GRAACH, the property of von KESSELSTATT.

Juliusspital
>Ancient charity at WÜRZBURG with top FRANKEN v'yds.

Kabinett
>The term for the driest and least expensive natural unsugared (QmP) wines.

Kaiserstuhl-Tuniberg (Bereich)
>Best v'yd. area of BADEN. Villages incl. IHRINGEN, ACHKARREN.

Kallstadt Rhpf. w. (r.) **→*** 71 75 76 78 79 81 82
>Village just n. of MITTEL-HAARDT. Fine rich wines. Top v'yd.: ANNABERG. Grosslages: Saumagen (***), Kobnert (**).

Kanzem M-S-R (Saar) w. **→*** 71 75 76 79 81 82
>Small but excellent neighbour of WILTINGEN. Top v'yds.: Sonnenberg, Altenberg. Grosslage: Scharzberg.

Kasel M-S-R (Ruwer) w. ** 71 75 76 79 81 82
>Village with attractive light wines. Best v'yd.: Nies'chen. Grosslage: Römerlay.

Keller Wine-cellar or winery.

Kerner
>Modern very flowery grape variety.

Kesselstatt, von
>The biggest private Mosel estate, 600 years old. Over 50 acres in GRAACH, PIESPORT, KASEL, MENNIG, WILTINGEN, etc. making light and fruity typical Mosels. Now belongs to Gunther Reh.

Kesten M-W w. *→*** 71 75 76 79 81 82
>Neighbour of BRAUNEBERG. Best wines (from Paulinshofberg v'yd.) similar. Grosslage: Kurfürstlay.

Kiedrich Rhg. w. **→**** 71 75 76 79 81 82
>Neighbour of RAUENTHAL; almost as splendid and high flavoured. Top v'yds.: Gräfenberg, Wasseros, Sandgrub. Grosslages: Heiligenstock and Steinmächer.

Klevner (or Clevner)
>Term for the PINOT BLANC grape used in BADEN-WÜRTTEMBERG. Red Klevner is supposedly Italian Chiavenna, an early-ripening black Pinot.

Klingelberger
>BADEN term for the RIESLING.

Kloster Eberbach
>Glorious 12th-century Abbey at HATTENHEIM, Rheingau, now State domain property and H.Q. of the German Wine Academy. See panel, p. 78.

Klüsserath M-M w. **→ ***   71 76 79 81 82
>Minor Mosel village worth trying in good vintages. Best v'yds.: Brüderschaft, Königsberg. Grosslage: St. Michael.

Kreuznach (Bereich)
>District name for the entire northern NAHE. See also Bad Kreuznach.

Kröv M-M w. *→*** 75 76 79 81 82
>Popular tourist resort famous for its Grosslage name: Nacktarsch, meaning "bare bottom".

Landespreismünze
>Prizes for quality at state, rather than national, level. Considered by some more discriminating than DLG medals.

Landgräflich Hessisches Weingut
>Wide-ranging 75-acre estate in JOHANNISBERG, WINKEL, etc.

Landwein
>A new (1982) category of superior TAFELWEIN from 15 designated regions. It must be TROCKEN or HALBTROCKEN. Similar to France's *vins de pays*.

Langenbach & Co.
>Well-known merchants of London and WORMS.

Lauerburg
>One of the three owners of the famous Doktor v'yd. in BERNKASTEL, with THANISCH and DEINHARD.

Liebfrauenstift
>26-acre v'yd. in the city of WORMS, said to be the origin of the name LIEBFRAUMILCH.

Liebfraumilch
>Legally defined as a QbA "of pleasant character" from RHEINHESSEN, RHEINPFALZ, NAHE or RHEINGAU, blended from RIESLING, SYLVANER or MÜLLER-THURGAU. Most is mild semi-sweet wine from Rheinhessen and Rheinpfalz.

Lieser   M-M w. *→   ******   71 75 76 79 81 82
>Little-known neighbour of BERNKASTEL. Grosslages: Beerenlay, Kurfürstlay.

Lorch   Rhg. w. (r.) *→** 71 76 79 81 82
>At extreme w. end of Rheingau. Secondary quality. Best grower: von Kanitz.

Löwenstein, Fürst
>66-acre FRANKEN estate: classic dry wines.

Maikammer Rhpf. w. (r.) *→   ******   76 79 81 82
>Village of n. SÜDLICHE WEINSTRASSE. Very pleasant wines incl. those from co-op at Rietburg. Grosslage: Mandelhöhe.

Maindreieck (Bereich)
>District name for central part of FRANKEN, incl. WÜRZBURG.

Mainviereck (Bereich)
>District name for minor w. part of FRANKEN.

Marcobrunn
>See Erbach

Markgräflerland (Bereich)
>Minor district s. of Freiburg (BADEN). GUTEDEL wine is delicious when drunk very young.

Martinsthal   Rhg. w. **→   *******   71 75 76 78 79 81 82
>Little-known neighbour of RAUENTHAL. Top v'yds.: Langenberg, Wildsau. Grosslage: Steinmächer.

Matuschka-Greiffenclau, Graf
>Owner of the ancient SCHLOSS VOLLRADS estate.

Maximin Grünhaus   M-S-R (Ruwer) w. **** 71 75 76 78 79 80 81 82
>Supreme RUWER estate of 52 acres at Mertesdorf.

Mennig   M-S-R (Saar) w.   ******   71 75 76 79 81 82
>Village between TRIER and the SAAR. Its Falkensteiner v'yd. is famous.

Mertesdorf
>See Maximin Grünhaus

Mittelheim   Rhg. w. **→   *******   71 75 76 78 79 81 82
>Minor village between WINKEL and OESTRICH. Top grower: WEGELER. Grosslage: Honigberg.

Mittel-Haardt
>The northern, best part, of RHEINPFALZ, incl. FORST, DEIDESHEIM, WACHENHEIM, etc.

Mittel-Mosel
>The central and best part of the Mosel, incl. BERNKASTEL, PIESPORT, etc.

Mittelrhein
>Northern Rhine area of secondary quality, incl. BACHARACH.

Morio Muskat
>Stridently aromatic grape variety popular in RHEINPFALZ.

Moselblümchen
>The "LIEBFRAUMILCH" of the Mosel, but on a lower quality level: TAFELWEIN not QbA.

Mosel-Saar-Ruwer
>Includes MITTEL-MOSEL, SAAR, RUWER and lesser areas.

Müller, Felix
>Fine small SAAR estate with delicate SCHARZHOFBERGER.

Müller-Thurgau
>Fruity, low-acid grape variety; the commonest in RHEINPFALZ and RHEINHESSEN, but increasingly planted in all areas.

Mumm, von
>173-acre estate in JOHANNISBERG, RUDESHEIM, etc. Under the same control as SCHLOSS JOHANNISBERG.

Munster Nahe w. `*→***` **71 75 76** 78 79 81 82
>Best village of n. NAHE, with fine delicate wines. Top grower: State Domain. Grosslage: Schlosskapelle.

Nackenheim Rhh. w. `*→***` **71 75 76** 79 81 82
>Neighbour of NIERSTEIN; best wines (Engelsberg, Rothenberg) similar. Grosslages: Spiegelberg (***), Gutes Domtal (*).

Nahe
>Tributary of the Rhine and quality wine region. Balanced, fresh and clean but full-flavoured wines. Two Bereiche: KREUZNACH and SCHLOSS BÖCKELHEIM.

Neef M-S-R w. `*→` `**` 71 76 79 *81* 82
>Village of lower Mosel with one fine v'yd.: Frauenberg.

Neipperg, Graf
>62-acre top WÜRTTEMBERG estate at Schwaigern.

Nell, von
>40-acre family estate at TRIER and AYL, etc.

Neumagen-Dhron M-M w. `**→***` 71 75 76 78 79 81 82
>Neighbour of PIESPORT. Top v'yd.: Hofberger. Grosslage: Michelsberg.

GERMANY'S QUALITY LEVELS
The range of qualities in ascending order is
1) Tafelwein; sweetish light wine of no special character.
2) Landwein: dryish tafelwein with some regional style.
3) Qualitätswein: dry or sweetish wine with sugar added to increase the strength but tested for quality and with distinct local and grape character.
4) Kabinettwein: dry or dryish natural (unsugared wine) of distinct personality – can be very fine.
5) Spätlese: stronger, often sweeter than Kabinett. Full bodied.
6) Auslese: sweeter, sometimes stronger than Spätlese, often with honey-like flavours, intense and long.
7) Beerenauslese: very sweet and usually strong, intense, can be superb.
8) Trockenbeerenauslese: intensely sweet and aromatic, often low strength.
9) Eiswein: (Beeren- or Trockenbeerenauslese) concentrated, sharpish and very sweet. Extraordinary and everlasting.

Neustadt
>Central city of Rheinpfalz, with famous wine school.

Niederhausen Na. w. `**→` `****` 71 75 76 79 81 82
>Neighbour of SCHLOSS BÖCKELHEIM and H.Q. of Nahe State Domain. Wines of grace and power. Top v'yds. incl. Hermannshöhle, Steinberg. Grosslage: Burgweg.

Niedermennig
>See Mennig

Niederwalluf
>See Walluf

Nierstein (Bereich)
>Large e. RHEINHESSEN district of very mixed quality.

Nierstein Rhh. w. `*→***` 71 75 76 78 79 81 82
>Famous but treacherous name. 1,300 acres incl. superb v'yds.: Hipping, Orbel, Pettenthal, etc., and their Grosslages Rehbach, Spiegelberg, Auflangen: ripe, racy wines. But beware Grosslage Gutes Domtal: no guarantee of anything.

Nobling

Promising new grape variety in BADEN.

Norheim   Nahe w. *→*** 71 75 76 79 81 82

Neighbour of NIEDERHAUSEN. Top v'yds.: Klosterberg, Kafels, Kirschheck. Grosslage: Burgweg.

Oberemmel   M-S-R (Saar) w. **→*** 71 75 76 79 81 82

Next village to WILTINGEN. Very fine wines from Rosenberg, Hütte, etc. Grosslage: Scharzberg.

Obermosel (Bereich)

District name for the upper Mosel above TRIER. Generally poor wines from the Elbling grape.

Ockfen   M-S-R (Saar) w. **→*** 71 75 76 79 81 82

200-acre hill with superb fragrant austere wines. Top v'yds.: Bockstein, Herrenberg. Grosslage: Scharzberg.

Oechsle

Scale for sugar-content of grape-juice (see page 21).

Oestrich   Rhg. w. **→*** 71 75 76 81 82

Big village; good but rarely top grade. V'yds. incl. Doosberg, Lenchen. Grosslage: Gottesthal.

Oppenheim   Rhh. w. *→*** 71 75 76 79 81 82

Town s. of NIERSTEIN, best wines (Kreuz, Sackträger) similar. Grosslages: Guldenmorgen (***) Krotenbrunnen (**).

Originalabfüllung

Bottled by the grower. An obsolete term.

Ortenau (Bereich)

District just s. of Baden-Baden. Soft wines to drink young. Best village DURBACH.

Palatinate

English for RHEINPFALZ.

Perlwein

Semi-sparkling wine.

Pfalz   See Rheinpfalz

Pieroth

Major wine-sales company; also has small vineyard holdings.

Piesport   M-M w. **→**** 71 75 76 78 79 81 82

Tiny village with famous amphitheatre of vines giving fine gentle fruity wine. Top v'yds.: Goldtröpfchen, Gunterslay, Falkenberg. Treppchen is on flatter land and inferior. Grosslage: Michelsberg.

Plettenberg, von

Fine 100-acre Nahe estate at BAD KREUZNACH.

Pokalwein

Café wine. A pokal is a big glass.

Portugieser

Second-rate red-wine grape.

Prädikat

Special attributes or qualities. See QmP.

Prüfungsnummer

The official identifying test-number of a quality wine.

Prüm, J. J.

Superlative 34-acre Mosel estate in WEHLEN, GRAACH, BERNKASTEL. Rich, long-lived wines.

Prüm, S. A., Erben

Small separate part of the Prüm family estate making fine Wehleners, etc.

Qualitätswein bestimmter Anbaugebiete (QbA)

The middle quality of German wine, with added sugar but strictly controlled as to grape areas, etc.

Qualitätswein mit Prädikat (QmP)

Top category, incl. all wines ripe enough to be unsugared, from KABINETT to TROCKENBEERENAUSLESE.

Randersacker   Franc. w. **★★→★★★ 71 76 79 81 82**
Leading village for distinctive dry wine. Top v'yds. incl. Teufelskeller. Grosslage: Ewig Leben.

Rauenthal   Rhg. w.   ★★★   → ★★★★ **71 75 76 78 79 *81* 82**
Supreme village for powerful spicy wine. Top v'yds. incl. Baiken, Gehrn, Wulfen. Grosslage: Steinmacher. The State Domain is an important grower.

Rautenstrauch Erben
Owners of the splendid Karthäuserhof, EITELSBACH.

Rheinart Erben
Distinguished 26-acre Saar estate. Fine OCKFENER BOCK-STEIN. Now owned by H. SCHMITT SÖHNE.

Rheinburgengau (Bereich)
District name for the v'yds. of the MITTELRHEIN round the famous Rhine gorge. Moderate quality only.

Rheingau
The best v'yd. region of the Rhine, near Wiesbaden. 5,000 acres. Classic, substantial but subtle RIESLING. Bereich name, JOHANNISBERG.

Rheinhessen
Vast region (30,000 acres of v'yds.) between Mainz and the NAHE, most second-rate, but incl. NIERSTEIN, OPPENHEIM, etc.

Rheinpfalz
Even vaster 35,000-acre v'yd. region s. of Rheinhessen. Wines inclined to sweetness. (See Mittel-Haardt and Südliche Weinstrasse.) This and the last are the chief sources of LIEBFRAUMILCH.

Rhodt
Village of SÜDLICHE WEINSTRASSE with well-known co-operative. Agreeable fruity wines. Grosslage: Ordensgut.

Rieslaner
Cross between RIESLING and SYLVANER; a good grape in FRANCONIA and BADEN.

Riesling
The best German grape: fine, fragrant, fruity, long-lived.

Ritter zu Groenesteyn, Baron
Fine 37-acre estate in KIEDRICH and RÜDESHEIM.

Roseewein
Rosé wine.

Rotenfelser Bastei
See Traisen

Rotwein   Red wine.

Rüdesheim   Rhg. w. ★★→★★★ **71 75 76 79 *81* 82**
Rhine resort with 650 acres of excellent v'yds.; the three best called Berg. . . . Full-bodied wines. Grosslage: Burgweg.

Rüdesheimer Rosengarten
Rüdesheim is also the name of a NAHE village near BAD KREUZNACH. Do not be misled by the ubiquitous blend going by this name. It has nothing to do with Rheingau RÜDESHEIM.

Ruländer
The PINOT GRIS: grape giving soft heavy wine. Best in BADEN.

Ruppertsberg   Rhpf. w. ★★→   ★★★   **71 75 76 79 80 81 82**
Southern village of MITTEL-HAARDT. Top v'yds. incl. Gaisbohl, Hoheburg. Grosslage: Hofstück.

Ruwer
Tributary of Mosel near TRIER. Very fine delicate wines. Villages incl. EITELSBACH, MERTESDORF, KASEL.

Saar   Tributary of Mosel s. of RUWER. Brilliant austere wines. Villages incl. WILTINGEN, AYL, OCKFEN, SERRIG. Grosslage: Scharzberg.

Saar-Ruwer (Bereich)
District incl. the two above.

Salem, Schloss
>113-acre estate of Margrave of Baden on L. Constance in S. Germany. MÜLLER-THURGAU and WEISSHERBST.

St. Ursula
>Well-known merchants at BINGEN; owners of VILLA SACHSEN.

Scharzberger
>Grosslage name of WILTINGEN and neighbours.

Scharzhofberger   Saar w. ★★★★ 71 75 76 77 78 79 *80 81* 82
>Superlative 30-acre SAAR v'yd.: austerely beautiful wines, the perfection of RIESLING. Do not confuse with the last.

Schaumwein
>Sparkling wine.

Scheurebe
>Fruity aromatic grape used in RHEINPFALZ.

Schillerwein
>Light red or rosé QbA, speciality of WÜRTTEMBERG.

Schlossabzug
>Bottled at the Schloss (castle).

Schloss Böckelheim   Nahe w. ★★→★★★★ 71 75 76 79 81 82
>Village with the best NAHE v'yds., incl. Kupfergrübe, Felsenberg. Firm yet delicate wine. Grosslage: Burgweg.

Schloss Böckelheim (Bereich)
>District name for the whole southern NAHE.

Schloss Johannisberg   Rhg. w. ★★★→★★★★
>Famous RHEINGAU estate of 66 acres belonging to the Oetke family and now run in conjunction with VON MUMM. Polished, elegant wine.

Schloss Reinhartshausen
>Fine 99-acre estate in ERBACH, HATTENHEIM, etc. much improved since 1976.

Schloss Vollrads   Rhg. w. ★★★→★★★★ 71 75 76 78 79 *81* 82
>Great estate at WINKEL, since 1300. 81 acres producing classical RHEINGAU RIESLING, esp. since 1977. TROCKEN wines a speciality.

Schmitt, Gustav Adolf
>Fine old 124-acre family estate at NIERSTEIN.

Schmitt, Franz Karl
>Even older 74-acre ditto.

Schmitt H., Söhne
>One of the largest merchant-houses of the Mosel, at LONGUICH, also with three small estates.

Schönborn, Graf von
>One of the biggest and best Rheingau estates, based at HATTENHEIM. Full-blooded wines. Also very good SEKT.

Schoppenwein
>Café wine: i.e. wine by the glass.

Schorlemer, Freiherr von
>Important MOSEL estate of 116 acres in 5 parts, based at LIESER, known for crisp, delicate wines. Now controlled by Meyer-Horne, merchants at BERNKASTEL.

Schubert, von
>Owner of MAXIMIN GRÜNHAUS.

Schweigen   Rhpf. w. ★→ ★★ 76 79 81 82
>Southernmost Rheinpfalz village with big co-operative, Deutsches WEINTOR. Grosslage: Guttenberg.

Sekt   German (QbA) sparkling wine.

Serrig   M-S-R (Saar) w. ★★→★★★ 71 75 76 79 *81* 82
>Village known for "steely" wine, excellent in hot years. Top growers: VEREINIGTE HOSPITIEN and State Domain. Grosslage: Scharzberg.

Sichel H., Söhne
>Famous wine-merchants of London and Mainz.

Silvaner
>Common German white grape, best in FRANKEN.

Simmern, von
>94-acre family estate at HATTENHEIM since 1464 and in ELTVILLE, RAUENTHAL, etc. Fine, relatively light wines.

Sonnenuhr
>"Sun-dial." Name of several famous v'yds., esp. one at WEHLEN.

Spätburgunder
>PINOT NOIR: the best red-wine grape in Germany.

Spätlese
>"Late gathered." One better (stronger/sweeter) than KABINETT.

Spindler
>Fine 33-acre family estate at FORST, Rheinpfalz.

Staatsweingut (or Staatliche Weinbaudomäne)
>The State wine estate or domain.

Staufenberg, Schloss
>65-acre DURBACH estate of the Margrave of Baden. Fine "Klingelberger" (RIESLING).

Steigerwald (Bereich)
>District name for e. part of FRANKEN.

Steinberg   Rhg. w. ★★★→★★★★71 75 76 78 79 81 82
>Famous 62-acre v'yd. at HATTENHEIM walled by Cistercians 700 yrs. ago. Now property of the State.

Steinwein
>Wine from WÜRZBURG's best v'yd., Stein. The term is loosely used for all Franconian wine.

Stuttgart
>Chief city of WÜRTTEMBERG, producer of some pleasant wines (esp. Riesling), recently beginning to be exported.

Südliche Weinstrasse (Bereich)
>District name for the s. RHEINPFALZ.

Tafelwein
>"Table wine." The vin ordinaire of Germany. Can be blended with other EEC wines. But Deutscher Tafelwein must come from Germany alone. (See also LANDWEIN.)

Thanisch, Dr.
>32-acre BERNKASTEL family estate of top quality, incl. part of Doktor v'yd.

Traben-Trarbach   M-W w.   ★★ 76 79 81 82
>Secondary wine-town, some good light wines. Top v'yds. incl. Schlossberg, Ungsberg. Grosslage: Schwarzlay.

Traisen   Na. w.   ★★★ 71 75 76 79 81 82
>Small village incl. superlative Bastei v'yd., making wine of great concentration and class.

Traminer
>See Gewürztraminer

Trier   M-S-R w. ★★→★★★★
>Important wine city of Roman origin, on the Mosel, adjacent to RUWER, now incl. AVELSBACH and EITELSBACH. Grosslage: Römerlay.

Trittenheim   M-M w.   ★★ →★★★ 71 75 76 79 81 82
>Attractive light wines. Top v'yds. Apotheke, Altärchen, Grosslage: Michelsberg.

Trocken
>Dry. On labels Trocken *alone* means with a statutory maximum of unfermented sugar (9 grams per litre). But see next entry. See also Halbtrocken.

Trockenbeerenauslese
>The sweetest and most expensive category of wine, made from selected withered grapes. See also Edelfäule.

Trollinger
Common red grape of WÜRTTEMBERG: locally very popular.

Ungstein Rhpf. w. **→ `★★★` 71 75 76 78 79 81 82
MITTEL-HAARDT village with fine harmonious wines. Top v'yd.
Herrenberg. Top grower Führmann (Weingut Pfeffingen).
Grosslage Hönigsackel.

Ürzig M-M w. `★★★` 71 75 76 79 81 82
Village famous for lively spicy wine. Top v'yd.: Würzgarten.
Grosslage: Schwarzlay.

Vereinigte Hospitien
"United Hospitals." Ancient charity at Trier with large holdings in SERRIG, WILTINGEN, TRIER, PIESPORT, etc.

Verwaltung
Property.

Villa Sachsen
75-acre BINGEN estate belonging to ST. URSULA Weingut.

Wachenheim Rhpf. w. `★★★` → ★★★★ 71 75 76 79 81 82
840 acres, incl. exceptionally fine Rieslings. V'yds. incl.
Gerümpel, Böhlig, Rechbächel. Top grower: Bürklin-Wolf.
Grosslages: Schenkenbohl, Schnepfenflug, Mariengarten.

Waldrach M-S-R (Ruwer) w. `★★` 75 76 79 *81* 82
Some charming light wines. Grosslage: (Trierer) Römerlay.

Walluf Rhg. w. `★★` 75 76 79 *81* 82
Neighbour of ELTVILLE; formerly Nieder- and Ober-Walluf.
Good but not top wines. Grosslage: Steinmächer.

Walporzheim-Ahrtal (Bereich)
District name for the whole AHR valley.

Wawern M-S-R (Saar) w. **→ ★★★ 71 76 79 *81* 82
Small village with fine Rieslings. Grosslage: Scharzberg.

Wegeler Erben
138-acre Rheingau estate owned by DEINHARD'S. V'yds. in
OESTRICH, MITTELHEIM, WINKEL, GEISENHEIM, RÜDESHEIM, etc.

Wehlen M-M w. `★★★` → ★★★★ 71 75 76 79 81 82
Neighbour of BERNKASTEL with equally fine, somewhat
richer, wine. Best v'yd.: Sonnenuhr. Top growers: Prüm
family. Grosslage: Münzlay.

Weil, Dr.
Fine 46-acre private estate at KIEDRICH. Currently below
form.

Weingut
Wine estate. Can only be used on the label by estates that
grow all their own grapes.

Weinkellerei
Wine cellars or winery.

Weinstrasse
"Wine road." Scenic route through v'yds. Germany has
several, the most famous in RHEINPFALZ.

Weintor, Deutsches
See Schweigen

Weissenheim-am-Sand Rhpf. w. (r.) ★→ ★★ 76 79 81 82
Big northern Pfalz village on sandy soil. Light wines.

Weissherbst
Rosé of QbA standard or above, even occasionally BEERENAUS-
LESE, the speciality of BADEN and WÜRTTEMBERG.

Werner, Domdechant
Fine 32-acre family estate on the best slopes of HOCHHEIM.

Wiltingen Saar w. ★★→ ★★★★ 71 75 76 79 *81* 82
The centre of the Saar. 790 acres. Beautiful subtle austere
wine. Top v'yds. incl. SCHARZHOFBERGER, Braune Kupp,
Braunfels, Klosterberg. Grosslage (for the whole Saar):
Scharzberger.

Winkel Rhg. w. ★★★→ ★★★★ 71 75 76 79 81 82
> Village famous for fragrant wine, incl. SCH. VOLLRADS. V'yds. incl. Hasensprung, Jesuitengarten. Grosslage: Hönigberg.

Wintrich M-M w. ★★→ ★★★ 71 75 76 79 81 82
> Neighbour of PIESPORT; similar wines. Top v'yds.: Grosser Herrgott, Ohligsberg, Sonnenseite. Grosslage: Kurfürstlay.

Winzergenossenschaft
> Wine-growers' co-operative, usually making good and reasonably priced wine.

Winzerverein
> The same as the last.

Wonnegau (Bereich)
> District name for s. RHEINHESSEN.

Worms Rhh. w. ★★
> City with the famous LIEBFRAUENSTIFT v'yd.

Württemberg
> Vast s. area little known for wine outside Germany. Some good RIESLINGS, esp. from Neckar valley. Also TROLLINGER.

Würzburg Frank. ★★→ ★★★★ 71 75 76 78 79 81 82
> Great baroque city on the Main, centre of Franconian (FRANKEN) wine: fine, full-bodied and dry. Top v'yds.: Stein, Leiste, Schlossberg. No Grosslage. See also Maindreieck.

ZBW (Zentralkellerei Baden-Württemberg)
> Germany's (and Europe's) biggest ultra-modern co-operative, at Breisach, BADEN, with 23,000 grower-members, producing 80 per cent of Baden's wine at all quality levels.

Zell M-S-R w. ★→ ★★ 76 79 81 82
> Lower Mosel village famous for its Grosslage name Schwarze Katze ("Black Cat"). No fine wines.

Zell (Bereich)
> District name for the whole lower Mosel from Zell to Koblenz.

Zeltingen-Rachtig M-M w. ★★ → ★★★★ 71 75 76 79 81 82
> Important Mosel village next to WEHLEN. Typically lively but full-bodied wine. Top v'yds.: Sonnenuhr, Schlossberg. Grosslage: Münzlay.

THE STRENGTH OF WINE *The alcoholic strength of wine varies considerably. Alcohol provides much of the feeling of "body" in strong wines, but needs to be balanced by the flavouring elements: sugar, acidity, tannin and assorted "extract". Without this richness of flavour it would be fierce and unpleasant.*
Typical alcoholic strengths (% by volume), as found in a laboratory analysing commercial samples, are:

German Tafelwein 8–11   *German Kabinett* 8–9
German Auslese 10–10.5   *German Beerenauslese* 12.8–14
French vin de table 9–12   *Red Bordeaux* 10.5–13
Bordeaux cru classé 11–12   *Beaujolais-Villages* 10–10.5
Muscadet 12   *Alsace Riesling* 10.5–11.5
Chablis Premier Cru 10.5–12.7   *Beaune* 11–14   *Chambertin* 12.4
Châteauneuf-du-Pape 12.6+   *Montrachet* 12.6
California Zinfandel 12–16   *California Chardonnay* 10.5–13.5
California Cabernet 11.44   *Australian Cabernet/Shiraz* 13.8
Barolo 12–14   *Chianti* 12–13   *Valpolicella* 11.7
Rioja reserva 12.5   *Sauternes* 12–15   *Château Yquem* 13.5–16
Fino sherry 18–20   *Oloroso sherry* 18–20   *Vintage port* 19–20

Italy

Valle d'Aosta
Vd'A

M.

Turin ●

Piemonte
Piem

Liguria

Genoa ●

Italy is the world's biggest wine producer with one of the biggest per capita consumptions: 100 bottles a year. She is so at home with wine that she can seem alarmingly casual about it. Yet year by year over the last decade her wines have been attracting more international attention. A great change is afoot.

The chief clue to Italian wine is the DOC system, an approximate equivalent of France's Appellations Controlées, which has been taking shape since the 1960s. Most of Italy's worthwhile wines now have defined areas and standards under the new system. A few, like Chianti Classico, it must be said, had them long before. A few, however, have not—and DOCs have been granted to many areas of only local interest: so the mere existence of a DOC proves little. The entries in this book ignore a score of unimportant DOCs and include considerably more non-DOCs. They also include a large number of grape-name entries.

Italian wines are named in a variety of ways: some geographical like French wines, some historical, some folklorical, and many of the best from their grapes. These include old "native" grapes such as Barbera and Sangiovese and more and more imported "international" grapes from France and Germany. Many of the DOCs, particularly in the north-east, are area names applying to widely different wines from as many as a dozen different varieties. No overall comment on the quality of such a diversity is really possible, except to say that general standards are rising steadily and a growing number of producers are emerging as outstanding by international standards.

Another rather disconcerting aspect of Italian wine is clear from the following pages: in many cases the same name applies to wine which can be red or white or in between, sweet or dry or in between, still or sparkling or in between. This must be taken into account when interpreting the necessarily cryptic grades of quality and vintage notes. Vintage notes are given when specific information has been available. Where there is no comment the best plan is to aim for the youngest available white wine and experiment with the oldest available red . . . within reason.

The map is the key to the province names used for locating each entry.

Abbreviations of province names shown in bold type are used in the text.

The following abbreviations are used in the Italian section
Pa.   passito
Pr.   Province
Com. commune
f.   fortified
See also key to symbols opposite
Contents

Abboccato
>   Semi-sweet.

Aglianico del Vulture   Bas. DOC r. (s/sw. sp.)   ★★★   73 75 77 78 79
81
>   Among the best wines of s. Italy. Ages well. Called Vecchio
>   after 3 yrs., Riserva after 5 yrs.

Alba   Major wine-centre of PIEMONTE.

Albana di Romagna   Em-Ro. DOC w. dr. s/sw. (sp.) ★★ 78 79 80 82
>   Produced for several centuries in Romagna from Albana
>   grapes. Cold fermentation now robs it of much character.

Alcamo   Sic. DOC w. dr. ★
>   Soft neutral whites from w. Sicily. Rapitalà is the best brand.

Aleatico
>   Red, slightly muscat-flavoured grape.

Aleatico di Gradoli   Lat. DOC r. sw. or f. ★★
>   Aromatic, fruity, alcohol 17·5%. Made in Viterbo.

Aleatico di Puglia   Apu. DOC r. sw. or f. ★★
>   Aleatico grapes make good dessert wine over a large area.
>   Two types have 15% or 18·5% alcohol.

Alezio   Apu. DOC r. p. dr. ★★
>   New Salento DOC for Negro Amaro wines.

Allegrini
>   Well-known producer of Veronese wines, incl. VALPOLICELLA.

Alto Adige   Tr-AAd. DOC r. p. w. dr. sw. sp. ★★
>   A DOC covering some 17 different wines named after their
>   grape varieties in 33 villages round Bolzano.

Amabile
>   Semi-sweet, but usually sweeter than ABBOCCATO.

Amaro   Bitter.

Amarone   See Recioto.

Antinori
>   A long-established Tuscan house of repute producing first-
>   rate, if not truly typical, CHIANTI and ORVIETO.

Asti   Major wine-centre of PIEMONTE.

Asti Spumante   Piem. DOC w. sp.   ★★★   NV
>   Sweet and very fruity muscat sparkling wine. Low in alcohol.

Attems, Count
>   Leading producer and Consorzio president of COLLIO. Good
>   PINOT GRIGIO, MERLOT, etc.

Badia a Coltibuono   71 75 77 78 79 80 81 82
>   Fine Chianti-maker at Gaiole with a restaurant and remark-
>   able collection of old vintages.

Banfi, Villa
>   Major American importers of Italian wine, esp. LAMBRUSCO.

Barbacarlo (Oltrepo' Pavese)   Lomb. DOC r. dr. or sw. ★★→★★★ 78
79 81 82
>   Delicately flavoured with bitter after-taste, made in the Com.
>   of Broni in the Pr. of Pavia.

Barbaresco   Piem. DOCG r. dr. ★★★→★★★★ 71 74 76 78 79 80 81
>   Neighbour of BAROLO from the same grapes but lighter,
>   ageing sooner. At best subtle and fine. At 3 yrs. becomes
>   Riserva, 4 yrs. Riserva Speciale. Best producers incl. GAJA.

Barbera
>   Dark acidic red grape, a speciality of Piemonte also used in
>   Lombardy, Veneto, Friuli and other n. provinces. Its best
>   wines are:

Barbera d'Alba   Piem. DOC r. dr. ★★ 74 78 79 80 81 82
>   Round ALBA NEBBIOLO is sometimes added. Clean, tasty, frag-
>   rant red improves for 3–4 yrs.

Barbera d'Asti   Piem. DOC r. dr.   ★★   78 79 80 81 82
>   Reputedly the best of the Barberas; all Barbera grapes; dark,
>   grapy and appetizing. Ages up to 7–8 yrs.

Barbera del Monferrato Piem. DOC r. dr. ∗ **78 79 81 82**
From a large area in the Pr. of Alessandria and ASTI. Pleasant, slightly fizzy, sometimes sweetish.

Bardolino Ven. DOC r. dr. (p.) ∗∗ D.Y.A.
Pale, light, slightly bitter red from e. shore of La. Garda. Bardolino Chiaretto is even paler and lighter.

Barolo Piem. DOCG r. dr. ∗∗∗→∗∗∗∗ **71 74** 78 79 80 81 82
Small area s. of Turin with one of the best Italian red wines, dark, rich, alcoholic (minimum 12°), dry but deep in flavour. From NEBBIOLO grapes. Ages for up to 15 yrs, Riserva after 3.

Bell 'Agio Brand of sweet white MOSCATO from BANFI.

Bertani
Well-known producers of quality Veronese wines (VAL-POLICELLA, SOAVE, etc.).

Bertolli, Francesco
Among the best-known producers of CHIANTI CLASSICO. Cellars at Castellina in Chianti, n. of Siena. Ambra is their standard branded range.

Bianco White.

Bianco di Pitigliano Tusc. DOC w. dr ✲ D.Y.A.
A soft, fruity, lively wine made near Grosseto.

Bianco Vergine della Valdichiana Tusc. DOC w. dr. ∗∗
D.Y.A.
Pale dry satisfying light wine from Arfezzo. But what music in the name.

Bigi Famous producers of ORVIETO and other wines of Umbria and Tuscany.

Biondi-Santi
One of the leading producers of BRUNELLO with cellars in Montalcino (Siena).

Boca Piem. DOC r. dr. ∗∗ **74 78 79** 80 81 82
From same grape as BAROLO in n. of PIEMONTE, Pr. of Novara.

Bolla Famous Veronese firm producing VALPOLICELLA, SOAVE, etc.

Bonarda
Minor red grape widely grown in PIEMONTE and Lombardy.

Bonarda (Oltrepo' Pavese) Lomb. DOC r. dr. ∗∗ **78 79 81** 82
Soft, fresh, pleasant red from s. of Pavia.

Bosca Wine-producers from PIEMONTE known for their ASTI SPUMANTE and Vermouths.

Botticino Lomb. DOC r. dr. ∗∗ **79 80 81** 82
Strong, full-bodied rather sweet red from Brescia.

Brachetto d'Acqui Piem. DOC r. sw. (sp.) ∗ D.Y.A.
Sweet sparkling red with pleasant muscat aroma.

Bricco Manzoni Piem. r. ∗∗∗ **76 78 79 80** 81 82
Excellent red of blended BARBERA and NEBBIOLO from Monforte d'Alba.

Brolio The oldest (c. 1200) and most famous CHIANTI CLASSICO estate now owned by Seagrams. Good whites as well as red.

Brunello di Montalcino Tusc. DOCG r. dr. ∗∗∗∗ **70 71 75** 77 78 79 80 81 82
Italy's most expensive wine. Strong, full-bodied, high-flavoured and long-lived. After 5 yrs. is called Riserva. Produced for over a century 15 miles s. of Siena.

Cabernet
Bordeaux grape much used in n.e. Italy and increasingly in Tuscany and the south. See place names, e.g.:

Cabernet di Pramaggiore Ven. DOC r. dr. ∗∗ **77 78 79** 82
Good, herb-scented, rather tannic, middle-weight red. Riserva after 3 yrs.

Cacchiano, Castello di
First-rate CHIANTI CLASSICO estate at Gaiole, owned by RICASOLI.

Calcinaia
First-class CHIANTI CLASSICO estate for centuries in the Capponi family.

Caldaro or Lago di Caldaro Tr-AAd. DOC r. dr. ∗∗ 78 79 80 82
Light, soft, slightly bitter-almond red. Classico from a smaller area is better. From s. of Bolzano.

Calissano
A long-established House of PIEMONTE producing ASTI SPUMANTE, Vermouths and red wines of that region.

Caluso Passito Piem. DOC w. sw. (f.) ∗∗ 71 74 76 78 79
Made from selected Erbaluce grapes left to partly dry; delicate scent, velvety taste. From a large area in the Pr. of Turin and Vercelli.

Cannonau di Sardegna Sard. DOC r. (p.) dr. or s/sw. ∗∗ 77 78 79 81
One of the good wines of the island capable of ageing.

Cantina
1. Cellar or winery. 2. Cantina Sociale = growers' co-op.

Capena Lat. DOC w. dr. s/sw ∗ D.Y.A.
A sound wine for daily drinking from n. of Rome.

Capri Widely abused name of the famous island in the Bay of Naples. No guarantee of quality.

Carema Piem. DOC r. dr. ∗∗ 71 74 78 79 80 82
Old speciality of northern PIEMONTE. NEBBIOLO grapes traditionally fermented Beaujolais-style before crushing. (See France: Macération carbonique.) More conventional today.

Carmignano Tusc. DOC r. dr. ∗∗→ ▢∗∗∗ 75 77 78 79 80 81 82
Section of CHIANTI using 10% of CABERNET to make good wine.

Carso Fr.-VG. DOC r. w. dr. ∗∗
New DOC near Trieste includes good Malvasia.

Casa fondata nel ...
Firm founded in ...

Castel del Monte Apu. DOC r. p. w. dr. ∗∗ 73 77 78 79 80 81
Dry, fresh, well-balanced southern wines. The red becomes Riserva after 3 yrs. Rosé most widely known.

Castel San Michele Tr-AAd. r. dr. ▢∗∗ 76 78 79 80 82
A good red made of Cabernet and Merlot grapes by the Trentino Agricultural College near Trento.

CAVIT
CAntina VITicultori, a co-operative of co-operatives near Trento, producing large quantities of table wine.

Cellatica Lomb. DOC r. dr. ∗∗ 79 80 81 82
Light red with slightly bitter after-taste of Schiava grapes, from Brescia.

Ceretto High-quality grower of BARBARESCO, BAROLO, etc.

Ceretto, Castello di
CHIANTI CLASSICO estate owned by Emilio Pucci.

Cerveteri Lat. DOC w. dr. s/sw. ∗ 79 80 81 82
Sound wines produced n.w. of Rome between Lake Bracciano and the Tyrrhenian Sea.

Chianti Tusc. DOC r. dr. ▢∗∗ 75 77 78 79 80 81 82
The lively local wine of Florence. Fresh but warmly fruity when young, usually sold in straw-covered flasks. Ages moderately. Montalbano, Rufina and Colli Fiorentini, Senesi, Aretini, Colline Pisane are sub-districts.

Chianti Classico Tusc. DOC r. dr. ▢∗∗∗ 71 75 77 78 79 80 81 82
Senior Chianti from the central area. Many estates make fine powerful scented wine. Riservas (after 3 yrs.) often have the bouquet of age in oak. The neck-label is a black rooster.

Chianti Putto
Often high-quality Chianti from a league of producers outside the Classico zone. Designated by a neck-label of a pink and white cherub.

Chiaretto
> Very light reds, almost rosé (the word means "claret") produced around Lake Garda. See Riviera del Garda.

Cinqueterre Lig. DOC w. dr. or sw. or pa. ★★
> Fragrant, fruity white made for centuries near La Spezia. The PASSITO is known as Sciacchetrà.

Cinzano Major Vermouth company also known for its ASTI SPUMANTE from PIEMONTE.

Cirò Cal. DOC r. (p. w.) dr. ★★ 73 74 77 78 79 81
> The wine of the ancient Olympic games. Very strong red, fruity white (to drink young).

Classico
> Term for wines from a restricted, usually central, area within the limits of a DOC. By implication, and often in practice, the best of the region.

Clastidio Lomb. r. (p.) w. dr. ★★ 78 79 81 82
> Pleasant, sour touch to the white. The red full, slightly tannic.

Collavini, Cantina
> High-quality producers of GRAVE DEL FRIULI wines: PINOT GRIGIO, RIESLING, MERLOT, PINOT NERO, etc.

THE BEST-KNOWN ITALIAN WINES, REGION BY REGION, ARE:

Piemonte: Barolo, Barbaresco, Barbera, Dolcetto, Gattinara, Nebbiolo, Asti Spumante.
Liguria: Cinqueterre, Rosso di Dolceacqua.
Trentino-Alto Adige: Teroldego, Caldaro, Santa Maddalena, Merlot, Pinot Bianco, Gewüztraminer, etc.
Lombardy: Valtelina, Oltrepo Pavese.
Veneto: Soave, Valpolicella, Recioto, Bardolino, Prosecco, etc.
Friuli-Venezia-Giulia: Collio, Pinot Grigio, Merlot Tokai, etc.
Emilia-Romagna: Albana, Lambrusco, Sangiovese.
Tuscany: Chianti, Brunello, Vino Nobile di Montepulciano.
Umbria: Orvieto, Rubesco di Torgiano.
Marches: Verdicchio, Rosso Conero, Rosso Piceno.
Latium: Frascati, Marino.
Abruzzi/Molise: Montepulciano.
Campania: Lacryma Christi, Taurasi.
Apulia: Castel del Monte.
Basilicata: Aglianico del Vulture.
Calabria: Cirò.
Sicily: Marsala, Corvo, Etna.
Sardinia: Nuraghus, Cannonau, Monica, Vermentino.

Colli Means "hills" in many wine-names.
Colli Albani Lat. DOC w. dr. or s/sw. (sp.) ★★ D.Y.A.
> Soft fruity wine of the Roman hills.

Colli Bolognesi Em-Ro. DOC r. p. w. dr. ★★ D.Y.A. (w.). 78 79 80 82 (r.)
> From the hills s.w. of Bologna. Six possible grape varieties.

Colli Euganei Ven. DOC r. w. dr. or s/sw. (sp.) [★] 78 79 81 82
> A DOC applicable to 7 wines produced s.w. of Padua. Red is adequate; white soft and pleasant. The table wine of Venice.

Colli Orientali del Friuli Fr-VG. DOC r. w. dr. or sw. ★★ 78 79 81 82
> 12 different wines are produced under this DOC on the hills e. of Udine and named after their grapes.

Collio (Goriziano) Fr-VG. DOC r. w. dr. ★★→★★★ 79 82
> 12 different wines named after their grapes from a small area between Udine and Gorizia nr. the Yugoslav border.

Colli Perugini Umbr. DOC r. p. w. ★
> New DOC for light wines in the hills of Perugia.

Conterno, Aldo
Highly regarded grower of BAROLO, etc.
Contratto
Piemonte firm known for BAROLO, ASTI SPUMANTE, etc.
Cora   A leading House producing ASTI SPUMANTE and Vermouth from PIEMONTE.
Cori   Lat DOC w. r. dr./sw. ☐ ⋆ **80 81 82**
Soft and well-balanced wines made 30 miles s. of Rome.
Cortese di Gavi   See Gavi
Cortese (Oltrepo' Pavese)   Lomb. DOC w. dr. ⋆ D.Y.A.
Delicate fresh white from w. Lombardy.
Corvo   Sic. r. w. dr. ⋆⋆ **74 75 77 78 79** 81
Popular Sicilian wines. Sound dry red, pleasant soft white.
D'Ambra
Well-known producer of ELBA and other wines of that island.
Dolce   Sweet.
Dolceacqua   See Rossese di Dolceacqua
Dolcetto
Common low-acid red grape of PIEMONTE, giving its name to:
Dolcetto d'Acqui   Piem. DOC r. dr. ⋆ D.Y.A.
Good standard table wine from s. of ASTI.
Dolcetto d'Alba   Piem. DOC r. dr. ⋆⋆ **80 82**
Among the best Dolcetti, with a trace of bitter-almond. Superiore after 1 yr.
Dolcetto di Ovada   Piem. DOC r. dr. ⋆⋆ **78 79 80** 82
The sturdiest and longest-lived of Dolcetti.
Donnaz   Vd'A. DOC dr. ⋆⋆ **74** 78 **79** 82
A mountain NEBBIOLO, fragrant, pale and faintly bitter. Aged for a statutory 3 yrs.
Donnici   Cal. DOC r. dr. ⋆
Middle-weight southern red from Cosenza.
Elba   Tusc. r. w. dr. (sp.) ☐ ⋆ **77 79 80** 81 82
The island's white is admirable with fish. Good dry red.
Enfer d'Arvier   Vd'A. DOC r. dr. ⋆⋆ **78 79** 82
An Alpine speciality: pale, pleasantly bitter, light red.
Enoteca
Italian for "wine library", of which there are many in the country, the most comprehensive being the Enoteca Italica Permanente of Siena. Chianti has one at Greve.
Erbaluce di Caluso   Piem. DOC w. dr. ⋆ D.Y.A.
Pleasant fresh hot-weather wine. See also CALUSO PASSITO.
Est! Est!! Est!!!   Lat. DOC w. dr. or s/sw. ⋆⋆ D.Y.A.
Famous soft fruity white from Montefiascone, n. of Rome. The name is more remarkable than the wine.
Etna   Sic. DOC r. p. w. dr. ☐ ⋆⋆ **77** 79 81 82
Wine from the volcanic slopes. The red is warm, full, balanced and ages well; the white is distinctly grapy.
Falerio dei Colli Ascolani   Mar. DOC w. dr. ☐ ⋆ D.Y.A.
Made in the Pr. of Ascoli Piceno. Pleasant, fresh, fruity; a wine for the summer.
Falerno   Camp. r. w. dr. ⋆⋆ **77 78 79** 80 81 82
One of the best-known wines of ancient times. Strong red, fruity white, improving in quality.
Fara   Piem. DOC r. dr. ☐ ⋆⋆ **74** 78 **79** 80 82
Good NEBBIOLO wine from Novara, n. PIEMONTE. Fragrant; worth ageing. Small production.
Faro   Sic. DOC r. dr. ⋆⋆ **79** 81
Sound strong Sicilian red, made in sight of the Straits of Messina.
Favonio   Apu. r. w. dr. ☐ ⋆⋆⋆ **78 79 80** 81 82
Revolutionary estate e. of Foggia using CABERNET, CHARDONNAY and PINOT BIANCO.

Fazi-Battaglia
> Well-known producer of VERDICCHIO, etc.

Ferrari
> Firm making one of Italy's best dry sparkling wines by the champagne method nr. Trento, Trentino-Alto Adige.

Fiano di Avellino   Cam. w. dr. *** 79 80 81 82
> Considered the best white of Campania.

Fiorano   Lat. r. w. dr. s/sw. ** 74 75 77 78 79 80 81 82
> Interesting reds of Cabernet Sauvignon and Merlot.

Florio   The major producer of Marsala, owning several brands, controlled by CINZANO.

Fontana Candida
> One of the biggest producers of FRASCATI.

Fontanafredda
> Leading producer of Piemontese wines, incl. BAROLO.

Fonterutoli
> High-quality CHIANTI CLASSICO estate at Castellina.

Fracia   Lomb. r. dr. ** 75 78 79 80 82
> Good light but fragrant red from VALTELLINA. DOC wine made by Negri.

Franciacorta Pinot   Lomb. DOC w. (p.) dr. (sp.) ⏥ ** D.Y.A.
> Agreeable soft white and good sparkling wines made of PINOT BIANCO, NERO or GRIGIO.

Franciacorta Rosso   Lomb. DOC r. dr. ⏥ ** 79 81 82
> Lightish red of mixed CABERNET and BARBERA from Brescia.

Franco Fiorina
> Highly regarded producer of BAROLO, BARBARESCO, etc.

Frascati   Lat. DOC w. dr. s/sw. sw. (sp.) *→ ⏥ ** 81 82
> Best-known wine of the Roman hills: soft, ripe, golden, tasting of whole grapes. Most is pasteurized and neutral today: look for dated wines from small producers (e.g. Colli di Catone). The sweet is known as Cannellino.

Frecciarossa   Lomb. r. w. dr. ** 78 79 81 82
> Sound wines from an estate nr. Casteggio in the Oltrepo' Pavese; the white is better known.

Freisa d'Asti   Piem. DOC r. dr. s/sw. or sw. (sp.) ** 81 82
> Usually sweet, often sparkling red, said to taste of raspberries and roses.

Frescobaldi
> Leading pioneers of CHIANTI PUTTO at Nipozzano, e. of Florence. Also elegant white POMINO.

Friuli-Venezia Giulia
> The north-eastern province on the Yugoslav border. Many wines, esp. COLLIO.

Frizzante
> Semi-sparkling or "pétillant", a word used to describe wines such as LAMBRUSCO.

Gaja   Old family firm at BARBARESCO. Top-quality Piemonte wines. Pioneer with carbonic maceration to make VINÒT.

Galestro   Tusc. w. dr. **
> New name for superior very light white from Chianti country.

Gambellara   Ven. DOC w. dr. or s/sw. (sp.) * 77 78 79 80 82
> Neighbour of SOAVE. Dry wine similar. Sweet (known as RECIOTO DI GAMBELLARA), agreeably fruity. Also VINSANTO.

Gancia   Famous ASTI SPUMANTE house from Piemonte, also produces vermouth.

Garganega   The principal white grape of SOAVE.

Gattinara   Piem. DOC r. dr. *** 70 74 76 78 79 80 82
> Excellent big-scale BAROLO-type red from n. PIEMONTE. Made from NEBBIOLO, locally known as Spanna.

Gavi   Piem. w. dr. ∗∗→ ∗∗∗ **79 80 81 82**

At best almost burgundian dry white. Gavi dei Gavi from Rovereto di Gavi Ligure is best. Needs two or three years ageing.

Geografico, Chianti

Good-quality Chianti Classico from a major growers' co-operative near Gaiole.

Ghemme   Piem. DOC r. dr. [∗∗] **74 78 79** 80 82

Neighbour of GATTINARA, capable of Bordeaux-style finesse.

Ghiaie della Furbia   Tusc. r. dr. ∗∗∗ **78 79 81**

Bordeaux-style Cabernet blend from the admirable Tenuta di Capezzana, CARMIGNANO.

Giacobazzi

Well-known producers of Lambrusco wines with cellars in Nonantola and Sorbara, near Modena.

Giacosa, Bruno

Old family business making excellent Barolo and other Piemonte wines at Neive (Cuneo).

Gradi   Degrees (of alcohol) i.e. percent by volume.

Grave del Friuli   Fr-VG. DOC r. w. dr. ∗∗ **77 78 79 82**

A DOC covering 14 different wines named after their grapes, from near the Yugoslav border. Good MERLOT and CABERNET.

Greco di Tufo   Camp. DOC w. dr. (sp.) [∗∗] **79 80 81 82**

One of the best whites of the south, fruity and slightly bitter.

Grignolino d'Asti   Piem. DOC r. dr. ∗ **80 81 82**

Pleasant lively standard wine of PIEMONTE.

Grumello   Lomb. DOC r. dr. ∗∗ **75 78 79** 80 82

NEBBIOLO wine from VALTELLINA, can be delicate and fine.

Gutturnio dei Colli Piacentini   Em-Ro. DOC r. dr. (s/sw.) ∗∗ **78 79 80** 82

Full-bodied wine of character from the hills of Piacenza. Named after a large Roman drinking cup.

Inferno   Lomb. DOC r. dr. [∗∗] **75 78 79** 80 82

Similar to GRUMELLO and like it classified as VALTELLINA Superiore.

Ischia   Camp. DOC (r.) w. dr. ∗ **79 80 81 82**

The wine of the island off Naples. The slightly sharp white Superiore is best; ideal with fish.

Isonzo   Fr-VG. DOC r. w. dr. ∗ **79 82**

DOC covering 10 varietal wines in the extreme north-east.

Kalterersee

German name for Lago di CALDARO.

Lacryma Christi del Vesuvio   Camp. r. p. w. (f.) dr. (sw.) ∗ **81 82**

Famous but frankly ordinary wines in great variety from the slopes of Mount Vesuvius.

Lago di Caldaro

See Caldaro

Lagrein   Tr-AAd. DOC r. p. dr. ∗∗ **78 79 80 82**

Lagrein is a Tyrolean grape with a bitter twist. Good fruity light wine. Rosé called Kretzer.

Lamberti

Producers of SOAVE, VALPOLICELLA and BARDOLINO at Lazise on the e. shore of La. Garda.

Lambrusco   DOC (or not) r. p. (w.) s/sw. ∗ D.Y.A.

Bizarre but popular fizzy red, generally drunk secco (dry) in Italy but a smash hit in its sweet version in the USA.

Lambrusco di Sorbara   Em-Ro. DOC r. (w.) dr. or s/sw. sp. ∗∗∗ D.Y.A.

The best of the Lambruscos. From near Modena.

Lambrusco Grasparossa di Castelvetro Em-Ro. DOC r. dr. or s/sw. sp. ∗∗ D.Y.A
 Similar to above. Highly scented, pleasantly acidic; often drunk with rich food.

Lambrusco Salamino di Santa Croce Em-Ro. DOC r. dr. or s/sw. sp. ∗ D.Y.A
 Similar to above. Fruity smell, high acidity and a thick "head".

Langhe The hills of central PIEMONTE.

Latisana Fr-VG. DOC r. w. dr. ∗∗ 79 82
 DOC for 7 varietal wines from some 50 miles n.e. of Venice.

Lessona Piem. DOC r. d. ∗∗ 74 76 78 79 80 81 82
 Soft, dry, claret-like wine produced in the province of Vercelli from Nebbiolo, Vespolina and Bonarda grapes.

Liquoroso Strong and usually sweet, e.g. like Tuscan Vinsanto.

Locorotondo Apu. DOC w. dr. (sp.) ∗ D.Y.A.
 A pleasantly fresh southern white.

Lugana Lomb. DOC w. dr. (sp.) ∗∗∗ D.Y.A.
 One of the best white wines of s. La. Garda: fragrant, smooth, full of body and flavour. Có de Fer is a good producer.

Lungarotti
 Leading producer of TORGIANO wine, with cellars and an outstanding Wine Museum near Perugia.

Most Italian wines have a simple name, in contrast to the combination village and vineyard names of France and Germany.

SOAVE CLASSICO

VINO A DENOMINAZIONE DI ORIGINE CONTROLLATA

IMBOTTIGLIATO DAL PRODUTTORE ALL 'ORIGINE CANTINA SOCIALE DI SOAVE

Soave is the name of this wine. It is qualified only by the word Classico, a legal term for the central (normally the best) part of many long-established wine regions. "Denominazione di Origine Controllata" is the official guarantee of authenticity. Imbottigliato . . . all 'origine means bottled by the producer. Cantina Sociale di Soave means the growers' co-operative of Soave.

Malfatti
 Recent go-ahead estate with modern methods, near Lecce, Apulia, producing Bianco, Rosso and SALICE SALENTINO.

Malvasia Important white or red grape for luscious wines, incl. Madeira's Malmsey. Used all over Italy for dry and sweet, still and sparkling wines.

Malvasia di Bosa Sard. DOC w. dr. sw. ∗∗ 79 81
 A wine of character. Strong and aromatic with a slightly bitter after-taste.

Malvasia di Cagliari Sard. DOC w. dr. s/sw. or sw. (f. dr. s.) ∗∗ 78 79 81
 Interesting strong Sardinian wine, fragrant and slightly bitter.

Malvasia di Casorzo d'Asti Piem. DOC r. sw. sp. ∗∗ D.Y.A.
 Fragrant grapy sweet red, sometimes sparkling.

Malvasia di Castelnuovo Don Bosco Piem. DOC r. sw. (sp.) ∗∗
 Peculiar method of interrupted fermentation gives very sweet aromatic red.

Malvasia delle Lipari Sic. DOC w. sw. (pa. f.) ∗∗∗ 77 78 79 81
 Among the very best Malvasias, aromatic and rich, produced on the Lipari or Aeolian Islands n. of Sicily.

Malvoisie de Nus   Vd'A. w. dr. s/sw. ★★★
>   Rare Alpine white, with a deep bouquet of honey. Small production and high reputation. Can age remarkably well.

Mamertino   Sic. w. s/sw. ★★ **75 76 77 78** 79 80 81
>   Made near Messina since Roman times. Sweet-scented, rich in glycerine. Mentioned by Caesar in *De Bello Gallico.*

Manduria (Primitivo di)   Apu. DOC r. s/sw. (f. dr. or sw.) ★★
>   Heady red, naturally strong but often fortified. From nr. Taranto. Primitivo is a southern grape.

Mantonico   Cal. w. dr. or sw. f. ★★ **75 77 78 79** 81
>   Fruity deep amber dessert wine from Reggio Calabria. Can age remarkably well. Named from the Greek for "prophetic".

Marino   Lat. DOC w. dr. or s/sw. (sp.)   ★   D.Y.A.
>   A neighbour of FRASCATI with similar wine, often a better buy.

Marsala   Sic. DOC br. dr. s/sw. or sw. f. ★★★ NV
>   Dark sherry-type wine invented by the Woodhouse Brothers from Liverpool in 1773; excellent apéritif or for dessert. The dry ("virgin"), sometimes made by the solera system, must be 5 years old.

Marsala Speciali
>   These are Marsalas with added flavours of egg, almond, strawberry, etc.

Martina Franca   Apu. DOC w. dr. (sp.) ★ D.Y.A.
>   Agreeable but rather neutral southern white, first cousin to LOCOROTONDO.

Martini & Rossi
>   Well-known vermouth House also famous for its fine wine museum in Pessione, nr. Turin.

Marzemino (del Trentino)   Tr.-AAd. DOC r. dr. ★ **80 82**
>   Pleasant local red of Trento. Fruity fragrance; slightly bitter taste. Mozart's Don Giovanni liked it.

Masi, Cantina
>   Well-known specialist producers of VALPOLICELLA, RECIOTO, SOAVE, etc., incl. fine red Campo Fiorin.

Mastroberardino
>   The leading wine-producer of Campania, incl. TAURASI and LACRYMA CHRISTI DEL VESUVIO.

Melini   Long-established important producers of CHIANTI CLASSICO at Pontassieve. Inventors of the standard *fiasco*, or litre flask.

Melissa   Cal. DOC r. w. dr. ★★ **77 78 79** 81
>   Mostly made from Gaglioppo grapes in the Pr. of Catanzaro. Delicate, balanced, ages rather well.

Meranese di Collina   Tr.-AAd. DOC r. dr. ★ **79 80** 81 **82**
>   Light red of Merano, known in German as Meraner Hügel.

Merlot
>   Adaptable red Bordeaux grape widely grown in n.e. Italy and elsewhere.

Merlot di Aprilia   Lat. DOC r. dr. ★ **80 81** 82
>   Harsh at first, softer after 2–3 yrs.

Merlot Colli Berici   Ven. DOC r. dr. ★ **78 79 81** 82
>   Pleasantly light and soft.

Merlot Colli Orientali del Friuli   Fr-VG. DOC r. dr. ★★ **79 81 82**
>   Pleasant herby character, best at 2–3 yrs (Riserva).

Merlot Collio Goriziano   Fr-VG. DOC r. dr. ★★ **79 82**
>   Grassy scent, slightly bitter taste. Best at 2–3 yrs.

Merlot Grave del Friuli   Fr-VG. DOC r. dr. ★★ **79 82**
>   Pleasant light wine, best at 1–2 yrs.

Merlot Isonzo   Fr-VG. DOC r. dr. ★★ **79 82**
>   A DOC in Gorizia. Dry, herby, agreeable wine.

Merlot del Piave   Ven. DOC r. dr. ★★ 78 79 82
Sound tasty red, best at 2–4 yrs.
Merlot di Pramaggiore   Ven. DOC r. dr. ★★ 78 79 82
A cut above other Merlots; improves in bottle. Riserva after 2 yrs.
Merlot (del Trentino)   Tr-AAd. DOC r. dr.   ★   78 79 80 82
Full flavour, slightly grassy scent, Riserva after 2 yrs.
Monica di Cagliari   Sard. DOC r. dr. or sw. (f. dr. or sw.) ★★ 78 79 81
Strong spicy red, often fortified and comparable with Spanish MALAGA. Monica is a Sardinian grape.
Monica di Sardegna   Sard. DOC r. dr. ★ 79 81
Dry version of above, not fortified.
Moniga (del Garda)
Village at s.w. end of Lake Garda, known for good fresh CHIARETTO (D.Y.A.).
Montecarlo   Tusc. DOC w. dr. r. ★★ 80 81 82
One of Tuscany's best whites, smooth and delicate, achieving a Graves-like style after 3–4 years. Now applies to a red too.
Montecompatri Colonna   Lat. DOC w. dr. or s/sw. ★ D.Y.A.
A neighbour of FRASCATI. Similar wine.
Montepaldi
Well-known producers and merchants of CHIANTI CLASSICO at San Casciano Val di Pesa. Owned by the Corsini family.
Montepulciano, Vino Nobile di
See Vino Nobile di Montepulciano.
Montepulciano d'Abruzzo (or Molise)   Abr&M. DOC r. p. dr.   ★★★   74 77 78 79 80 81
One of Italy's best reds, from Adriatic coast round Pescara. Soft, slightly tannic, reminiscent of MARSALA when aged.
Monterosso (Val d'Arda)   Em-Ro. DOC w. dr. or sw. (sp.) ★ D.Y.A.
Agreeable and fresh minor white from Piacenza.
Moscato
Fruitily fragrant grape grown all over Italy.
Moscato d'Asti   Piem. DOC w. sw. sp. ★★ NV
Low-strength sweet fruity sparkler made in bulk. ASTI SPUMANTE is the superior version.
Moscato dei Colli Euganei   Ven. DOC w. sw. (sp.) ★★ D.Y.A.
Golden wine, fruity and smooth, from nr. Padua.
Moscato d'Asti Naturale   Piem. DOC w. sw. ★ D.Y.A.
The light and fruity base wine for Moscato d'Asti.
Moscato di Noto   Sic. DOC w. s/sw. or sw. or sp. or f. ★ NV
Light sweet still and sparkling versions, or strong Liquoroso. Noto is near Siracusa.
Moscato (Oltrepo' Pavese)   Lomb. DOC w. sw. (sp.) ★★ D.Y.A.
The Lombardy equivalent of Moscato d'Asti.
Moscato di Pantelleria   Sic. DOC w. sw. (sp.) (f. pa.) ★★★
Italy's best muscat, from the island of Pantelleria close to the Tunisian coast; rich, fruity and aromatic. Ages well.
Moscato di Siracusa   Sic. DOC w. sw.   ★★   NV
Amber dessert wine reputedly from Syracuse. Can be superb.
Moscato di Sorso Sennori   Sard. DOC w. sw. (f.)   ★   D.Y.A.
Strong golden dessert wine from Sassari, n. Sardinia.
Moscato di Trani   Apu. DOC w. sw. or f. ★ 77 78 79 81
Another strong golden dessert wine, sometimes fortified, with "bouquet of faded roses".
Moscato (Trentino)   Tr-AAd. DOC w. sw. ★ D.Y.A.
Typical muscat: high strength for the north.
Nasco di Cagliari   Sard. DOC w. dr. or sw. (f. dr. or sw.) ★ 78 79 81
Sardinian speciality, light bitter taste, high alcoholic content.
Nebbiolo
The best red grape of PIEMONTE and Lombardy.

Nebbiolo d'Alba   Piem. DOC r. dr. s/sw. (sp.)   ★★   74 76 78 79 80
81 82
>Like light-weight BAROLO; often easier to appreciate than the
>more powerful classic wine.

Nipozzano, Castello di
>The most important CHIANTI producer outside the Classico
>zone, to the n. near Florence. Owned by FRESCOBALDI.

Nozzole
>Famous estate in the heart of CHIANTI CLASSICO n. of Greve.

Nuraghe Majore   Sard. w. dr. ★★ D.Y.A.
>Sardinian white: delicate, fresh, among the island's best.

Nuragus di Cagliari   Sard. DOC w. dr.   ★   D.Y.A.
>Lively Sardinian white, not too strong.

Oliena   Sard. r. dr. ★★
>Interesting strong fragrant CANNONAU red; a touch bitter.

Oltrepo' Pavese   Lomb. DOC r. w. dr. sw. sp. ★→★★
>DOC applicable to 7 wines produced in the Pr. of Pavia,
>named after their grapes.

Orvieto   Umb. DOC w. dr. or s/sw. ★★→★★★ D.Y.A.
>The classical Umbrian golden-white, smooth and substantial,
>though the dry version is sometimes flat and rather dull.
>O. Classico is superior.

Ostuni   Apu. DOC r. or w. dr. ★★
>Rather delicate, dry, balanced; produced in the Pr. of Brindisi.

Parrina   Tusc. r. or w. dr. ★★ 81 82
>Light red and fresh appetizing white from n. Tuscany.

Passito
>Strong sweet wine from grapes dried either in the sun or
>indoors.

Per' e Palummo   Camp. r. dr. ★★ 78 79 81 82
>Excellent red produced on the island of Ischia; delicate,
>slightly grassy, a bit tannic, balanced.

Petit Rouge   Vd'A.   ★★
>Good dark lively REFOSCO-like red.

Pian d'Albola
>Renowned old CHIANTI CLASSICO estate.

Piave   Ven. DOC r. or w. dr.   ★★   78 79 82 (w. D.Y.A.)
>Flourishing DOC covering 8 wines, 4 red and 4 white, named
>after their grapes.

Picolit (Colli Orientali del Friuli)   Fr-VG. DOC w. s/sw. or sw.
★★★★ 77 78 79 82
>Known as Italy's Château d'Yquem. Delicate bouquet, well
>balanced, high alcohol. Ages up to 6 years, but overpriced.

Piemonte
>The most important Italian region for quality wine. Turin
>is the capital, Asti the wine-centre. See Barolo, Barbera,
>Grignolino, Moscato, etc.

Pieropan
>Outstanding producers of SOAVE.

Pinocchio   Tusc. r. w. ★
>Long-established brand notable for its variable nose.

Pinot Bianco
>Rather neutral grape popular in n.e., good for sparkling wine.

Pinot Bianco (dei Colli Berici)   Ven. DOC w. dr. ★★ D.Y.A.
>Straight satisfying dry white.

Pinot Bianco (Colli Orientali del Friuli)   Fr-VG. DOC w. dr. ★★
79 82
>Good white; smooth rather than showy.

Pinot Bianco (Collio Goriziano)   Fr-VG. DOC w. dr. ★★ 79 82
>Similar to the above.

Pinot Bianco (Grave del Friuli)   Fr-VG. DOC w. dr. ★★ 82
>Same again.

Pinot Grigio
Tasty, low-acid white grape popular in n.e.

Pinot Grigio (Collio Goriziano)   Fr-VG. DOC w. dr. ** **79 82**
Fruity, soft, agreeable dry white. The best age well.

Pinot Grigio (Grave del Friuli)   Fr-VG. DOC w. dr. ** D.Y.A.
Hardly distinguishable from the above.

Pinot Grigio (Oltrepo' Pavese)   Lomb. DOC w. dr. (sp.)   ******   **79 81 82**
Lombardy's P.G. is considered best.

Pinot Nero Trentino   Tr-AAd. DOC r. dr. ****** **78 79 80** 82
Pinot Nero (Noir) gives lively burgundy-scented light wine in much of n.e. Italy, incl. Trentino. Riserva after 2 yrs.

Pio Cesare
A producer of quality red wines of PIEMONTE, incl. BAROLO.

Poggio al Sole
Up-and-coming CHIANTI CLASSICO estate.

Pomino   Tusc. DOC (r.) w. dr. (br.) ***
Fine white, partly Chardonnay, and a Sangiovese/Cabernet blend. Also Vinsanto. From FRESCOBALDI.

Primitivo di Apulia   Apu. r. dr. ******
One of the best southern reds. Fruity when young, soft and full-flavoured with age (see also MANDURIA).

Prosecco di Conegliano   Ven. DOC w. dr. or s/sw. (sp.) *** D.Y.A.
Popular sparkling wine of the n.e. Slight fruity bouquet, the dry pleasantly bitter, the sw. fruity; the best are known as Superiore di Cartizze. Best producer: Carpene-Malvolti.

Raboso (del Piave)   Ven. r. dr. ** **75 76 78 79** 82
Powerful but sharp country red; needs age.

Ramandolo   See Verduzzo Colli Orientali del Friuli.

Ravello   Camp. r. p. w. dr. ** **77 78 79 81** 82
Among the best wines of Campania: full dry red, fresh clean white. Caruso is the best-known brand.

Recioto
Wine made of half-dried grapes. Speciality of Veneto.

The 1982 vintage was most favourable for red wines in n. and central Italy, esp. in Piemonte, Lombardy and Tuscany. The extreme summer heat caused some problems with white wines and, combined with drought, ruined the harvest in parts of the south.

Recioto di Gambellara   Ven. DOC w. s/sw. sp. *
Sweetish golden wine, often half-sparkling.

Recioto di Soave   Ven. DOC w. s/sw. (sp.) ** **76 77 78 79** 82
Soave made from selected half-dried grapes; sweet, fruity, fresh, slightly almondy: high alcohol.

Recioto della Valpolicella   Ven. DOC r. s/sw. sp. ** **74 77 78 79** 82
Strong rather sweet red, sometimes sparkling.

Recioto Amarone della Valpolicella   Ven. DOC r. dr. **** **74 77 78 79** 82
Dry version of the above; strong concentrated flavour, rather bitter. Impressive and expensive.

Refosco (Colli Orientali del Friuli)   Fr-VG. DOC r. dr. ** **78 79** 82
Full-bodied dry red; Riserva after 2 yrs. Refosco is said to be the same grape as the MONDEUSE of Savoie (France).

Refosco (Grave del Friuli)   Fr-VG. DOC r. dr. ** **78 79** 82
Similar to above but slightly lighter.

Regaleali   Sic. w. r. p. ***** **76 77 78 79** 81 82
Among the better Sicilian table wines, produced between Caltanissetta and Palermo.

Ribolla (Colli Orientali del Friuli) Fr-VG. DOC w. dr. ∗ D.Y.A.
> Clean and fruity n.e. white.

Ricasoli
> Famous Tuscan family, "inventors" of CHIANTI, whose Chianti is named after their BROLIO estate and castle.

Riecine Tusc. ⟦∗∗∗⟧ **75 77 78 79** 81 82
> First-class CHIANTI CLASSICO estate at Gaiole started by an Englishman. First wine 1975.

Riesling
> Normally refers to Italian Riesling (R. Italico or "Welschriesling"). German Riesling, uncommon, is R. Renano.

Riesling Alto Adige DOC w. dr. ∗∗
> Can often be Italy's best Riesling.

Riesling (Oltrepo' Pavese) Lomb. DOC w. dr. (sp.) ∗∗
> The Lombardy version, quite light and fresh. Occasionally sparkling. Keeps well. Made of both types of Riesling.

Riesling (Trentino) Tr-AAd. DOC w. dr. ∗∗ D.Y.A.
> Delicate, slightly acid, very fruity. Can be Müller-Thurgau.

Riserva
> Wine aged for a statutory period in barrels.

Riunite
> Cantine Sociali, a Co-operative cellar near Reggio Emilia producing large quantities of LAMBRUSCO.

Rivera
> Important and reliable wine-makers at Andria, near Bari, with good red and CASTEL DEL MONTE rosé.

Riviera del Garda Chiaretto Ven. and Lom. DOC p. dr. ∗∗ D.Y.A.
> Charming cherry-pink, fresh and slightly bitter, from s.w. Garda esp. round Moniga del Garda.

Riviera del Garda Rosso Ven. DOC r. dr. ∗∗ **79 80 81 82**
> Red version of the above; ages surprisingly well.

Rosato
> Rosé.

Rosato del Salento Apu. p. dr. ∗→∗∗ D.Y.A.
> Strong but refreshing southern rosé from round Brindisi.

Rossese di Dolceacqua Lig. DOC r. dr. ∗∗ **75 78 79 81** 82
> Well-known fragrant light red of the Riviera with typical touch of bitterness. Superiore is stronger.

Rosso Red.

Rosso delle Colline Lucchesi Tusc. DOC r. dr. ∗∗ **77 78 79 81 82**
> Produced round Lucca but not greatly different from CHIANTI.

Rosso Conero Mar. DOC r. dr. ∗∗ **77 78 79 81** 82
> Substantial CHIANTI-style wine from the Adriatic coast.

Rosso Piceno Mar. DOC r. dr. ∗→∗∗ **77 78 79** 81 82
> Adriatic red with a touch of style. Can be Superiore.

Rubesco
> See Torgiano

Rubino di Cantavenna Piem. DOC r. dr. ∗∗
> Lively red, principally BARBERA, from a well-known co-operative s.e. of Turin.

Rufina
> A sub-region of CHIANTI in the hills e. of Florence.

Ruffino
> Well-known CHIANTI merchants.

Runchet (Valtellina) Lomb. DOC r. dr. ∗∗
> Soft bouquet, slightly tannic, drink relatively young.

Salice Salentino Apu. DOC r. ∗∗ **73 75 77 78 79** 80 81
> Strong red from Negroamaro grapes, Riserva after 2 yrs., ages to smooth full wine. Leading maker: Leone de Castris.

Sangiovese
> Principal red grape of CHIANTI, used alone for:

Sangiovese d'Aprilia   Lat. DOC r. or p. dr. * D.Y.A.
> Strong dry rosé from s. of Rome.

Sangiovese di Romagna   Em-Ro. DOC r. dr. ** 78 79 80 82
> Pleasant standard red; gains character with a little age.

Sangue di Giuda (Oltrepo' Pavese)   Lomb. DOC r. dr. or s/sw. **
> "Judas' blood". Strong soft red of w. Lombardy.

San Severo   Apu. DOC r. p. w. dr. * 79 80 81
> Sound neutral southern wine; not particularly strong.

Santa Maddalena   Tr-AAd. DOC r. dr. [**] 79 80 82
> Perhaps the best Tyrolean red. Round and warm, slightly almondy. From Bolzano.

Sassella
> A CHIANTI CLASSICO estate of MELINI producing an excellent single-vineyard wine.

Sassella (Valtellina)   Lomb. DOC r. dr. *** 75 78 79 80 82
> Considerable NEBBIOLO wine, tough when young. Known since Roman times, mentioned by Leonardo da Vinci.

Sassicaia   Tusc. r. dr. [****] 70 72 75 76 77 78 79 80 81 82
> Perhaps Italy's best red wine, produced from CABERNET grapes in the Tenuta San Guido of the Incisa family, at Bolgheri near Livorno, since 1968 and cellared by ANTINORI. Tiny production.

Sauvignon
> The Sauvignon Blanc: excellent white grape used in n.e.

Sauvignon (Colli Berici)   Ven. DOC w. dr. ** D.Y.A.
> Delicate, slightly aromatic, fresh white from near Vicenza.

Sauvignon (Colli Orientali del Friuli)   Fr-VG. DOC w. dr. ** D.Y.A.
> Full, smooth, freshly aromatic n.e. white.

Sauvignon (Collio Goriziano)   Fr-VG. DOC w. dr. ** D.Y.A.
> Very similar to the last; slightly higher alcohol.

Savuto   Cal. DOC r. p. dr. ** 77 78 79 81
> The ancient Savuto produced in the Pr. of Cosenza and Catanzaro. Fragrant juicy wine.

A new top category, DOCG, Denominazione Controllata e Garantita, is gradually being added to the Italian wine classification. It is awarded only to certain wines from top-quality zones which have been bottled and sealed with a government seal by the producer. The first five areas to be "guaranteed" are Barolo, Barbaresco, Brunello di Montalcino Chianti and Vino Nobile di Montepulciano. Albana di Romagna has applied to be the first white. But it should be remembered that several of Italy's best wines are not covered by the DOC system. Examples are Sassicaia, Tignanello, Venegazzú, Bricco Manzoni.

Schiava
> Good red grape of Trentino-Alto Adige with characteristic bitter after-taste.

Sciacchetrá
> See Cinqueterre

Secco   Dry.

Sella & Mosca
> Major Sardinian growers and merchants at Alghero.

Settesoli
> Sicilian growers' co-operative with range of adequate table wines.

Sforzato (Valtellina)   Lomb. DOC r. dr. *** 70 71 75 78 79 80 82
> Valtellina equivalent of RECIOTO AMARONE made with partly dried grapes. Velvety, strong, ages remarkably well. Also called Sfursat.

Sfursat
> See SFORZATO.

Sizzano   Piem. DOC r. dr. ** **74 78 79** 80 82
> Attractive full-bodied red produced at Sizzano in the Pr. of Novara, mostly from NEBBIOLO.

Soave   Ven. DOC w. dr. *** D.Y.A.
> Famous, if not very characterful, Veronese white. Fresh with attractive texture. Classico is more restricted and better.

Solopaca   Camp. DOC r. w. dr. * **78 79 81** 82
> Comes from nr. Benevento, rather sharp when young, the white soft and fruity.

Sorni   Tr-AAd. r. w. dr. ** D.Y.A.
> Made in the Pr. of Trento. Light, fresh and soft. Drink young.

Spanna   See GATTINARA.

Spumante
> Sparkling.

Squinzano   Apu. DOC r. p. dr. * **77 78 79** 80 81
> Strong southern red from Lecce. Riserva after 2 yrs.

Stravecchio   Very old.

Sylvaner
> German white grape successful in ALTO ADIGE and elsewhere.

Sylvaner (Alto Adige)   Tr-AAd. DOC w. dr. ** D.Y.A.
> Pleasant grapy well-balanced white.

Sylvaner (Terlano)   Tr-AAd. DOC w. dr. [**] D.Y.A.
> Attractive lively and delicate wines.

Sylvaner (Valle Isarco)   Tr-AAd. DOC w. dr. ** D.Y.A.
> Like the last. Perhaps better.

Taurasi   Camp. DOC r. dr. [**] **73 75 77 78** 81 82
> The best Campanian red, from Avellino. Bouquet of cherries. Harsh when young, improves with age. Riserva after 4 yrs.

Terlano   Tr-AAd. DOC w. dr. [**] **79 82**
> A DOC applicable to 7 white wines from the Pr. of Bolzano, named after their grapes. Terlaner in German.

Termeno   Tr-AAd. r. w. dr. **
> Village nr. Bolzano. Tramin in German, reputedly the origin of the TRAMINER. Its red is light and slightly bitter.

Teroldego Rotaliano   Tr-AAd. DOC r. p. dr. ** **77 78 79 80 82**
> The attractive local red of Trento. Blackberry-scented, slight bitter after-taste, ages moderately.

Tignanello   Tusc. r. dr. [***] **71 75 77** 78 79 80 81 82
> One of the new style of Bordeaux-inspired Tuscan reds, made by ANTINORI. Small production.

Tocai Friulano   (Collio) ** D.Y.A.
> North-east Italian white grape; no relation of Hungarian or Alsace Tokay.

Tocai di Lison   Ven. DOC w. dr. ** D.Y.A.
> From Treviso, delicate smoky/fruity scent, fruity taste. Classico is better.

Tocai (Colli Berici)   Ven. DOC w. dr. *
> Less character than the last.

Tocai (Grave del Friuli)   Fr-VG. DOC w. dr. ** D.Y.A.
> Similar to TOCAI DI LISON, generally rather milder.

Tocai di S. Martino della Battaglia   Lomb. DOC w. dr. ** D.Y.A.
> Small production s. of La. Garda. Light, slightly bitter.

Torbato di Alghero   Sard. w. dr. (Pa.) ** D.Y.A.
> Good n. Sardinian table wine, also PASSITO of high quality.

Torgiano, Rubesco di   Umb. DOC r. w. dr. [***] **71 73 74 75 77 78** 79 80 81 82
> Excellent red from near Perugia comparable with CHIANTI CLASSICO. Riserva Monticcio is superb. Keep 10 years. White Torre di Giano is also good, but not as outstanding as the red.

Torricella Tusc. w. dr. ★★★
> Remarkable aged dry white from BROLIO.

Traminer Aromatico Tr-AAd. DOC w. dr. ★★ D.Y.A.
> Delicate, aromatic, rather soft Gewürztraminer.

Trebbiano
> The principal white grape of Tuscany found all over Italy. Ugni Blanc in French.

Trebbiano d'Abruzzo Abr&M. DOC w. dr. ★ D.Y.A.
> Gentle, rather neutral, slightly tannic. From round Pescara.

Trebbiano d'Aprilia Lat. DOC w. dr. ★ D.Y.A.
> Heady, mild-flavoured, rather yellow. From s. of Rome.

Trebbiano di Romagna Em-Ro. DOC w. dr. or s/sw. (sp.) ★ D.Y.A.
> Clean, pleasant white from near Bologna.

Trentino Tr-AAd. DOC r. w. dr. or sw. ★→★★
> DOC applicable to 10 wines named after their grapes.

Uzzano, Castello di
> Fine old estate at Greve. First-class CHIANTI CLASSICO.

Valcalepio Lomb. DOC r. w. dr. ★ 79 80 82
> From nr. Bergamo. Pleasant red; lightly scented, fresh white.

Valdadige Tr-AAd. DOC r. w. dr. or s/sw. ★
> Name for the ordinary table wines of the Adige valley — in German Etschtal.

Val d'Arbia Tusc. DOC w. dr. ★ D.Y.A.
> Another new DOC for a pleasant white from Chianti country.

Valgella (Valtellina) Lomb. DOC r. dr. ★★ 75 78 79 80 82
> One of the VALTELLINA NEBBIOLOS: good dry red, growing nutty with age. Riserva at 4 yrs.

Valle Isarco Tr-AAd. DOC w. dr. ★→★★
> A DOC applicable to 5 varietal wines made n.e. of Bolzano.

Italian bottle shapes

1 Orvieto 2 Chianti 3 Verdicchio 4 Barolo

Valpolicella Ven. DOC r. dr. ★★★ 78 79 82
> Attractive light red from nr. Verona; most attractive when young. Delicate nutty scent, slightly bitter taste. Classico more restricted; Superiore has 12% alcohol and 1 yr. of age.

Valtellina Lomb. DOC r. dr. ★★→★★★
> A DOC applicable to wines made principally from Chiavennasca (NEBBIOLO) grapes in the Pr. of Sondrio, n. Lombardy. V. Superiore is better.

Velletri Lat. DOC r. w. dr. or s/sw. ★★
> Agreeable Roman dry red and smooth white. Drink young.

Vendemmia Harvest or vintage.

Venegazzu' Ven. r. w. dr. sp. ★★★ 71 76 78 79 82
> Remarkable rustic Bordeaux-style red produced from CABERNET grapes nr. Treviso. Rich bouquet, soft, warm taste, 13.5% alcohol, ages well. Also sparkling white.

Verdicchio dei Castelli di Jesi Mar. DOC w. dr. (sp.) ★★★ D.Y.A.
> Ancient, famous and very pleasant fresh pale white from nr. Ancona. Goes back to the Etruscans. Classico is more restricted. Comes in amphora-shaped bottles.

Verdicchio di Matelica   Mar. DOC w. dr. (sp.) ★★ D.Y.A.
>Similar to the last, though less well known.

Verdiso
>Native white grape of n.e., used with PROSECCO.

Verduzzo (Colli Orientali del Friuli)   Fr-VG. DOC w. dr. s/sw. or sw. ★★ 79 81 82
>Full-bodied white from a native grape. The best sweet is called Ramandolo.

Verduzzo (Del Piave)   Ven. DOC w. dr. ★★ D.Y.A.
>Similar to the last but fresh and dry.

Vermentino   Lig. w. dr.   ★★   D.Y.A.
>The best dry white of the Riviera: good clean seafood wine made at Pietra Ligure and San Remo.

Vermentino di Gallura   Sard. DOC w. dr. ★★ D.Y.A.
>Soft, dry, rather strong white from n. Sardinia.

Vernaccia di Oristano   Sard. DOC w. dr. (sw.) (f.)   ★★★   74 75 77 78 79
>Sardinian speciality, like light sherry, a touch bitter, full-bodied and interesting. Superiore with 15.5% alcohol and 3 yrs. of age.

Vernaccia di San Gimignano   Tusc. DOC w. dr. (f.) ★★ 80 81 82
>Distinctive strong high-flavoured wine from nr. Siena. Michelangelo's favourite. Riserva after 1 yr.

Vernaccia di Serrapetrona   Mar. DOC r. dr. s/sw. sw. sp. ★★ D.Y.A.
>Comes from the Pr. of Macerata; aromatic bouquet, pleasantly bitter after-taste.

Vicchiomaggio
>Important CHIANTI CLASSICO estate near Greve.

Vignamaggio
>Historic and beautiful CHIANTI CLASSICO estate near Greve.

Villa Ronche
>Reputable producer of GRAVE DEL FRIULI, esp. for CABERNET, MERLOT, REFOSCO.

Vino da arrosto
>"Wine for roast meat", i.e. good robust dry red.

Vino da pasto
>Table wine: i.e. nothing special.

Vino Nobile di Montepulciano   Tusc. DOCG r. dr. ★★★ 70 73 75 77 78 79 81 82
>Impressive traditional Chianti-like red with bouquet and style. Aged for 3 yrs. Riserva; for 4 yrs. Riserva Speciale. Best estates incl. Boscarelli, Avignonesi.

Vinòt   Italy's first "new wine", inspired by Beaujolais Nouveau. From GAJA.

V.I.D.E.   ʼ
>An association of better-class Italian producers for marketing their estate wines.

Vinsanto or **Vin Santo**
>Term for certain strong sweet wines esp. in Tuscany: usually PASSITI.

Vinsanto di Gambellara   Ven. DOC w. sw. ★★
>Powerful, velvety, golden: made near Vicenza and Verona.

Vinsanto Toscano   Tusc. w. s/sw. ★★→★★★
>Aromatic bouquet, rich and smooth. Aged in very small barrels known as Carratelli.

VQPRD
>Often found on the labels of DOC wines to signify "Vini di Qualita Prodotti in Regioni Delimitate", or quality wines from restricted areas in accordance with E.E.C. regulations.

Zagarolo   Lat. DOC w. dr. or s/sw. ★★ D.Y.A.
>Neighbour of FRASCATI, similar wine.

Spain & Portugal

The following additional abbreviations are used in the Spanish section (see p. 117):

R'a.A.   Rioja Alta
R'a.Al. Rioja Alavesa
Res.   Reserva
g. see Vino generoso

Abbreviations of regional names shown in bold type are used in the text.

The very finest wines of Spain and Portugal are respectively sherry and port and madeira, which have a section to themselves on pages 122 to 127.

Spain's table wines divide naturally into those from the Mediterranean climate of the centre, south and east and those from the Atlantic climate of the north and west. The former are strong and with rare exceptions dull. The latter include the very good wines of Rioja, certainly, with the Penedès in Catalonia, the most important quality table-wine region of the peninsula.

Rainy north-west Spain and northern Portugal make similar fresh and slightly fizzy wines. Central Portugal has an excellent climate for wines like full-bodied Bordeaux.

The old and outdated Portuguese system of controlled appellation is being progressively overhauled. Small areas of dwindling interest are being supplemented with promising new "determinate areas". The Spanish system dates from the post-war era and, although much amended in recent years, is for the moment over-optimistic, delimiting some areas of purely domestic interest.

The listing here includes the best and most interesting types and regions of each country, whether legally delimited or not. Geographical references (see map) are to the traditional division of Spain into the old kingdoms, and the major provinces of Portugal.

Spain

Alavesas, Bodegas   R'a. Al. r. (w. dr.) res. ★★→★★★ **68 70 73 74 75**
The pale orange-red Solar de Samaniego is one of the most delicate of the soft, fast-maturing Alavesa wines.

Albariño del Palacio   Gal. w. dr. ★★
Flowery "green wine" from FEFIÑANES near Cambados, made with the Albariño grape, the best of the region.

Alella   Cat. r. (p.) w. dr. or sw. ★★
Small demarcated region just n. of Barcelona. Makes pleasantly fresh and fruity wines in limited amounts. (See Marfil.)

Alicante   Lev. r. (w.) ★
Demarcated region. Its wines tend to be "earthy", high in alcohol and heavy.

Almansa   Lev. r. ★
Demarcated region w. of ALICANTE, with similar wines.

Aloque   N. Cas. r.   ⟦★⟧   D.Y.A.
A light (though not in alcohol) variety of VALDEPEÑAS, made by fermenting together red and white grapes.

Almendralejo   Ext. r. w. ★
Commercial wine centre of the Extremadura. Much of its produce is distilled to make the spirit for fortifying sherry.

Alvear, S.A.   And. g.   ⟦★★★⟧
The largest producer of excellent sherry-like aperitif and dessert wines from MONTILLA-MORILES.

Ampurdán
See PERELADA.

Año   4° Año (or Años) means 4 years old when bottled.

Banda Azul   R'a. A. r.   ⟦★★⟧   **75 76**
Big-selling wine from Bodegas Paternina, S.A., much improved over recent years.

Benicarló   Lev. r. ★
Town on the Mediterranean. Its strong red wines were formerly used for adding colour and body to Bordeaux.

Berberana, Bodegas   R'a. A. r. (w. dr.) res. ★→★★★ **70 72 74 75 76** 78
Best are the fruity, full-bodied reds: the 3° año Carta de Plata, the 5° año Carta de Oro and the smooth velvety reservas.

Beronia, Bodegas   R'a. A. r. res. ★★→★★★ **77**
A small new bodega making excellent reds in the traditional oaky style.

Bilbainas, Bodegas   R'a. A. r. (p.) w. dr. sw. or sp. res.   ⟦★★⟧   →★★★ **66 69 70 72 73 75 76**
Large bodega in HARO, making a wide range of reliable wines, including Viña Pomal, Viña Zaco, Vendimia Especial Reserves and "Royal Carlton" by the champagne method.

Blanco   White.

Bodega
1. a wineshop; 2. a concern occupied in the making, blending and/or shipping of wine.

Campanas, Las   Nav. r. (w.)   ⟦★★⟧
Small wine area near Pamplona. Clarete Campanas is a sturdy red. Mature 5° año Castillo de Tiebas is like a heavy RIOJA Reserva.

Campo Viejo, Bodegas   R'a. A. r. (w. dr.) res.   ⟦★⟧   →★★★ **64 66 70 71** 78
Branch of Savin s.a., one of Spain's largest wine companies. Makes the popular 2° año San Asensio and some big, fruity red reservas.

Cañamero   Ext. w. ★
Remote village near Guadalupe whose wines grow FLOR and acquire a sherry-like taste.

Caralt, Cavas Conde de   Cat. sp. ★★
"CAVA" sparkling wines from SAN SADURNÍ DE NOYA.

Cariñena   Ara. r. (p.w.) ⌈ * ⌉
>   Demarcated region and large-scale supplier of strong wine for
>   everyday drinking.

Casar de Valdaigo   O.Cas. r. w. dr. **
>   Producer in El Bierzo, n. of Leon, with a light, very dry clarete
>   of fair quality.

Castillo Ygay
>   See Marqués de Murrieta.

Cava   1. an establishment making sparkling wines by the cham-
>   pagne method; 2. a Spanish name for such wines.

Cenicero
>   Wine township in the RIOJA ALTA.

Cepa   Wine or grape variety.

Chacolí   Gui. (r.) w. *
>   Alarmingly sharp "GREEN WINE" from the Basque coast, con-
>   taining only 8% to 9% alcohol.

Champaña
>   "Champagne": i.e. Spanish sparkling wine.

Clarete
>   Light red wine (occasionally dark rosé).

Codorníu, S.A.   Cat. sp. ⌈ *** ⌉
>   Largest and best known of the firms in SAN SADURNI DE NOYA
>   making good wines by the champagne method. Ask for the
>   extra dry Non Plus Ultra, and better still the vintage version.

Compañía Vinícola del Norte de España (C.V.N.E.)   R'a.A. r. (p.)
w. dr. or sw. res. ⌈ ** → *** ⌉ **66 70 73 74 75 76** 78
>   The 3° año is among the best of young red Riojas and Monopol
>   one of the best dry whites. Excellent red Imperial and Viña
>   Real reservas. C.V.N.E. is pronounced "Coonie."

Consejo Regulador
>   Official organization for the defence, control and promotion
>   of a DENOMINACIÓN DE ORIGEN.

Cosecha
>   Crop or vintage.

Criado y embotellado por . . .
>   Grown and bottled by . . .

Crianza
>   Literally, "nursing", the ageing of wine. New or unaged wine
>   is "sin crianza".

Cumbrero
>   See Montecillo, Bodegas.

Domecq Domain   R'a.A. r. ** **73 74 76**
>   A reliable red Rioja made by Pedro Domecq in their new
>   bodega near Laguardia.

Denominación de origen
>   Officially regulated wine region. (See introduction p. 111.)

Dulce   Sweet.

Elaborado y añejado por . . .
>   Made and aged by . . .

Elciego
>   Village in the Rioja Alavesa surrounded by vineyards.

Espumoso
>   Sparkling.

Faustino Martinez, S.A.   R'a.Al. r. w. dr. (p.) res. ⌈ ** ⌉ → *** **64
74 76**
>   Good red wines and the dry, light, fruity new-style white
>   Faustino VII.

Fefiñanes Palacio   Gal. w. res. ***
>   Best of all the ALBARIÑO wines, though hardly "green", since it
>   is aged for 2–6 years.

Ferrer, José L.   Mallorca r. res. ★
> His wines, made in Binisalem, are the only ones of any distinction from Mallorca.

Flor   A wine yeast peculiar to sherry and certain other wines that oxidize slowly and tastily under its influence.

Franco-Españolas, Bodegas   R'a.A. r. w. dr. or sw. res. ★→ ★★ **64 68 70** 73
> Reliable wines from LOGROÑO. Bordon is a fruity red. The sweet white Diamante is a favourite in Spain.

Freixenet, S.A., Cavas   Cat. sp. ★★→ ★★★
> Cava, next in size to CODORNIU, making a range of good sparkling wines by the champagne method.

Fuenmayor
> Wine township in the RIOJA ALTA.

Gaseoso
> A cheap sparkler made by pumping carbon dioxide into wine.

Gonzalez y Dubosc, S.A., Cavas   Cat. sp. ★★→ ★★★
> Its pleasant sparkling wines, sold in the UK as JEAN PERICO, are made in the cavas of SEGURA VIUDAS.

Gran Vas
> Pressurized tanks (*cuves closes*) for making inexpensive sparkling wines; also used to describe this type of wine.

Green Wines
> Galicia makes some fresh and fizzy wines like Portuguese VINHOS VERDES.

Haro   The wine centre of the RIOJA ALTA.

Huelva   And. r. w. br. ★→ ★★
> Demarcated region w. of Cadiz. White table wines and sherry-like *generosos*, formerly sent to JEREZ for blending.

Jean Perico
> See Gonzalez y Dubosc

Jerez de la Frontera
> The city of sherry. (See p. 122.)

Jumilla   Lev. r. ★ (w. dr. p.) ★
> Demarcated region in the mountains north of MURCIA. Its full-bodied wines approaching 18% of alcohol are now being lightened by selection of the grapes and improved methods of fermentation.

La Bastida, Cooperativa Vinícola de   R'a.Al. r. res. ★★→ ★★★ 66 70 75 78
> Very drinkable Manuel Quintano and fruity, well-balanced Montebuena, Gastrijo and Castillo Labastida reservas and gran reservas.

Laguardia
> Picturesque walled town at the centre of the wine-growing district of LA RIOJA ALAVESA.

Lan, Bodegas   R'a.A. r. (p.w.) ★★ **73 75** 78
> A huge new bodega, lavishly equipped and making red Riojas of medium quality.

La Rioja Alta, Bodegas   R'a.A. r. (p.) w. dr. (or sw.) res. ★★→ ★★★ **64 68 70 73 76** 78
> Excellent wines, esp. the red 3° año Viña Alberdi, the velvety 5° año Ardanza, the lighter 6° año Arana, the fruity Reserva 904 and dry white Metropol Extra.

León   O.Cas. r. p. w. ★→ ★★
> Northern region becoming better known. Its wines, particularly those from the unfortunately named V.I.L.E. (e.g. Rey León, the young Coyanza and Don Suero reserva), are light, dry and refreshing.

Logroño
> Principal town of the RIOJA region.

López de Heredia, S.A. R'a.A. r. (p.) w. dr. or sw. res. ★★→ ★★★★
68 70 73 76 78

Old established bodega in HARO with typical and good dry red
Viña Tondonia of 6° año or more. Its wines are exceptionally
long-lasting, and the Tondonia whites are also impressive,
like old-fashioned Graves.

Malaga And. br. sw. ★★→★★★

Demarcated region around the city of Malaga. At their best,
its dessert wines yield nothing to tawny port.

Mallorca

No wine of interest except from José FERRER.

Mancha/Manchuela N.Cas. r. w. ★

Large demarcated region n. and n.e. of VALDEPEÑAS, but
wines without the light and fresh flavour of the latter.

Marqués de Cáceres, Bodegas R'a.A. r. w. dr. ★★→★★★ 70 71
73 75 78

Good red Riojas of various ages made by French methods and
also a surprisingly light and fragrant white (D.Y.A.).

Marqués de Monistrol, Bodegas Cat. w. r. (dr. or sw.) sp. res.
★★→★★★

A family firm, just taken over by Martini & Rossi. Refreshing
whites, esp. the Vin Nature, a good red reserva and an odd
sweet red wine.

Marqués de Murrieta, S.A. R'a.A. r. w. dr. res. ★★→ ★★★★ 34 60
64 68 70 74 75 76 78

Highly reputed bodega near LOGROÑO. Makes 4° año Etiqueta
Blanca, superb red Castillo Ygay and a dry fruity white.

Marqués de Riscal, S.A. R'a.Al. r. (p. and w. dr.) res. ★★→★★★★ 64
65 68 71 73 75 76 78

The best-known bodega of the RIOJA ALAVESA. Its red wines
are relatively light and dry. Recently up to its old standards.

RIOJA VINTAGES
*Thanks to a more consistent climate and the blending of a proportion
of wine from better vintages in poor years, Riojas do not vary to the
same extent as the red wines from Bordeaux and Burgundy. The 71
and 77 vintages were a disaster, owing to high rainfall and the onset of
rot and oidium. Of other recent years, the best were: 52 55 58 64 66 68
70 73 76, 78, 80 and 81. (Those in bold type were outstanding.)*

*Riojas are put on the market when they are ready to drink. The best
reservas of the best vintages, however, have very long lives and improve
with more bottle age. Certain '64s, for example (even white wines) are
still improving.*

Mascaró, Cavas Cat. sp. (w. dr. r.) ★★→ ★★★

Maker of some of the best Spanish brandy, good sparkling
wine and a refreshing dry white Viña Franca.

Masía Bach Cat. r. p. w. dr. or sw. ★★ →★★★ 70 74 78

Extrisimo Bach from SAN SADURNÍ DE NOYA, luscious and
oaky, is one of the best sweet white wines of Spain.

Marfíl Cat. r. (p.) w. ★★

Brand name of Alella Vinicola (Bodegas Cooperativas), best
known of the producers in ALELLA. Means "ivory".

Méntrida N.Cas. r. w. ★

Demarcated region w. of Madrid, supplying everyday wine to
the capital.

Monopole

See Compania Vinicola del Norte de España.

Montánchez Ext. r. g. ★

Village near Mérida, interesting because its red wines grow
FLOR yeast like FINO sherry.

Montecillo, Bodegas   R'a.A. r. w. (p.)   ⸢**⋆⋆**⸥   73 75 76 78
> Rioja bodega owned by Osborne (see Sherry), best known for
> its red and dry white Cumbrero, most reasonably priced and
> currently among the best of the 3° año wines.

Montecristo, Bodegas
> Well-known brand of MONTILLA-MORILES wines, owned by
> RUMASA.

Monterrey   Gal. r. ⋆
> Demarcated region near the n. border of Portugal, making
> wines like those of VERIN.

Montilla-Moriles   And. g.   ⸢**⋆⋆⋆**⸥
> Demarcated region near Cordoba. Its crisp, sherry-like FINO
> and AMONTILLADO contain 14% to 17.5% natural alcohol and
> remain unfortified and singularly toothsome.

RIOJA'S CHARACTERISTIC STYLE

*To the Spanish palate the taste of luxury in wine is essentially the taste
of oak. Oak contains vanillin, the taste of vanilla. Hence the
characteristic vanilla flavour of all mature Spanish table wines of
high quality — exemplified by the reservas of Rioja (red and white).*

*Historically the reason for long oak-ageing was to stabilize the best
wines while their simple fruity flavours developed into something more
complex and characteristically winy. Today fashion has turned
against such treatment for white wines. We tend to prefer them grapy.
But the marriage of ripe fruit and oak in red Rioja is still highly
appreciated.*

Muga, Bodegas   R'a.A. r. (w.) res. (sp.)   ⸢**⋆⋆⋆**⸥   70 73 76
> Small family firm in HARO, making some of the best
> red Rioja now available by strictly traditional methods in
> oak. Its wines are light but intensely aromatic, with long
> complex finish. The best is Prado Enea.

Navarra   Nav. r. (w.) ⋆→⋆⋆
> Demarcated region; mainly sturdy red wines but some good
> reservas.

Olarra, Bodegas   R'a.A. r. (w. p.) ⋆⋆→⋆⋆⋆ 70 73 75 76 78
> A new and vast bodega near LOGROÑO, one of the show-pieces
> of RIOJA, making good red and white wines and excellent
> Cerro Añon reservas.

Paternina, S.A., Bodegas   R'a.A. r. (p.) w. dr. or sw. res. ⋆→⋆⋆⋆ 28
59 67 71 73 76 78
> Bodega at Ollauri and a household name. Its best wines are
> the red Viña Vial and the magnificent older reservas.

Pazo   Gal. r. p. w. dr. ⋆
> Brand name of the co-operative at RIBEIRO, making wines
> akin to Portuguese VINHOS VERDES. The rasping red is the
> local favourite. The pleasant fizzy white is safer.

Peñafiel   O.Cas. r. and w. dr. ⋆⋆
> Village on the R. Duero near Valladolid. Best wines are fruity
> reds from the cooperativa de Ribero del Duero, including the
> altogether outstanding 5° año Protos.

Penedès   Cat. r. w. dr. sp. ⋆→⋆⋆⋆
> Demarcated region including Vilafranca del Penedès, SAN
> SADURNI DE NOYA and SITGES. See also Torres.

Perelada   Cat. (r. p.) w. sp. ⋆⋆
> In the demarcated region of Ampurdán on the Costa Brava.
> Best known for sparkling wines made both by the champagne
> and tank or *cuve close* system.

Priorato   Cat. br. dr. r. **

> Demarcated region, an enclave in that of TARRAGONA, known for its alcoholic "rancio" wines and also for almost black full-bodied reds, often used for blending. Lighter blended Priorato is a good carafe wine in Barcelona restaurants.

Protos   See Peñafiel

Raimat   Cat. r. w. p. *→**

> Sound but unexciting wines from old v'yds. near Lérida recently replanted by CODORNÍU.

Reserva

> Good-quality wine matured for long periods in cask. Gran Reserva, in Rioja, must spend at least 7 years in the bodega.

Ribeiro   Gal. r. (p.) w. dr. *→**

> Demarcated region on the n. border of Portugal — the heart of the "GREEN WINE" country.

Rioja   O.Cas. r. p. w. sp. esp. **64 66 68 70 73 75 76** 78 80 81

> This upland region along the R. Ebro in the n. of Spain produces most of the country's best table wines in some 50 BODEGAS DE EXPORTACIÓN. It is sub-divided into:

Rioja Alavesa

> North of the R. Ebro, the R'a.Al. produces fine red wines, mostly the lighter CLARETES.

Rioja Alta

> South of the R. Ebro and w. of LOGROÑO, the R'a.A. grows most of the finest red and white wines; also some rosé.

Rioja Baja

> Stretching e. from LOGROÑO, the Rioja Baja makes coarser red wines, high in alcohol and often used for blending.

Riojanas, Bodegas   R'a.A. r. (w. p.) res. **→*** **34 42 56 64 66 68 70 73 74 75** 78

> One of the older bodegas, making a good traditional Viña Albina. Monte Real reservas are big, mellow, above average.

Rioja Santiago, S.A.   R'a.A. r. (w. dr. or sw. p.) res. *→*** 78

> Bodega at HARO with well-known wines. The flavour sometimes suffers from pasteurization, and appropriately, as it now belongs to Pepsi-Cola, it makes the biggest-selling bottled SANGRÍA. Top red: Gran Enologica.

Rosado   Rosé.

Rueda   O.Cas. br. w. dr. *→**

> Small area w. of Valladolid. Traditional producer of flor-growing sherry-like wines up to 17° of alcohol, now making fresh young whites including that of the MARQUÉS DE RISCAL.

Rumasa

> This great and now troubled Spanish conglomerate has absorbed many bodegas, incl. Williams and Humbert, Garvey, Paternina, Franco-Españolas and, in England, Augustus Barnett.

Salceda, S.A., Bodegas Viña   R'a.Al. r. res. **→*** 73

> Makes fruity, well-balanced red wines.

Sangre de Toro

> Brand name for a rich-flavoured red wine from TORRES S.A.

Sangría

> Cold red wine cup with citrus fruit, ice and brandy.

Sanlúcar de Barrameda

> Centre of the Manzanilla district. (See Sherry p. 122.)

San Sadurní de Noya   Cat. sp.   **→***

> Town s. of Barcelona, hollow with cellars where dozens of firms produce sparkling wine by the champagne method. Standards are high, even if the ultimate finesse is lacking.

Sarría, Senorío de Nav. r. (p. w. dr.) res. `** → ***` 70 73 74 75 78
The model winery of H. Beaumont y Cía. near Pamplona produces wines up to RIOJA standards.

Scholtz, Hermanos, S.A. And. br. `** →` `***`
Makers of the best MALAGA, including a good, dry 10-year-old amontillado. Best is the dessert Solera Scholtz 1885.

Seco Dry.

Segura Viudas Cavas Cat. sp. `** →` `***`
Cava making excellent sparkling wines by the champagne method. Part of the RUMASA group.

Siglo Popular sack-wrapped RIOJA brand of Bodegas Age. Medium quality.

Sitges Cat. w. sw. `**`
Coastal resort s. of Barcelona noted for sweet dessert wine made from Moscatel and Malvasia grapes.

Solar de Samaniego
See Alavesas, Bodegas

Tarragona Cat. r. w. dr. or sw. br. `* → ***`
1. Table wines from the demarcated region; of little note. 2. Dessert wines from firms such as de Muller, comparable with good cream sherries. 3. The town makes vermouth and Chartreuse and exports cheap blended wine.

Tierra de Medina O.Cas. w. `* → **`
Area w. of Valladolid including the wine villages of La Nava and RUEDA.

Tinto Red.

Toro O.Cas. r. `* → **`
Town, 150 m. n.w. of Madrid, and its powerful (to 16°) wine. Leading producer Bodegas Mateos. His 3 año is good.

Torres, Bodegas Cat. r. w. dr. or semi-sw. p. res. `** → ****` 70 71 73 74 75 76 77 78
Distinguished family firm making the best wines of Penedés, esp. the flowery white Viña Sol and Gran Viña Sol, the semi-dry Esmeralda, the red Tres Torres and Gran Sangredetoro, the beautiful Gran Coronas reservas, and the red Santa Digna (alias Viña Magdala) from the Pinot Noir grape.

Utiel-Requena Lev. r. (w.) p.
Demarcated region w. of Valencia. Apart from sturdy reds and chewy vino de doble pasta for blending, it makes some deliciously light and fragrant rosé.

Valbuena O.Cas. r. `*** 75` 77
Made with the same grapes as VEGA SICILIA but sold as 3° año or 5° año.

Valdeorras Gal. r. w. dr. `* → **`
Demarcated region e. of Orense. Dry and refreshing wines.

Valdepeñas N.Cas. r. (w.) `* → **`
Demarcated region near the border of Andalucia. The supplier of most of the carafe wine to Madrid. Its wines, though high in alcohol, are sometimes surprisingly light in flavour.

Valencia Lev. r. w. `*`
Demarcated region producing earthy high-strength wine.

Vega Sicilia O.Cas. r. res. `****` 41 48 53 59 61 64 66 67
One of the very best Spanish wines, full-bodied, fruity and almost impossible to find. Containing up to 16% alcohol. Valbuena is (excellent) second quality – currently **75**, 77.

Vendimia
Vintage.

Verín Gal. r. `*`
Town near n. border of Portugal. Its wines are the strongest from Galicia, without a bubble, and up to 14% alcohol.

Vicente, Suso y Pérez, S.A. Ara. r. `**`
A bodega s. of Sarragossa producing superior Cariñena.

Viña   Literally, a vineyard. But wines such a Tondonia (LOPEZ DE HEREDIA) or Zaco (BILBAINAS) are not necessarily made with grapes exclusively from the vineyard named.

Vino Blanco
> White wine.

Vino comun/corriente   Ordinary wine.

> **clarete**   Light red wine.
>
> **dulce**   Sweet wine.
>
> **espumoso**   Sparkling wine.
>
> **generoso**   Apéritif or dessert wine rich in alcohol.
>
> **rancio**   Maderized (brown) white wine.
>
> **rosado**   Rosé wine.
>
> **seco**   Dry wine.
>
> **tinto**   Red wine.
>
> **verde**   Wine akin to Portuguese VINHO VERDE.

Yecla   Lev. r. w. ⋆
> Demarcated region n. of Murcia. Its co-operative, "La Purisima", is said to be Spain's biggest. Its wines, once heavyweight bruisers, have been lightened for export.

Ygay   See Marqués de Murrieta

Portugal

For Port and Madeira see pages 122 to 127.

Adega   A cellar or winery.

Aguardente
> The Portuguese word for brandy, made by a multiplicity of firms. Safest to ask for Adega Velha from Aveleda or one from a port concern.

Alentejo   Alen. r. ⋆→⋆⋆
> Vast and long-neglected area s. of the R. Tagus, now being developed as a wine region, chiefly for red wine.

Algarve   Alg. r. w. ⋆
> Newly demarcated region in the holiday area. It wines are nothing to write home about.

Aliança, Caves   r. w. dr. sp. res. ⋆⋆→⋆⋆⋆
> Large Oporto-based firm, making sparkling wine by the champagne method and a variety of reds and whites, including mature DÃOS.

Amarante
> Sub-region in the VINHOS VERDES area. Rather heavier and stronger wines than those from farther n.

Aveleda   Douro a. dr. ⋆⋆
> A first-class "GREEN WINE" made on the Aveleda estate of the Guedes family, proprietors of SOGRAPE. Sold dry in Portugal but sweetened for export.

Bairrada   Bei. Lit. r. w. dr. and sp. ⋆→ ⋆⋆
> Newly demarcated region supplying much of Oporto's (often good) carafe wine and some excellent red GARRAFEIRAS. Also good-quality sparkling wines by the champagne method.

Barca Velha   ('Ferreirinha') Trás-os-M. r. res. ⋆⋆⋆⋆ 57 64 65 66
> One of Portugal's best wines, made in very limited quantity by the port firm of Ferreira. Fruity and fine with deep bouquet.

Barrocão, Cavas do   Bei. Lit. r. w. dr. res. ⋆→ ⋆⋆⋆
> Based in the BAIRRADA, the firm blends good red DÃOS and makes first-rate old Bairrada garrafeiras, such as **60** and 64.

Basto   A sub-region of the VINHOS VERDES area on the R. Tamego, producing more astringent red wine than white.

Borba Alen. r. ★

Small "determinate area" near Evora, making some of the best wine from the ALENTEJO.

Braga Sub-region of the VINHOS VERDES area, good for both red and white wines.

Buçaco B'a.Al. r. (p.) w. res. ★★★★   r. 51 53 57 58 60 63 67 70 72 75 77; w. 56 65 66 70 72 75

The legendary speciality of the luxury Buçaco hotel near Coimbra, not seen elsewhere. Incredible quality.

Bucelas Est'a. w. dr. ★★★

Tiny demarcated region just n. of Lisbon. João Camilo Alves Lda. and Caves Velhas make delicate, perfumed wines with 11% to 12% alcohol.

Camarate Est'a. r. ★★

Reliable CLARETE from FONSECA at Azeitão, s. of Lisbon.

Carcavelos Est'a. br. sw. ★★★

Minute demarcated region w. of Lisbon. Its excellent sweet wines average 19% alcohol and are drunk cold as an apéritif or with dessert.

Cartaxo Rib. r. w. ★

A district in the Ribatejo n. of Lisbon, now a "determinate area" making everyday wines popular in the capital.

Casal García Douro w. dr. ★

One of the biggest-selling "GREEN WINES" in Portugal, made by SOGRAPE.

Casal Mendes M'o. w. dr. ★★

The "GREEN WINE" from Caves Aliança.

Casaleiro

Trade mark of Caves Dom Teodosio—João T. Barbosa, who make a variety of reliable wines: DÃO, VINHOS VERDES, etc.

Cepa Velha M'o. (r.) w. dr. ★★★

Brand name of Vinhos de Monção, Lda. Their Alvarinho, from the grape of that name, is one of the best "GREEN WINES".

Clarete

Light red wine.

Colares Est'a. r. ★★★

Small demarcated region on the coast w. of Lisbon. Its classical dark red wines, rich in tannin, are from vines which survived the phylloxera epidemic. Drink the oldest available.

Conde de Santar B'a.A. r. (w. dr.) res. ★★→★★★

The only estate-grown DAO, later matured and sold by Carvalho, Ribeiro & Ferreira. The reservas are fruity, full-bodied and exceptionally smooth.

Dão B'a.Al. r. w. res. ★→ ★★★

Demarcated region round Viseu on the R. Mondego. Produces some of Portugal's best table wines: solid reds of some subtlety with age: substantial dry whites. All are sold under brand names. 1970 was the best year of the last decade.

Douro

The n. river whose valley produces port and more than adequate (though undemarcated) table wines.

Evel Trás-os-M. r. ★→★★

Reliable middle-weight red made near VILA REAL by Real Companhia Vinícola do Norte de Portugal. Ages well in bottle.

Faisca Est'a. p. ★

Big-selling sweet carbonated rosé from J. M. da Fonseca.

Fonseca, J. M. da

See Camarate and Moscatel de Setúbal.

Gaeiras Est'a. r. ★★

Dry, full-bodied and well-balanced red made in the neighbourhood of Óbidos.

Garrafeira
>The "private reserve" aged wine of a merchant; usually his best, though often of indeterminate origin.

Gatão M'o. w. dr. ★★
>Reliable "GREEN WINE" from the firm of Borges & Irmão, fragrant but sometimes a little sweetened.

Grão Vasco B'a.A. r. w. res. ★★→ ★★★
>One of the best brands of DÃO, blended and matured at Viseu by SOGRAPE. Fine red reservas; fresh young white (D.Y.A.).

Green Wine (Vinho verde)
>Wine made from barely ripe grapes and undergoing a special secondary fermentation, which leaves it with a slight sparkle. Ready for drinking in the spring after the harvest. It may be white or red.

Lagoa See Algarve.

Lagosta M'o. w. dr. ★★
>Well-known "GREEN WINE" from the Real Companhia Vinícola do Norte de Portugal.

Lancers Est'a. p. ★
>Sweet carbonated rosé extensively shipped to the USA by J. M. da Fonseca.

Lima Sub-region in the n. of the VINHOS VERDES area making mainly astringent red wines.

Madeira Island br. dr./sw. ★★→ ★★★★
>Producer of the famous apéritif and dessert wines. See pages 122 to 127.

Magrico M'o. w. dr. ★★
>At a time when many VINHOS VERDES are being slightly sweetened for export, this is a genuinely dry "GREEN WINE".

Mateus Rosé Trás-os-M. p. (w.) ★
>World's biggest-selling medium-sweet carbonated rosé, made by SOGRAPE at VILA REAL.

Monção
>Sub-region of the VINHOS VERDES area on R. Minho, producing the best of "GREEN WINES" from the ALVARINHO grape.

Moscatel de Setúbal Est'a. br. ★★★
>Small demarcated region s. of the R. Tagus, where J. M. da Fonseca make an aromatic dessert muscat, 6 and 25 years old.

Palacio de Brejoeira M'o. (r.) w. dr. ★★★
>Outstanding estate-made "GREEN WINE" from Monção, with astonishing fragrant nose and full, fruity flavour.

Penafiel Sub-region in the s. of the VINHOS VERDES area.

Periquita Est'a. r. ★★
>One of Portugal's more robust reds, made by J. M. da Fonseca at Azeitão s. of Lisbon from a grape of that name.

Pinhel B'a.Al. (r.). w. sp. ★
>Undemarcated region e. of the DÃO, making similar wine, mostly processed into sparkling.

Ponte de Lima, cooperativa de M'o. r. ★★
>Maker of one of the best bone dry *red* VINHOS VERDES.

Quinta de S. Claudio M'o. w. dr. ★★★
>Estate at Esposende and maker of the best "GREEN WINE" outside MONÇÃO.

Quinta do Corval Trás-os-M. r. ★★
>Estate near Pinhão making good light CLARETES.

Raposeira B'a.Al. sp. ★★
>One of the best-known Portuguese sparkling wines, made by the champagne method at Lamego. Ask for the *bruto* (extra dry).

Santola B'a. Al. w. dr. ★★
>A refreshing dry "GREEN WINE" from Vinhos Messias.

Serradayres Est'a. r. (w.) res. ☐ ★★→ ★★★ ☐

> Blended Ribatejo table wines from Carvalho, Ribeiro & Fer-
> reira, Lda. Sound and very drinkable.

Setúbal

> See Moscatel.

Sogrape

> Sociedade Comercial dos Vinhos de Mesa de Portugal. Largest
> wine concern in the country, making VINHOS VERDES, DÃO,
> MATEUS ROSÉ, VILA REAL red, etc.

Terras Altas B'a.Al. r. w. res. ★★

> Good DÃO wines made by J. M. da Fonseca.

Vila Real Trás-os-M. r. ★→ ☐ ★★ ☐

> Town in a new "determinate area" of the upper DOURO, now
> making some good red table wine.

Vinho branco White wine.

> **consumo** Ordinary wine.
>
> **doce** Sweet wine.
>
> **espumante** Sparkling wine.
>
> **garrafeira** A reserve with long bottle age.
>
> **generoso** Apéritif or dessert wine rich in alcohol.
>
> **maduro** A normal, mature table wine—as opposed to a
> VINHO VERDE.
>
> **rosado** Rosé wine.
>
> **seco** Dry wine.
>
> **tinto** Red wine.
>
> **verde** See under Green Wines.

Vinhos Verdes M'o. and D'o. r. ★ w. dr. ★→ ★★★

> Demarcated region between R. Douro and n. frontier with
> Spain, producing "GREEN WINES".

Sherry, Port & Madeira

The original, classical sherries of Spain, ports of Portugal
and madeiras of Madeira are listed in the A–Z below. Their
many imitators in South Africa, California, Australia,
Cyprus, Argentina are not. References to them will be
found under their respective countries.

The map on page 111 locates the port and sherry districts.
Madeira is an island 400 miles out in the Atlantic from the
coast of Morocco, a port of call for west-bound ships: hence its
traditional market in North America.

In this section most of the entries are shippers' names
followed by a brief account of their wines. The names of
wine-types are included in the alphabetical listing.

Amontillado

> In general use means medium sherry; technically means a
> wine which has been aged to become more powerful and
> pungent. A FINO can be amontillado.

Amoroso

> Type of sw. sherry, not much different from a sweet OLOROSO.

Barbeito

> Shippers of good-quality Madeira, including the driest and
> best apéritif Madeira, "Island Dry".

Bertola

> Sherry shippers, owned by the giant Rumasa group, best
> known for their Bertola Cream Sherry.

Blandy

> Old family firm of Madeira shippers at Funchal. Duke of
> Clarence Malmsey is their most famous wine.

Blazquez
> Sherry bodega at JEREZ with outstanding FINO. "Carta Blanca", and "Carta Oro" amontillado "al natural" (unsweetened).

Brown sherry   British term for a style of dark sweet sherry.

Bual   One of the grapes of Madeira, making a soft smoky sweet wine, not as sweet as Malmsey.

Caballero
> Sherry shippers best known for Gran Señor Choice Old Cream. Their best FINO is Don Guisa.

Calem   Old Portuguese house with a good reputation, owning the excellent Quinta da Foz. Vintages: 50, 54, 58, 60, 63, 70, 75, 77, 78.

Cockburn
> British-owned port shippers with a range of good wines. Fine vintage port from very high v'yds. can look deceptively light when young, but has great lasting power. Vintages: **55 60** 63 67 70 75.

Cossart Gordon
> Leading firm of Madeira shippers founded 1745, best known for their "Good Company" range of wines but also producing old vintages and soleras.

Cream sherry
> A style of fairly pale sweet sherry made by sweetening a blend of well-aged OLOROSOS.

Crofts   One of the oldest firms shipping vintage port: 300 years old in 1978. Bought early this century by Gilbey's. Well-balanced vintage wines last as long as any. Vintages: **55 60** 63 **66** 70 75 77, and lighter vintage wines under the name of their Quinta da Roeda in several other years ('80). Also now in the sherry business with Croft Original (pale cream), Delicado (fino).

Crusted
> Term for a vintage-style port, but blended from several vintages not one, bottled young and aged in bottle, so forming a "crust" in the bottle. Needs decanting.

Cuvillo
> Sherry bodega at Puerto de Santa Maria best known for their Cream, dry Oloroso Sangre y Trabajadero and Fino "C" and a fine Palo Cortado.

Delaforce
> Port shippers owned by International Distillers and Vintners, particularly well known in Germany. "His Eminence" is an excellent tawny. "Vintage Character" is also good. Vintage wines are very fine, among the lighter kind: **55 58 60** 63 **66** 70 75 77. "Quinta da Corte" in 1980.

Domecq
> Giant family-owned sherry bodegas at JEREZ. Double Century Original Oloroso is their biggest brand, La Ina their excellent FINO, Guitar a new pale cream. Other famous wines incl. Celebration Cream, Botaina (old amontillado) and Rio Viejo (dry oloroso). Now also in Rioja (p. 117).

Dow   Old name used on the British market by the port shippers Silva & Cosens, well known for their relatively dry vintage wines, said to have a faint "cedarwood" character. Vintages: **55 57 58 60** 63 66 70 75 77 80.

Dry Sack   See Williams & Humbert.

Duff Gordon
> Sherry shippers best known for their El Cid AMONTILLADO. Owned by the big Spanish firm Bodegas Osborne.

Duke of Wellington
> Luxury range of sherries from Bodegas Internacionales, owned by RUMASA.

Eira Velha, Quinta da

  Small port estate with old-style vintage wines shipped by HARVEY's of Bristol. Vintages: 72 78.

Ferreira

  Portuguese-owned port growers and shippers (since 1751) well-known for old tawnies and good, relatively light, vintages: **60 63 66** 70 75 77 80. Also Special Reserve (vintage character) Donna Antonia.

Findlater's

  Old established London wine merchant shipping his own very successful brand of medium sherry: Dry Fly amontillado.

Fino   Term for the lightest and finest of sherries, completely dry, very pale and with great delicacy. Fino should always be drunk cool and fresh: it deteriorates rapidly once opened. TIO PEPE is the classic example.

Flor   The characteristic natural yeast which gives FINO sherry its unique flavour.

Fonseca

  British-owned port shipper of high reputation. Robust, deeply coloured vintage wine, sometimes said to have a slight "burnt" flavour. Vintages: **55 60** 63 **66** 70 75 77. Also excellent Vintage Character "Bin 27".

Garvey's

  Famous old sherry shippers at JEREZ owned by RUMASA. Their finest wines are Fino San Patricio, Tio Guillermo Dry Amontillado and Ochavico Dry Oloroso. San Angelo Medium Amontillado is their most popular. Also Bicentenary Pale Cream.

Gonzalez Byass

  Enormous concern shipping the world's most famous and one of the best sherries: Tio Pepe. Other brands incl. La Concha Medium Amontillado, Elegante Dry Fino, San Domingo Pale Cream, Romano Cream.

Gould Campbell   See Smith Woodhouse.

Graham

  Port shippers famous for one of the richest and sweetest of vintage ports, largely from their own Quinta Malvedos, also excellent brands, incl. Ruby, Late Bottled 10- and 20-year-old Tawny. Vintages: **55 58 60 63** 66 70 75 77 80.

Harvey's

  World-famous Bristol shippers of Bristol Cream and Bristol Milk sweet sherries, Club Amontillado and Bristol Dry, which are medium. Luncheon Dry and Bristol Fino, which are dry and excellent Palo Cortado.

Henriques & Henriques

  Well-known Madeira shippers of Funchal. Their wide range includes a good dry apéritif wine: Ribeiro Seco.

Jerez de la Frontera

  Centre of the sherry industry, between Cadiz and Seville in s. Spain. The word sherry is a corruption of the name, pronounced in Spanish "Hereth". In French, Xérés.

Late-bottled vintage

  Port of a single good vintage kept in wood for twice as long as vintage port (about 5 years). Therefore lighter when bottled and ageing quicker.

Leacock   One of the oldest firms of Madeira shippers. Most famous wine is "Penny Black" Malmsey.

Lustau

  The largest independent family-owned sherry bodega in JEREZ, making many wines for other shippers, but with a very good "Dry Lustau" range (particularly the oloroso) and "Jerez Lustau" Palo Cortado.

Macharnudo

One of the best parts of the sherry v'yds., n. of Jerez, famous for wines of the highest quality, both FINO and OLOROSO.

Malmsey

The sweetest form of Madeira; dark amber, rich and honeyed yet with Madeira's unique sharp tang.

Manzanilla

Sherry, normally FINO, which has acquired a peculiar bracing salty character from being kept in bodegas at Sanlucar de Barrameda, on the Guadalquivir estuary near JEREZ.

Misa, Marques de

Old sherry bodega now in the RUMASA group.

Morgan

A subsidiary of Croft port, best known in France.

Offley Forester

Port shippers and owners of the famous Quinta Boa Vista. Their vintage wines tend to be round, "fat" and sweet, good for relatively early drinking. Vintages: **55 60 62 63 66 67** 70 72 75 77 (an exception to the "early-drinking" rule).

Oloroso

Style of sherry, heavier and less brilliant than FINO when young, but maturing to greater richness and roundness. Naturally dry, but generally sweetened for sale, as CREAM.

Osborne

Brandy well known, but good sherries include Fino Quinta, Coquinero, dry AMONTILLADO, 10 R.S. Oloroso.

Palo Cortado

A style of sherry close to OLOROSO but with some of the character of a FINO. Dry but rich and soft. Not often seen.

Palomino & Vergara

Sherry shippers of JEREZ, best known for Palomino Cream, Medium and Dry. Best FINO: Tio Mateo. RUMASA group.

Pemartin

Jerez bodega in the RUMASA group.

Puerto de Santa Maria

The port and second city of the sherry area with a number of important bodegas.

P.X.

Short for Pedro Ximenez, the grape used in JEREZ for sweetening blends. P.X. wine alone is almost like treacle.

Quarles Harris

One of the oldest port houses, since 1680, now owned by the Symington family (see WARRE). Vintages: **60 63** 66 70 75 77 80.

Quinta

Portuguese for "estate".

Quinta do Noval

Great Portuguese port house making splendidly dark, rich and full-bodied vintage port; a few pre-phylloxera vines still at the Quinta make a small quantity of "Nacional"—very dark, full and slow-maturing wine. Vintages: **55 58 60** 63 **66** 70 75 78.

Rainwater

A fairly light, not very sweet blend of Madeira—in fact of VERDELHO wine—popular in the USA and Canada.

Real Tesoro, Marques de

Sherry shippers of SANLUCAR and JEREZ, specializing in MANZANILLA, esp. "La Capitala".

Rebello Valente

Name used for the vintage port of ROBERTSON. Their vintage wines are light but elegant and well-balanced, maturing rather early. Vintages: **55 60 63 66 67** 70 75 77.

La Riva
> Distinguished firm of sherry shippers making one of the best FINOS, Tres Palmas, among many good wines.

Rivero Considerable sherry concern best known for CZ range.

Robertson
> Subsidiary of SANDEMAN'S, shipping REBELLO VALENTE vintage port and Gamebird Tawny and Ruby.

Fino sherries – the palest, driest and most delicate – need handling with more care than the older, heavier and/or sweeter amontillados and olorosos. They lose their vital freshness quite rapidly after bottling, and very rapidly indeed once the bottle is opened. For this reason the Spanish often use half-bottles. Buy fino in small quantities and use it straight away, keeping the bottle in the refrigerator if it is not finished at a sitting.

Rozes Port shippers controlled by Moët-Hennessy. Tawny very popular in France; also Ruby and 77.

Ruby The youngest (and cheapest) style of port: very sweet and red. The best are vigorous and full of flavour. Others can be merely strong and rather thin.

Ruiz Mateos
> The sherry bodega which gave its name to the mammoth Rumasa group of bodegas, banks, etc, now in financial trouble. Its Don Zoilo sherries are some of the most expensive and best. Ruiz Hermanos is a cheaper range.

Rumasa See Ruiz Mateos.

Rutherford & Miles
> Madeira shippers with one of the best known of all Bual wines: Old Trinity House.

Saccone & Speed
> British sherry shippers owned by Courage's the Brewers. Popular Troubador and Cuesta ranges and a good Fino.

Sanchez Romate
> Family company founded in 1781. Best known in Spanish-speaking world esp. for their brandy, Cardinal Mendoza. Makes good sherry—Fino Cristal, Oloroso Dona Juana, Amontillado N.P.U.

Sandeman
> Giant of the port trade and a major figure in the sherry one owned by Seagrams. "Partners" is their best-known tawny port; their vintage wines are robust—some of the old vintages were superlative [**55 58 60 63 66 67** 70 75 77 80]. Of the sherries, Medium Dry Amontillado is the best-seller, their Fino "Apitiv" is particularly good and Armada Cream and Dry Don Amontillado are both well known.

Sanlucar Seaside sherry-town (see Manzanilla) 15 miles from JEREZ.

Sercial Grape (reputedly a RIESLING) grown in Madeira to make the driest of the island's wines—a good apéritif.

Smith Woodhouse
> Port firm founded in 1784, now owned by the Symington family (see WARRE). GOULD CAMPBELL is a subsidiary. Wines include: Old Priory Vintage Character, Old Lodge Tawny, 70 75 77 80.

Solera System used in making both sherry and Madeira, also some port. It consists of topping up progressively more mature barrels with slightly younger wine of the same sort: the object to attain continuity in the final wine. Most commercial sherries are blends of several solera wines.

Tarquinio Lomelino

> Madeira shippers famous for their collection of antique wines. Their standard range is called Dom Henriques.

Tawny

> A style of port aged for many years in wood (in contrast to vintage port, which is aged in bottle) until tawny in colour.

Taylor

> One of the best port shippers, particularly for their full, rich, long-lived vintage wine and tawnies of stated age (40-year-old, 20-year-old, etc.). Their Quinta de Vargellas is said to give Taylor's its distinctive scent of violets. Vintages: **55 60** 63 **66** 70 75 77 80. Vargellas is shipped unblended in certain (lesser) vintages (67).

De Terry, Carlos y Javier

> Family-owned bodega at PUERTO DE SANTA MARIA with a good range of sherries.

Tio Pepe

> The most famous of FINO sherries (see GONZALEZ BYASS).

Valdespino

> Famous family-owned bodega at JEREZ, owner of the Inocente v'yd., making the excellent FINO of the same name. Tio Diego is their splendid dry AMONTILLADO, Solera 1842 a ditto oloroso, Matador the name of their popular range.

Varela

> Sherry shippers, members of the RUMASA group, best-known for their Varela Medium and Cream.

Verdelho

> Madeira grape making fairly dry wine without the distinction of SERCIAL. A pleasant apéritif.

Vintage Port

> The best port of exceptional vintages is bottled after only 2 years in wood and matures very slowly, for up to 20 years or even more, in its bottle. It always leaves a heavy deposit and therefore needs decanting.

Vintage port is almost as much a ritual as a drink. It always needs to be decanted with great care (since the method of making it leaves a heavy deposit in the bottle). The simplest and surest way of doing this is by filtering it through clean muslin or a coffee filter-paper into either a decanter or a well-rinsed bottle. All except very old ports can safely be decanted the day before drinking. At table the decanter is traditionally passed from guest to guest clockwise. Vintage port can be immensely long-lived. Particularly good vintages older than those mentioned in the text include 1950, 48, 45, 35, 34, 27, 20, 11, 08, 04.

Vintage Character

> Somewhat misleading term used for a good-quality full and meaty port like a first-class RUBY made by the solera system. Lacks the splendid "nose" of vintage port.

Warre Probably the oldest of all port shippers (since 1670), now owned by the Symington family. Fine long-maturing vintage wines, a good TAWNY, Nimrod and Vintage Character Warrior. Vintages: **55 58 60** 63 **66** 70 75 77.

White Port

> Port made of white grapes, golden in colour. Formerly made sweet, now more often dry: a good apéritif but a heavy one.

Williams & Humbert

> Famous and first-class sherry bodega now owned by the giant Rumasa group. Dry Sack (medium AMONTILLADO) is their best-selling wine. Pando is an excellent FINO. Canasta Cream and Walnut Brown are good in their class.

Central & South-east Europe

Weinviertel
Langenlois
Wachau • Vienna
Mátra
Somló
Sopron • Bud
Burgenland
AUSTRIA Graz • HUNGAR
Styria Balaton
Lutomer
Ljubljana • Vilanyi-Pecs
Slovenia Slavonia
Trieste • Vojvodi
Zagreb
Croatia
Bosnia-Herzegovina
Dalmatia YUGOSLAVIA
Split • Sarajevo
Monten
Dubrovnik •

Corf

The huge range of wines from the countries covered by this map offers some of the best value for money in the world today. Quality is moderate to high, tending to improve, and reliability on the whole is excellent.

The references are arranged country by country, with all geographical references back to the map on this page.

Labelling in all the countries involved except Greece is based on the German, now international, pattern of place-name plus grape-variety. The main grape-varieties are therefore included alongside areas and other terms in the alphabetical listings. Quality ratings in this section are given where there is enough information to warrant it.

Austria

Austria has recently become recognized as one of Europe's most reliable sources of fresh, fruity, dry wines and succulent sweet ones at very fair prices. Most of her practices and terms are similar to the German; the basic difference is a higher alcoholic degree in almost all her wine. The Austrian Wine Quality Seal (Weingutesiegel or WGS), in the form of a red, white and gold disc on the bottle, means the wine has met fixed standards, been officially tested and approved.

Recent vintages:

1982	Early harvest of record size, fewer sweet wines.
1981	Small crop, quality high, esp. sweet wines.
1980	A difficult vintage, as in most of Europe.
1979	Reduced crop; excellent quality.
1978	Average quantity and quality.

Apetlon Burgenland w. s./sw. or sw. * → ⟦ ** ⟧
> Village of the SEEWINKEL making tasty whites on sandy soil, incl. very good sweet wines.

Ausbruch
> Term used for very sweet wines between Beerenauslese and Trockenbeerenauslese (see Germany) in richness.

Baden Vienna (r.) w. dr. or sw. * → ***
> Town and area s. of VIENNA incl. GUMPOLDSKIRCHEN. Good lively high-flavoured wines, best from ROTGIPFLER and ZIERFÄNDLER grapes.

Blaufränkisch
> The GAMAY grape.

Blue Danube
> Popular GEWÜRZTRAMINER/WÄLSCHRIESLING blend from LENZ MOSER.

Bouvier
> Native Austrian grape giving soft but aromatic wine.

Burgenland Burgenland r. w. dr. sw. * → ⟦ **** ⟧
> Region on the Hungarian border with ideal conditions for sweet wines. "Noble rot" occurs regularly and Ausleses are abundant. (See Rust, etc.)

Dürnstein w. dr. sw. ** → ***
> Wine centre of the WACHAU with a famous ruined castle and important WINZERGENOSSENSCHAFT. Some of Austria's best whites, esp. Rheinriesling and GRÜNER VELTLINER.

Eisenstadt Burgenland (r.) w. dr. or sw. ** → ****
> Town in BURGENLAND and historic seat of the ESTERHAZYS.

Esterhazy
> Quasi-royal family whose AUSBRUCH and other BURGENLAND wines are of superlative quality.

Grinzing Vienna w. ** D.Y.A.
> Suburb of VIENNA with delicious lively HEURIGE wines.

Grüner Veltliner
> Austria's most characteristic white grape (31% of her white v'yds.) making short-lived but marvellously spicy and flowery, racy and vital wine.

Gumpoldskirchen Vienna (r.) w. dr. or sw. ** → ***
> Pretty resort s. of VIENNA with wines of great character.

Heiligenkreuz, Stift
> Cistercian Monastery at THALLERN making some of Austria's best wine, particularly from a fine steep v'yd.: Wiege.

Heurige
> Means both new wine and the tavern where it is drunk.

Kahlenberg Vienna w. ** D.Y.A.
> Village and v'yd. hill n. of VIENNA, famous for HEURIGEN.

Kamp Langenlois (r.) w. dr. or sw. *→ **
>Tributary of the Danube (Donau) giving its name to wines from its valley, n. and e. of the WACHAU, incl. pleasant Veltliner (see Grüner Veltliner) and RIESLING.

Klöch Steiermark (r.) p. w. *→ **
>The chief wine town of Styria, the s.e. province. No famous wines, but agreeable ones, esp. Traminer.

Klosterneuberg Danube r. w. *→ ***
>District with a famous monastery and major producer, also a wine college and research station, just n. of VIENNA.

Krems Danube w. *→ ***
>Town and district just e. of the WACHAU with good GRÜNER VELTLINER and Rheinriesling (see Riesling) esp. from Austria's biggest WINZERGENOSSENSCHAFT.

Langenlois Langenlois r. w. *→ **
>Chief town of the KAMP valley with many modest and some good wines, esp. peppery GRÜNER VELTLINER and Rheinriesling (see Riesling). Reds less interesting.

Lenz Moser
>Austria's best known and most progressive grower, invented a high vine system and makes good to excellent wine at Röhrendorf near KREMS, APETLON, MAILBERG and elsewhere.

Mailberg Weinviertel w. **
>Town of the WEINVIERTEL known for lively light wine, esp. LENZ MOSER's Malteser.

Morandell, Alois
>Big-scale Viennese wine-merchant.

Mörbisch Burgenland r. w. dr. or sw. *→ ***
>Leading wine-village of BURGENLAND. Good sweet wines. Reds and dry whites not inspiring.

Müller-Thurgau
>9% of all Austria's white grapes are Müller-Thurgau.

Muskat-Ottonel
>The strain of muscat grape grown in e. Europe, incl. Austria.

Niederösterreich
>Lower Austria: i.e. all the n.e. corner of the country.

Neuberger
>Popular white grape: pleasant wine in KREMS/LANGENLOIS but soft and coarse in BURGENLAND.

Neusiedlersee
>Shallow lake in sandy country on the Hungarian border, creating autumn mists and giving character to the sweet wines of BURGENLAND.

Nussdorf Vienna w. **
>Suburb of VIENNA with well-known HEURIGEN.

Oggau Burgenland (r.) w. sw. **→ ***
>One of the wine-centres of BURGENLAND, famous for Beerenausleses (see Germany) and AUSBRUCH.

Portugieser
>With BLAUFRÄNKISCH, one of the two main red-wine grapes of Austria, giving dark but rather characterless wine.

Retz Weinviertel (r.) w. *
>Leading wine-centre of the WEINVIERTEL, known for pleasant GRÜNER VELTLINER, etc.

Ried Vineyard: when named it is usually a good one.

Riesling
>German Riesling is always called Rheinriesling. "Riesling" is Wälschriesling.

Rotgipfler
>Good and high-flavoured grape peculiar to BADEN and GUMPOLDSKIRCHEN. Used with ZIERFÄNDLER to make lively whites. Very heavy/sweet on its own.

Ruländer
> The PINOT GRIS grape.

Rust Burgenland (r.) w. dr. or sw. *→ ***
> Most famous wine centre of BURGENLAND, long and justly famous for its AUSBRUCH, often made of mixed grapes.

St. Laurent
> Traditional Austrian red grape, faintly muscat-flavoured.

Schilcher
> Pleasant sharp rosé, speciality of STYRIA.

Schloss Grafenegg
> Famous property of the Metternich family near KREMS. Good standard white and excellent Ausleses.

Schluck
> Name for the common white wine of the WACHAU, good when drunk very young. Also a good brand of GRÜNER VELTLINER from LENZ MOSER.

Seewinkel
> "Sea corner": the sandy district around the NEUSIEDLERSEE.

Sepp Hold
> Well-known EISENSTADT grower and merchant.

Siegendorf, Klosterkeller
> First-class private BURGENLAND wine estate.

Sievering Vienna w. **
> Suburb of VIENNA with notable HEURIGEN.

Spätrot Another name for ZIERFÄNDLER.

Spitzenwein
> Top wines—as opposed to TISCHWEIN: ordinary table wines.

Steiermark (Styria)
> Province in the s.e., not remarkable for wine but well-supplied with it.

Stift
> The word for a monastery. Monasteries have been, and still are, very important in Austria's wine-making, combining tradition and high standards with modern resources.

Thallern Vienna (r.) w. dr. or sw. ** → ***
> Village near GUMPOLDSKIRCHEN and trade-name of wines from Stift HEILIGENKREUZ.

Tischwein
> Everyday wine, as opposed to SPITZENWEIN.

Traiskirchen Vienna (r.) w. **
> Village near GUMPOLDSKIRCHEN with similar wine.

Veltliner
> See Grüner Veltliner

Vöslau Baden r. (w.) *
> Spa town s. of BADEN (and WIEN) known for its reds made of PORTUGIESER and BLAUFRÄNKISCH: refreshing but no more.

Wachau
> District on the n. bank of the Danube round DÜRNSTEIN with cliff-like slopes giving some of Austria's best whites, esp. Rheinriesling (see Riesling) and GRÜNER VELTLINER.

Weinviertel
> "The wine quarter": name given to the huge and productive district between VIENNA and the Czech border. Mainly light white wines.

Wien (Vienna)
> The capital city, with 1,800 acres of v'yds. in its suburbs to supply its cafés and HEURIGEN.

Winzergenossenschaft
> Growers' co-operative.

Zierfändler
> White grape of high flavour peculiar to the BADEN area. Used with ROTGIPFLER.

Hungary

The traditional and characteristic firmness and strength of character which can make Hungarian wine the most exciting of Eastern Europe have been modified by modern ideas. Average quality is still high; whites are lively and reds made to last, but much of the drama has gone—at least from the standard exported lines. Visitors to the country will find plenty of excellent wine.

Aszu
> Word meaning "syrupy" applied to very sweet wines, esp. Tokay (TOKAJI), where the "aszu" is late-picked and "nobly rotten" as in Sauternes. (See p. 47.)

Badacsony   Balaton w. dr. sw. `**→***`
> 1,400 ft. hill on the n. shore of La. BALATON whose basalt soil can give rich high-flavoured wines, among Hungary's best.

Balatonfüred   Balaton (r.) w. dr. sw. `**`
> Town on the n. shore of La. BALATON e. of BADACSONY. Good but softer, less fiery wines.

Balaton   Balaton r. w. dr. sw. `*` → `***`
> Hungary's inland sea and Europe's largest lake. Many wines take its name and most are good. The ending "i" (e.g. Balatoni, Egri) is the equivalent of -er in German names, or in Londoner.

Bársonyos-Császár
> Wine-district of n. Hungary. MÓR is its best-known centre.

Bikavér
> "Bull's Blood"—or words to that effect. The historic name of the best-selling red wine of EGER: full-bodied and well-balanced, improving considerably with age.

Csopak
> Village next to BALATONFÜRED, with similar wines.

Debrö   Mátraalya w. sw. `***`
> Important centre of the MÁTRAALYA famous for its pale, aromatic and sweet HÁRSLEVELÜ.

Eger   Mátraalya r. w. dr. sw. `*→` `**`
> Best-known MÁTRAALYA wine-centre: fine baroque city of cellars full of BIKAVÉR. Also delicate white LEANYKA and dark sweetish MERLOT, known as MÉDOC NOIR.

Eszencia
> The fabulous quintessence of Tokay (TOKAJI): intensely sweet grape-juice of very low, if any, alcoholic strength, reputed to have miraculous properties. Now almost unobtainable.

Ezerjó
> The grape grown at MÓR to make one of Hungary's best dry white wines: potentially distinguished, fragrant and fine.

Furmint
> The classic grape of Tokay (TOKAJI), with great flavour and fire, also grown for table wine on La. BALATON, sometimes with excellent results.

Hajós   Mecsek r. `*`
> Town in s. Hungary becoming known as a centre for good CABERNET SAUVIGNON reds.

Hárslevelü
> The "lime-leaved" grape used at DEBRÖ to make good gently sweet wine.

Kadarka
> The commonest red grape of Hungary, grown in vast quantities for everyday wine on the plains in the s.; also used at EGER; capable of ample flavour and interesting maturity.

Kékfrankos
> Hungarian for GAMAY, literally "blue French". Makes good light red at SOPRON on the Austrian border.

Kéknelyü
> High-flavoured white grape making the best and "stiffest" wine of Mt. BADACSONY. It should be fiery and spicy stuff.

Leanyka
> East-European white grape better known in Romania but making admirable pale soft wine at EGER.

Mátraalya
> Wine-district in the foothills of the Matra range in n. Hungary, incl. DEBRÖ and EGER.

Mecsek
> District in s. Hungary known for the good reds of VILÁNY and whites of PÉCS.

Médoc Noir
> Possibly MERLOT, used to make sweet red at EGER.

Monimpex
> The Hungarian state export monopoly, with great cellars at Budafok, near Budapest.

Mór North Hungary w. dr. ★★★
> Town in n. Hungary famous for its fresh dry EZERJÓ.

Muskotály
> Hungarian muscat, used to add aroma to Tokay (TOKAJI) and occasionally alone at EGER, where its wine is long-lived and worth tasting.

Nágyburgundi
> Literally "black burgundy"—the PINOT NOIR makes admirable wine in s. Hungary, esp. round VILÁNY.

Olasz Riesling
> The Hungarian name for the Italian, or Wälschriesling.

Pécs Mecsek (r.) w. dr. ⬚★⬚ → ★★
> Town in the Mecsek hills known in the West for its agreeable well-balanced (if rather sweet) Riesling.

Puttonyos
> The measure of sweetness in Tokay (TOKAJI). A 7-gal. container from which ASZU is added to SZAMORODNI. One "putt" makes it sweetish; 6 (the maximum) very sweet indeed.

Siller
> Pale red or rosé. Usually made from KADARKA grapes.

Somló North Hungary w. dr. ★★★
> Isolated small v'yd. district n. of BALATON making intense white wines of high repute from FURMINT and RIESLING.

Sopron Burgenland r. ★★
> Little Hungarian enclave in Burgenland s. of the Neusiedlersee (see Austria) specializing in KÉKFRANKOS (Gamay) red.

Szamorodni
> Word meaning "as it comes": i.e. fully fermented (therefore dry) wine from all the grapes not specially selected. Used to describe the unsweetened form of Tokay (TOKAJI).

Szürkebarát
> Literally means "grey friar": Hungarian for PINOT GRIS, which makes rich heavy wine in the BALATON v'yds.

Szekszárdi Vörós Mecsek r. ⬚★★⬚
> The red (KADARKA) wine of Szekszárd in south-central Hungary. Dark strong wine which needs age.

Tokaji (Tokay) Tokaji w. dr. sw. ⬚★★⬚ → ★★★★
> Hungary's famous strong sweet wine, comparable to an oxidized Sauternes, from hills on the Russian border in the n.e. See Aszu, Eszencia, Furmint, Puttonyos, Szamorodni.

Tramini
> The TRAMINER grape; little grown in Hungary.

Vilány Mecsek r. p. (w.) ******

Southernmost city of Hungary and well-known centre of red wine production. Vilányi Burgundi is largely PINOT NOIR—and very good.

Wälschriesling

Austrian name sometimes used for Olasz (Italian) Riesling.

Zöldszilváni

"Green Sylvaner"—i.e. Sylvaner. Grown round La. BALATON.

Romania

The wine industry is orientated towards Russia as its biggest customer, and consequently specializes in the sweet wines that Russians like. The need for foreign currency makes export to the West highly desirable, so the best qualities are available at subsidized prices. They include sound and good-value reds and whites, including dry ones, but at present nothing memorable.

Alba Iulia

Town in the TIRNAVE area in Transylvania, known for off-dry whites blended from Italian Riesling, FETEASCA and MUSKAT-OTTONEL.

AligotéThe junior white burgundy grape makes pleasantly fresh white wine in Romania.

Babeaşca

Traditional red grape of the FOCSANI area: agreeably sharp wine tasting slightly of cloves.

Banat The plain on the border with Serbia. Workaday Riesling and light red CADARCA.

Cabernet

Increasingly grown in Romania, particularly at DEALUL MARE, to make dark intense wines though sometimes too sweet for French-trained palates.

Cadarca

Romanian spelling of the Hungarian Kadarka.

Chardonnay

The great white burgundy grape is used at MURFATLAR to make honey-sweet dessert wine.

Cotesti

Part of the FOCSANI area making reds of PINOT NOIR, MERLOT, etc., and dry whites said to resemble Alsace wines.

Cotnari

Romania's most famous historical wine: light dessert wine from MOLDAVIA. Like very delicate Tokay.

Dealul Mare

Important up-to-date v'yd. area in the s.e. Carpathian foot-hills. Red wines from CABERNET, MERLOT, PINOT NOIR, etc.

Dobruja

Black Sea region round the port of Constanta. MURFATLAR is the main v'yd. area.

Dragaşani

Region on the R. Olt s. of the Carpathians, growing both traditional and "modern" grapes. Good MUSKAT-OTTONEL.

Feteasca

Romanian white grape of mild character, the same as Hungary's Leanyka (and some say Switzerland's Chasselas).

Focsani

Important eastern wine region including those of COTESTI, ODOBESTI and NICORESTI.

Grasa
> A form of the Hungarian Furmint grape grown in Romania and used in, among other wines, COTNARI.

Moldavia
> The n.e. province, now largely within the USSR.

Murfatlar
> Big modern v'yds. near the Black Sea specializing in sweet wines, incl. CHARDONNAY. Now also dry reds and whites.

Muskat-Ottonel
> The e. European muscat, at its best in Romania.

Nicoresti
> Eastern area of FOCSANI best known for its red BABEAŞCA.

Odobesti
> The central part of FOCSANI; mainly white wines of FETEASCA, RIESLING, etc.

Perla The speciality of TÎRNAVE: a pleasant blended semi-sweet white of RIESLING, FETEASCA and MUSKAT-OTTONEL.

Pitesti
> Principal town of the Arges region s. of the Carpathians. Traditionally whites from FETEASCA, TAMIÎOASA, RIESLING.

Premiat
> Reliable range of mid-quality wines for export.

Riesling
> Italian Riesling. Very widely planted. No exceptional wines.

Sadova
> Town in the SEGARCEA area exporting a rosé.

Segarcea
> Southern wine area near the Danube. Exports rather sweet CABERNET.

Tamiîoasa A traditional white-wine grape variety of no very distinct character.

Tîrnave
> Important Transylvanian wine region, known for its PERLA and MUSKAT-OTTONEL.

Valea Calugareasca
> "The Valley of the Monks", part of the DEALUL MARE v'yd. with a well-known research station. CABERNET, MERLOT and PINOT NOIR are generally made into heavy sweetish wines.

Yugoslavia

A well-established supplier of wines of international calibre at very reasonable prices. Yugoslav Riesling was the pioneer, now followed by Cabernet, Pinot Blanc and Traminer of equal quality as well as such worthwhile specialities as Zilavka and Prokupac. All parts of the country except the central highlands make wine, almost entirely in giant co-operatives. Tourists on the Dalmatian coast will find more original products—all well worth trying.

Amselfelder
> German marketing name for the Red Burgundac (Spät-burgunder or PINOT NOIR) wine of KOSOVO.

Babic
> Agreeable standard red of the Dalmatian coast.

Banat
> Sandy north-eastern area, partly in Romania, with up-to-date wineries making adequate RIESLING.

Beli Pinot
> The PINOT BLANC, a popular grape in SLOVENIA.

Bijelo White.

Blatina
>The red grape and wine of MOSTAR. Not in the same class as the white ZILAVKA.

Bogdanuşa
>Local white grape of the Dalmatian islands, esp. Hvar and Brac. Pleasant fresh faintly fragrant wine.

Burgundac Bijeli
>The CHARDONNAY, grown a little in SLAVONIA and VOJVODINA.

Cabernet
>See Grapes for red wine. Now introduced in many places with increasingly pleasant, occasionally exciting, results.

Crno Black—i.e. red wine.

Ćvićek
>Traditional pale red or dark rosé of SLOVENIA.

Dalmaciajavino
>Important co-operative based at Split and selling a full range of coastal and island wines.

Dalmatia
>The middle coast of Yugoslavia from Rijeka to Dubrovnik. Has a remarkable variety of wines of character.

Dingac
>Heavy sweetish red from the local PLAVAC grape, speciality of the mid-Dalmatian coast.

Faros
>Smooth and substantial age-worthy red from the island of Hvar.

Fruska Gora
>Hills in VOJVODINA, on the Danube n.w. of Belgrade, with a growing modern v'yd. and a wide range of wines, incl. good Traminer and Sauvignon Blanc.

Graşevina
>Slovenian for Italian Riesling (also called Wälschriesling, LASKI RIZLING, etc.). The normal Riesling of Yugoslavia.

Grk Strong almost sherry-like white from the Grk grape. Speciality of the island of Korcula.

Istria Peninsula in the n. Adriatic, Porec its centre, with a variety of pleasant wines, the MERLOT as good as any.

Jerusalem
>Yugoslavia's most famous v'yd., at LJUTOMER. Its best wines are late-picked Rieslings and more aromatic whites.

Kadarka
>The major red grape of Hungary, widely grown in SERBIA.

Kosovo
>Region in the s., between SERBIA and Macedonia, with modern v'yds. The source of AMSELFELDER and well-balanced, lively CABERNET.

Laski Rizling
>Yet another name for Italian Riesling.

Ljutomer (or Lutomer)-Ormoz
>Yugoslavia's best known and probably best wine district, in n.e. SLOVENIA, famous for its RIESLING: full-flavoured, full-strength and at its best rich and satisfying wine.

Malvasia
>White grape giving luscious heavy wine, used in w. SLOVENIA.

Marastina
>Strong dry white of the Dalmatian islands.

Maribor
>Important wine-centre of n. SLOVENIA. White wines incl. SIPON, Ruländer, etc., as well as RIESLING and Austrian BOUVIER (see Austria).

Merlot

    The Bordeaux red grape, grown in SLOVENIA and ISTRIA with reasonable results.

Mostar

    Islamic-looking little city inland from DALMATIA, making admirable dry white from the ZILAVKA grape. Also BLATINA.

Muskat-Ottonel

    The East European muscat, grown in VOJVODINA.

Navip The big growers' co-operative of SERBIA, with its headquarters at Belgrade.

Opol Pleasantly light pale red made of PLAVAĆ grapes round Split and Sibenik in DALMATIA.

Plavać Mali

    Native red grape of SLOVENIA and DALMATIA: makes DINGAC, POSTUP, OPOL, etc.

Plavina

    Light red of the DALMATIAN coast round Zadar.

Plovdina

    Native red grape of Macedonia in the s., giving mild wine. Grown and generally blended with PROKUPAC.

Portugizac Austria's Portugieser: plain red wine.

Posip Pleasant, not-too-heavy white wine of the Dalmatian islands, notably Korcula.

Postup

    Sweet and heavy DALMATIAN red from the Peljesac peninsula near Korcula. Highly esteemed locally.

Prokupac

    Principal native red grape of s. SERBIA and Macedonia: 85% of the production. Makes good dark rosé (RUZICA) and full-bodied red of character. Some of the best comes from ZUPA. PLOVDINA is often added for smoothness.

Prosek

    The dessert wine of DALMATIA, of stupefying natural strength and variable quality. The best is excellent, but hard to find.

Radgonska Ranina

    Ranina is Austria's BOUVIER grape (see Austria). Radgona is near MARIBOR. The wine is sweet and carries the trade name TIGROVO MLJEKO (Tiger's Milk).

Rajnski Rizling

    The Rhine Riesling, rare in Yugoslavia but grown a little in LJUTOMER-ORMOZ.

Refosco

    Italian grape grown in e. SLOVENIA and ISTRIA under the name TERAN.

Renski Rizling

    Alternative spelling for Rhine Riesling.

Riesling

    Without qualification means Italian Riesling.

Ruzica

    Rosé, usually from PROKUPAC. Darker than most; and better.

Serbia

    The e. state of Yugoslavia, with nearly half the country's v'yds., stretching from VOJVODINA to Macedonia.

Sipon Yugoslav name for the FURMINT grape of Hungary, also grown in SLOVENIA.

Slamnak A good late-harvest LUTOMER estate Riesling.

Slavonia

    Northern Croatia, on the Hungarian border between SLOVENIA and SERBIA. A big producer of standard wines, mainly white, including most "Yugoslav Riesling".

Slovenia
> The n.w. state, incl. Yugoslavia's most European-style v'yds. and wines: LJUTOMER, etc. Slovenija-vino, the sales organization, is Yugoslavia's biggest.

Teran Stout dark red of ISTRIA. See REFOSCO.

Tigrovo Mljeko
> See Radgonska Ranina

Tocai The PINOT GRIS, making rather heavy white wine in SLOVENIA.

Traminac
> The TRAMINER. Grown in SLOVENIA and VOJVODINA. Particularly successful in the latter.

Vojvodina
> An autonomous province of n. SERBIA with substantial, growing and improving v'yds. Wide range of grapes, both European and Balkan.

Zilavka
> The white wine of MOSTAR in Hercegovina. Can be one of Yugoslavia's best: dry, pungent and memorably fruity, with a faint flavour of apricots. Exported samples are disappointing.

Zupa Central SERBIAN district giving its name to above-average red and rosé (or dark and light red) of PROKUPAC and PLOVDINA: respectively Zupsko Crno and Zupsko Ruzica.

Bulgaria

A dramatic new entry into the world's wine-diet. State-run and state-subsidized wineries seem to have learnt a great deal from the New World and offer Cabernet and Chardonnay at bargain prices and in rapidly improving quality and variety.

Cabernet
> The Bordeaux grape is highly successful in n. Bulgaria. Dark, vigorous, fruity and well-balanced wine, needs aging.

Chardonnay
> The white burgundy grape is scarcely less successful . Very dry but full-flavoured wine improves with a year in bottle.

Dimiat
> The common native white grape, grown in the e. towards the coast. Agreeable dry white without memorable character.

Euxinograd
> Brand of blended white wine produced for export.

Fetiaska
> The same grape as Romania's Feteasca and Hungary's Leanyka. Rather neutral but pleasant pale wine, best a trifle sweet, sold as Donau Perle.

Gamza
> The common red grape, Hungary's Kadarka: gives fairly light but "stiff" and worthwhile wine. Recently a superior oak-aged version has appeared.

Hemus
> A pale medium to sweet muscat from KARLOVO.

Iskra The national brand of sparkling wine, normally sweet but of fair quality.

Karlovo
> Town in central Bulgaria famous for the "Valley of Roses" and its very pleasant white MISKET.

Mavrud
> Darkly plummy red from s. Bulgaria. Improves with age. Traditionally considered the country's best.

Melnik
>   City of the extreme s.e. Such concentrated MAVRUD that the
>   locals say it can be carried in a handkerchief.

Misket
>   Bulgaria's muscat: locally popular flavour in sweet whites.

Pamid
>   The light, pallid, everyday red of s. and central Bulgaria.

Rcatzitelli
>   One of Russia's favourite white grapes for strong sweet wine.
>   Grown in n.e. Bulgaria.

Riesling
>   Normally refers to Italian Riesling. Some Rhine Riesling is
>   grown but at present is made over-dry.

Saperavi
>   Russian red grape, presumably used for export to Russia: the
>   biggest export market.

Sonnenküste
>   Brand of medium-sweet white sold in Germany.

Sungurlare
>   Eastern town giving its name to a sweet MISKET, similar to
>   that of KARLOVO.

Sylvaner
>   Some pleasant dry SYLVANER is exported as "Klosterkeller".

Tamianka
>   Sweet white; sweeter than HEMUS.

Tirnovo
>   Strong sweet red wine.

Trakia "Thrace". Brand name of a good export range.

Vinimpex
>   The "State Commercial Enterprise for Export and Import of
>   Wines and Spirits".

Greece

Entry into the E.E.C. gives Greece the challenge of moder-
nizing and internationalizing a wine industry that has been
up a backwater for two thousand years, concentrating on
resin-flavoured white Retsina. (The resin is that of the
Aleppo pine.) To those unenthusiastic about Greek food its
strong flavour has at least one advantage. Recently there
have been signs of experiment and investment, which promise well for the future.

Achaia-Clauss
>   The best-known Greek wine-merchant, with cellars at
>   Patras, n. PELOPONNESE.

Attica Region round Athens, the chief source of RETSINA.

Boutari
>   Merchants in Macedonian wines, esp. good NAOUSSA.

Cambas, Andrew
>   Important Athenian wine-growers and merchants.

Carras, John
>   Hotelier at Chalkidiki, n. Greece, producing interesting new
>   red and white wines under the names Château Carras and
>   Caves du Meliton.

Castel Danielis
>   One of the best brands of dry red wine, from ACHAIA-CLAUSS.

Corfu
>   Adriatic island with wines scarcely worthy of it. Ropa is the
>   traditional red.

Courtakis, D.
Athenian merchant with good dark NEMEAN red.
Crete Island with the name for some of Greece's better wine, esp. Archanes, Daphnes, Peza and Sitia.
Demestica
A reliable standard brand of dry red and white from ACHAIA-CLAUSS.
Hymettus Standard brand of red and dry white without resin.
Kalligas
The leading merchant of KEPHALONIA. Good red Monte Nero.
Kephalonia
Ionian (western) island with good white Rombola. Also Mavrodaphne.
Kokkineli
The rosé version of RETSINA: like the white. Drink very cold.
Lindos
Name for the higher quality of RHODES wine, whether from Lindos itself or not. Acceptable; no more.
Malvasia
The famous grape is said to originate from Monemvasia in the S. PELOPONNESE.
Mantinia A fresh white from CAMBAS.
Mavro "Black"—the word for dark red wine.
Mavrodaphne
Literally "black laurel": dark sweet concentrated red; a speciality of the Patras region, n. PELOPONNESE.
Mavroudi
The red wine of Delphi and the n. shore of the Gulf of Corinth: dark and plummy.
Minos Popular Cretan brand; the Castello red is best.
Naoussa
Above-average strong dry red from Macedonia in the n.
Nemea
Town in the e. PELOPONNESE famous for its lion (a victim of Hercules) and its fittingly forceful MAVRO.
Peloponnese
The s. landmass of mainland Greece, with a half of the whole country's v'yds.
Pendeli
Reliable brand of dry red from ATTICA, grown and bottled by Andrew CAMBAS.
Retsina
White wine with pine resin added, tasting of turpentine and oddly appropriate with Greek food. The speciality of ATTICA. Drink it very cold.
Rhodes
Easternmost Greek island. Its sweet MALVASIAS are its best wines. LINDOS is the brand name for tolerable table wines.
Rombola (or Robola)
The dry white of Cephalonia; island off the Gulf of Corinth.
Samos
Island off the Turkish coast with a reputation for its sweet pale-golden muscat. The normal commercial quality is nothing much.
Santorin
Island north of Crete, making sweet Vinsanto from sun-dried grapes, and dry white Thira.
Tsantalis
Merchants of Thessaloniki with a wide range of table wines.
Verdea
The dry white of Zakinthos, the island just w. of the PELOPONNESE. The red is Byzantis.

Cyprus

A well-established exporter of strong wines of reasonable quality, best known for very passable Cyprus sherry, though old Commandaria, a treacly dessert wine, is the island's finest product. Until recently only traditional grape varieties of limited potential were available; now better kinds are beginning to improve standards.

Afames
> Village at the foot of Mt. Olympus, giving its name to one of the better red (MAVRON) wines.

Aphrodite
> Full-bodied medium-dry white from KEO, named after the Greek goddess of love.

Arsinöe
> Dry white wine from SODAP, named after an unfortunate female whom Aphrodite turned to stone.

Bellapais
> Rather fizzy medium-sweet white from KEO named after the famous abbey near Kyrenia.

Commandaria
> Good-quality brown dessert wine made since ancient times and named after a crusading order of knights. The best is superb, of incredible sweetness.

Emva Cream
> Best-selling sw. sherry from Etko, a HAGGIPAVLU subsidiary.

Haggipavlu
> Well-known wine-merchant at LIMASSOL. Trades as Etko.

Hirondelle
> The sweet white and some of the other wines of this popular brand are produced by Etko (see Emva).

Keo   One of the biggest firms in the wine trade at LIMASSOL.

Kokkineli
> Rosé: the name is related to "cochineal".

Kolossi
> Red and white table wines from SODAP.

Limassol
> "The Bordeaux of Cyprus". The wine-port in the s.

Loel   Major producer. Amathus and Kykko brands and Command Cyprus sherry.

Mavron
> The black grape of Cyprus (and Greece) and its dark wine.

Mosaic
> The brand-name of KEO's Cyprus sherries.

Othello
> Perhaps the best dry red: solid, satisfying wine from KEO.

Palomino
> Very drinkable dry white made of this grape.

Pitsilia
> Region s. of Mt. Olympus producing the best white and COMMANDARIA wines.

Rosella
> Brand of strong medium-sweet rosé.

St Panteleimon
> Brand of strong sweet white from Keo.

Sherry
> Cyprus makes a full range of sherry-style wines, the best (particularly the dry) of very good quality.

SODAP
> Major wine cooperative at LIMASSOL.

Xynisteri
> The native white grape of Cyprus.

North Africa & Asia

Algeria

The massive v'yds. of Algeria have dwindled in the last ten years from 860,000 acres to under 500,000. Red wines of some quality are made in the coastal hills of Tlemcen, Mascara, Haut-Dahra, Zaccar and Ain-Bessem. Most goes for blending today. The Soviet Union is the biggest buyer.

Israel

Israeli wine, since the industry was re-established by a Rothschild in the 1880s, has been primarily of Kosher interest until recently, when CABERNET, SAUVIGNON BLANC, SEMILLON, PETITE SIRAH and GRENACHE of fair quality have been introduced. Carmel is the principal brand. Galilee and Samson are two areas producing superior reds.

Lebanon

The small Lebanese wine industry, based on Ksara in the Bekaa valley n.e. of Beirut, has made red wine of real vigour and quality. Château Musar has recently made a great stir with splendid matured reds, largely of CABERNET SAUVIGNON.

Morocco

Morocco today makes North Africa's best wine from v'yds. along the Atlantic coast and round Meknes. In ten years the v'yds. have declined from 190,000 to 54,000 acres. Chante Bled and Tarik are the best reds, Gris de Guerrouane a very pale dry rosé. In Morocco they sell as Les Trois Domaines.

Tunisia

Tunisia now has 75,000 acres compared with 120,000 ten years ago. Her speciality is sweet muscat, but reasonable reds come from Carthage, Mornag and Cap Bon.

Turkey

Most of Turkey's huge v'yds. produce table grapes. But her wines, from Thrace, Anatolia and the Aegean, are remarkably good. Trakya (Thrace) white and Buzbag (Anatolian) red are the well-known standards of the State wineries. Doluca and Kavaklidere are private firms of good quality. Villa Doluca red from Thrace is remarkable: dry, full-bodied, deep-flavoured and vigorous.

USSR

With over 3 million acres of v'yds. the USSR is the world's fourth-biggest wine-producer—but almost entirely for home consumption. Ukraine (incl. the Crimea) is the biggest v'yd. republic, followed by Moldavia, the Russian Republic and Georgia. The Soviet consumer has a sweet tooth, for both table and dessert wines. Of the latter the best come from the Crimea (esp. Massandra). Moldavia and Ukraine use the same grapes as Romania, plus Cabernet, Riesling, Pinot Gris, etc. The Russian Republic makes the best Rieslings (esp. Arbau, Beshtau, Anapa) and sweet sparkling Tsimlanskoye "Champanski". Georgia uses mainly traditional grapes (esp. white Tsinandali and red Mukuzani) for good table wines.

Soviet wines are classified as ordinary (unmatured), "named" (matured in cask or vat) or "kollektsionye" (which are matured both in cask and bottle).

Japan

Japan has a small wine industry in Yamanashi Prefecture, w. of Tokyo. Standard wines are mainly blended with imports from Argentina, E. Europe, etc. Premium wines of Semillon, Cabernet and the local white grape, Koshu, are light but can be good, though expensive. Remarkable sweet wines with noble rot have been made in an area with high humidity. The main producers are Suntory, Mercian, Mann's.

California

California has been making wine for 150 years, but her modern wine industry has grown from scratch in scarcely more than 25. Today it leads the world in good-quality cheap wines and startles it with a handful of luxury wines of brilliant quality. In the last decade the industry has expanded and altered at a frenzied pace. The majority of the wineries listed here have a history shorter than ten years. Quality-ratings must therefore be tentative.

Grape-varieties (combined with brand-names) are the key to California wine. Since grapes in California play many new roles they are separately listed on pages 146-147.

Vineyard areas

Amador
County in the Sierra foothills e. of Sacramento. Grows fine Zinfandel, esp. in Shenandoah Valley.

Central Coast
A long sweep of coast with scattered wine activity, from San Francisco Bay s. to Santa Barbara.

Central Coast/Santa Barbara
Some of the most promising recent planting in the state is in the Santa Ynez Valley n. of Santa Barbara, where coastal fog gives particularly cool conditions.

Central Coast/Santa Cruz Mts.
Wineries are scattered round the Santa Cruz Mts. s. of San Francisco Bay, from Saratoga down to the HECKER PASS.

Central Coast/Hecker Pass
Pass through the Santa Cruz Mts. s. of San Francisco Bay with a cluster of small old-style wineries.

Central Coast/Salinas Valley/Monterey
The main concentration of new planting in the Central Coast: the Salinas Valley runs inland s.e. from Monterey.

Central Coast/San Luis Obispo
Edna Valley just s. of San Luis Obispo and new more scattered v'yds. nr. Paso Robles.

Livermore
Valley e. of San Francisco Bay long famous for white wines but now largely built over.

Lodi Town and district at the n. end of the San Joaquin Valley, its hot climate modified by a westerly air-stream.

Mendocino
Northernmost coastal wine country; a varied climate coolest in Anderson Valley nr. the coast, warm around Ukiah inland.

Napa The Napa Valley, n. of San Francisco Bay, well established as the top-quality wine area. Coolest at southern end (Carneros).

San Joaquin Valley
The great central valley of California, fertile and hot, the source of most of the jug wines and dessert wines in the State.

Sonoma
County n. of San Francisco Bay, between Napa and the sea. Most v'yds. are in the north (see below). A few, historically important, are in the Valley of the Moon in the south. Kenwood lies between the two.

Sonoma/Alexander Valley/Russian River
High-quality area from Alexander Valley (n. of Napa Valley) towards the sea (Russian River). Incl. Dry Creek Valley.

Temecula (Rancho California)
Very new small area in s. California, 25 miles inland halfway between San Diego and Riverside.

Recent Vintages

The Californian climate is far from being as consistent as its reputation. Although on the whole the grapes ripen regularly, they are subject to severe spring frosts in many areas, sometimes a wet harvest-time, and such occasional calamities as the two-year drought of 1975–7.

Wines from the San Joaquin Valley tend to be most consistent year by year. The vintage date on these, where there is one, is more important for telling the age of the wine than its character.

Vineyards in the Central Coast are mainly so new that no pattern of vintage qualities has yet emerged.

The Napa Valley is the one area where comment can be made on the last dozen vintages of the top varietal wines: Cabernet Sauvignon and Chardonnay.

	Chardonnay	Cabernet Sauvignon
1982	Problematical	Early-maturing
1981	Very early vintage; good if not too strong.	Promising
1980	Small crop; high alcohol. The best well-balanced.	Outstanding
1979	Excellent.	Rain; generally light.
1978	Very good if not too heady.	Excellent.
1977	Generally excellent.	Attractive: ageing well.
1976	Difficult: variable.	Small crop but splendid.
1975	Very good.	Delicate: charming.
1974	Good: ready.	Difficult: but many superb.
1973	Very good, but drink up.	Big and good.
1972	The best wines of a cool year.	Uneven: rain: many poor wines.
1971	Good balance: long lived.	Average.
1970	Good all round: not great: mature.	Best ever.
1969	Weak.	Good, not great. Drink soon.
1968	Well-balanced: now ageing.	Fine, well-balanced, now ageing.

California: grape varieties

Barbera
Darkly plummy variety from Piemonte (see Italy). Gives full-blooded and astringent wine in cool areas, good but softer wine in hot ones.

Cabernet Sauvignon
The best red-wine grape in California with a wide range of styles from delicately woody to overpoweringly fruity. The classic Napa grape.

Carignane
Bulk-producing red grape rarely used as a "varietal".

Charbono
Rare red grape of Italian origin needing long ageing.

Chardonnay
The best white-wine grape — indeed the best wine-grape — in California. Styles of making vary from merely clean and grapy to rich and complex like the best white burgundies.

Chenin Blanc
A work-horse white grape with a surprising turn of speed when made dry and in limited, concentrated quantities. But usually made soft and sweet.

Emerald Riesling
A Californian original in the German manner. Clean, flowery/fruity and a touch tart.

Flora California-bred white. Mildly flowery; best made sweet.

French Colombard
High-acid white coming into favour for clean semi-dry wines made more German-style than French.

Fumé Blanc
See Sauvignon Blanc.

Gamay (or Napa Gamay)
The red grape of Beaujolais. Never remarkable in California.

CALIFORNIAN VINTAGES TO NOTE
For Cabernets: **70 73 74 75 76 77 78 80**
For Pinot Noir: **70 74 75 76 78 79 80 81**
For Zinfandel: **70 74 76 77 78 80**
For Chardonnay: **71 73 75 76 77 78 79 80 81**
For Riesling: **73 76 77 78 79 80 81 82**
For Sauvignon Blanc: **78 80 81 82**
For Gewürztraminer: **78 79 80 81 82**

Gamay Beaujolais
Not the red grape of Beaujolais, but a selection of Pinot Noir capable of good Beaujolais-style reds in California.

Gewürztraminer
Generally softer and less aromatically thrilling in California than in France, but at best one of the real successes.

Green Hungarian
A minority interest: rather tasteless white. Can be lively.

Grenache
Used mainly for sweetish rosés in California.

Gray Riesling
Not a Riesling. Full-bodied but scarcely notable white.

Grignolino
Highly seasoned grape good for young reds and rosés.

Johannisberg Riesling
Real Rhine Riesling (also known as White Riesling). Often rather strong and bland in California, but at its best (esp. in Auslese-style wines) gloriously complex and satisfying.

Merlot The St-Emilion grape has a growing acreage in California. Very good heavy reds have been made.

Muscat   Light sweet pale gold muscat is one of California's treats.

Petite Syrah or **Syrah**
>The name of the Rhône's and Australia's great red grape has been wrongly applied to a poor one. Generally used in Burgundy blends. But the real one (Syrah) is present in small quantities, and has great promise. See Phelps, Estrella River.

Pinot Blanc
>Much in the shade of the better Chardonnay.

Pinot Noir
>Has yet to reach consummation in California. Most wine with the name is disappointing; a minute proportion thrilling.

Pinot St George
>Used by a few wineries to make a sound sturdy red.

Riesling
>See Johannisberg Riesling. Also Sylvaner.

Ruby Cabernet
>A California-bred cross between Carignan and Cabernet Sauvignon with enough of the character of the latter to be interesting. Good in hot conditions.

Sauvignon Blanc
>Excellent white grape used either Sancerre style (fresh, aromatic, effervescent) or Graves style (fat, chewable). The former usually called Fumé Blanc.

Semillon
>High-flavoured whites from the cooler areas; bland ones from hotter places. The most memorable are sweet.

Zinfandel
>California's own red grape, open to many interpretations from light-weight fruity to galumphing. Capable of ageing to great quality.

California wineries

Acacia   Napa. ✶✶✶✶ CH **80 81** PN **79 80 81**
>New Carneros winery (first wine 1979) specializing in CHAR-DONNAY and PINOT NOIR of marvellous promise.

Alexander Valley Vineyards   Alexander Valley.   ✶✶→✶✶✶ CH **80**
>New small winery. CHARDONNAY, JOH. RIESLING esp. good.

Almaden   Central Coast. ✶→ ✶✶ CS 79
>Big winery famous for pioneer varietal labelling and planting in Central Coast. Now owned by National Distillers. Best regular wines incl. GEWÜRZTRAMINER, CABERNET and Eye of the Partridge. Charles le Franc label for top wines.

Barengo   Lodi. ✶→✶✶
>Small firm making wines of character, especially ZINFANDEL.

Beaulieu   Napa. ✶✶ →✶✶✶✶ CS **74** 76 **77 78** 79
>Rightly famous medium-size growers and makers of esp. CABERNET. Top wine: De Latour Private Reserve Cabernet. Now owned by Heublein Corp.

Beringer   Napa. ✶✶→✶✶✶✶ CH **79 80** 81 CS **78** 79
>Century-old winery recently modernized by Nestlé Co. Increasingly fine wines incl. Auslese types.

Boeger   Amador. ✶→✶✶ CS 79
>Small winery in Sierra foothills. Good ZIN.

Brookside   S. California. ✶→✶✶
>Traditional dessert wine firm also making table varietals from TEMECULA under the Assumption Abbey label.

Bruce, David   Central Coast. ✶✶✶ CH **80** 81
>   Small luxury winery with heavy-weight old-style wines.

Buena Vista   Sonoma. ✶✶→✶✶✶ CH **80** CS 79
>   Historic pioneer winery with new owners and improving
>   recent record esp. in whites (RIESLING, FUMÉ BLANC). Reds
>   include old-style ZINFANDEL from its reputed original v'yd.

Burgess Cellars   Napa. ✶✶✶ CH **79 80** CS 78 79
>   Small hillside winery, originally called Souverain, making
>   good CHARDONNAY, late harvest RIESLING, CABERNET.

B.V.   Abbreviation of BEAULIEU VINEYARDS used on their labels.

Cakebread   Napa. ✶✶✶ CH **80** 81 CS 79
>   Started 1973. Increasing reputation, esp. for SAUVIGNON
>   BLANC and CABERNET (79 esp.); also CHARDONNAY, ZIN.

Calera   Monterey-San Benito. ✶✶ PN **79 80**
>   1975 winery growing good ZIN and ambitious with PINOT NOIR.

Callaway   S. California. ✶✶
>   Small new winery in new territory at TEMECULA. Early reds
>   are strong, dark, conservative; whites interesting.

Carneros Creek   Napa. ✶✶✶ CH **80 81** CS **74 75 77** 78 79
>   The first winery in the cool Carneros area between Napa and
>   San Francisco Bay. First PINOT NOIR ('77) was sensational.
>   Fine CHARDONNAY (Giles v'yd.), ZINFANDEL and CABERNET.

Cassayre-Forni   Napa. ✶✶→✶✶✶ CS 79 CH **81**
>   Small new Rutherford winery. Good CABERNET, ZIN and dry
>   CHENIN BLANC.

Caymus   Napa.   ✶✶✶   CS **74 75** 76 **77 78** 79
>   Small winery at Rutherford with white PINOT NOIR and nota-
>   ble CABERNET. Second label: Liberty School.

Chalone   Central Coast/Salinas.   ✶✶✶✶   CH **78 79 80** 81 PN **75 77** 78 **79**
>   Unique small hilltop v'yd/winery at the Pinnacles. French-
>   style CHARDONNAY and PINOT NOIR of superb quality.

Chappellet   Napa. ✶✶✶ CH **80** CS **74 75** 76 78 79
>   Small modern luxury winery and hillside v'yd. Good CABER-
>   NET SAUVIGNON and RIESLING, very good dry CHENIN BLANC.

Château Chevalier   Napa. ✶✶ CH **81** CS 78
>   Small estate in hills above St. Helena known for darkly
>   concentrated CABERNET and Edna Valley Chardonnay.

Château Montelena   Napa. ✶✶✶→✶✶✶✶ CH **77 78 79** 80 CS **74 75 77** 78 **79**
>   Small 1969 winery making very good distinctive CHARDON-
>   NAY and CABERNET SAUVIGNON.

Château St Jean   Sonoma. ✶✶✶✶ CH **78 79 80** 81
>   Impressive winery specializing in richly flavoured whites
>   from individual v'yds., incl. CHARDONNAY, PINOT BLANC and
>   esp. late harvest RIESLING. Now also sparkling wine.

Christian Brothers   Napa and San Joaquin.   ✶→✶✶✶
>   The biggest Napa winery, run by a religious order, shifting
>   from blends to named vintages, incl. excellent CABERNET,
>   useful FUMÉ BLANC, sweet white Ch. La Salle, very good
>   brandy and ZIN 'port'.

Clos du Bois   Sonoma. ✶✶→✶✶✶ CH **79 80** CS 78 79
>   Healdsburg winery of considerable grower in Dry Creek
>   Valley. Good GEWÜRZ and CABERNET.

Clos du Val   Napa. ✶✶✶→✶✶✶✶ CH **79 80** CS **74** 75 **76 77** 78 79 80
>   French-owned. Strong, rustic ZIN, fine delicate CABERNET.

Concannon   Livermore. Table ✶✶→✶✶✶
>   Substantial winery first famous for whites, but with reds now
>   prominent. Recently bought by Distillers' Company.

Congress Springs   Santa Clara/Santa Cruz. ✶✶
>   Tiny winery above Saratoga. Well-made whites, esp. SAUVIG-
>   NON BLANC, SEMILLON.

Conn Creek Napa. ★★→★★★ CH 79 80 CS 78 79

New winery built on Silverado Trail in 1979, has a growing reputation. Best known for CABERNET.

Cresta Blanca Mendocino. ★★

Old name from Livermore revived on the n. coast by new owners, GUILD. Husky ZIN and PETITE SYRAH. Mild whites.

Cuvaison Napa. ★★→★★★ CH 80 81 CS 78 79

Small winery with expert new direction. Shows promise. Austere CABERNET and CHARDONNAY for long ageing.

Davis Bynum Sonoma. ★→★★

Established maker of standard varieties, w. of Healdsburg.

Dehlinger Sonoma. ★★→ ★★★ CS 76 78 CH 77 79

Small winery and v'yd. w. of Santa Rosa. Promising CHARDON-NAY, CABERNET and ZIN since 1976.

DeLoach Vineyards Sonoma. ★★★ CH 80 81 PN 79 80

Russian River winery founded 1975 for CHARDONNAY, GEWÜRZ, P. NOIR. CABERNET will follow.

Diamond Creek. Napa. ★★★★ CS 74 75 76 77 78 79

Small winery since the 60s with austere, long-ageing CABER-NET from hills w. of Calistoga. Highly esteemed.

Domaine Chandon Napa. ★★★

Californian outpost of Moët & Chandon Champagne. Launched 1976. Early promise is being fulfilled.

Dry Creek Sonoma. ★★★ CH 78 79 80 81 CS 79

Small winery with high ideals, making old-fashioned dry wines, esp. whites, incl. CHARDONNAY, CHENIN BLANC and FUMÉ BLANC.

Durney Vineyard Central Coast/Monterey. ★★→★★★ CS 78 79

Good CABERNET from Carmel Valley, riper than most in Monterey. Also CHENIN BLANC. Since '76.

East-Side San Joaquin. ★

Progressive growers' co-operative best known for its Royal Host label. Good RUBY CABERNET, EMERALD RIESLING, ZIN.

Edmeades Mendocino. ★★ CS 78 79 CH 81

Tiny winery in Anderson Valley near Pacific. Known for CABERNET and a French Colombard Ice Wine.

Estrella River San Luis Obispo/Santa Barbara. ★★ CH 79 80

Impressive new winery with 700 acres. CHARDONNAY, RIES-LING, MUSCAT, SYRAH are promising.

Far Niente Napa. ★★★ CH 79 80 81

Founded 1885; reactivated in 1979. Chardonnay now; Caber-net to be released later.

Felton-Empire Vineyards Cent. Coast/Santa Cruz Mts. ★★★

The old Hallcrest property recently revived by new owners. Excellent RIESLING. A label to watch.

Fetzer Mendocino. ★★ CH 81 CS 79 80

Rapidly expanding 14-year-old winery with interesting but inconsistent wines, incl. CABERNET, SAUVIGNON BLANC, ZIN, RIESLING. Good-value jug wine.

Ficklin San Joaquin. ★★★

Family firm making California's best "port" and minute quantities of table wine.

Field Stone Sonoma (Alexander Valley). ★★

Small winery founded by mechanical harvester maker, pres-sing grapes in the v'yd. for whites and CABERNET rosé.

Firestone Central Coast/Santa Barbara. ★★★ CH 77 78 79

Ambitious 1973 winery in a new area n. of Santa Barbara. Cool conditions are producing very attractive wines, incl. PINOT NOIR, RIESLING, GEWÜRZ and esp. CHARDONNAY.

Flora Springs Wine Co. Napa. ★★★ CH 79 80 81 CS 80

Old stone cellar in St. Helena reopened in 1979. CABERNET, CHARDONNAY and SAUV. BLANC are all successful.

Foppiano   Sonoma. ★★
> Old winery at Healdsburg refurbished with vintage varieties
> incl. CHENIN BLANC, FUMÉ BLANC, CAB, ZIN, PETITE SYRAH.

Franciscan Vineyard   Napa.   ★★ CH 81 CS 77
> Rapidly growing enterprise with a meet-the-folks approach.
> Good ZINFANDEL, CABERNET, CHARDONNAY and RIESLING.

Franzia   San Joaquin. ★
> Large old winery now owned by Coca Cola Bottling Co. of N.Y.
> Various labels, but all say "made and bottled in Ripon".

Freemark Abbey   Napa. ★★★★ CH 76 77 78 79 80 CS 74 75 76 77 78
> Small connoisseur's winery with high reputation for CABER-
> NET, CHARDONNAY and RIESLING.

Gallo, E. & J.   San Joaquin.   ★→★★
> The world's biggest winery, pioneer in both quantity and
> quality. Family owned. Hearty Burgundy and Chablis Blanc
> set national standards. Varietals incl. SAUVIGNON BLANC,
> GEWÜRZ, RIESLING, CHARDONNAY, CABERNET.

Gemello   Santa Clara/Santa Cruz. ★★
> Old winery with reputation for reds, esp. PETITE SYRAH, ZIN.

Geyser Peak   Sonoma. ★★
> Old winery recently revived and expanded by Schlitz
> Brewery. More steady than inspired.

Giumarra   San Joaquin.   ★★
> Recent installation expanding rapidly. Attractive RUBY CAB.,
> CHENIN BLANC from family v'yds. in hottest part of valley.

Grand Cru   Sonoma. ★★→★★★ CS 78 79
> Small 1971 winery making good GEWÜRZ and increasingly
> CABERNET, CHENIN and SAUVIGNON BLANC.

Grgich-Hills Cellars   Napa. ★★★★ CH 77 78 79 80 Z 77 78 79
> Grgich (formerly of CH. MONTELENA) is wine-maker, Hills
> grows the grapes—esp. CHARDONNAY and RIESLING. Delicate,
> lively wines include ZINFANDEL.

Guild   San Joaquin. ★
> Big growers' co-operative famous for Vino da Tavola semi-
> sweet red and B. Cribari label. New line of varietals with
> Winemasters label incl. good ZINFANDEL.

Gundlach-Bundschu   Sonoma.   ★★★
> Very old small family winery revived by the new generation.
> Excellent CABERNET, MERLOT, ZIN and good whites: CHARDON-
> NAY, GEWÜRZ, RIESLING.

Hacienda   Sonoma. ★★→★★★ CH 81 CS 79
> Small winery at Sonoma specializing in high-quality CHAR-
> DONNAY and GEWÜRZ. Recently good CABERNET.

Hanzell   Sonoma. ★★★ CH 77 78 79 80 PN 77 78 79
> Small   winery   which   revolutionized   Californian
> CHARDONNAYS in the '50s under its founder, now in
> new hands. PINOT NOIR is a huge wine, to keep.

Harbor Winery   Yolo county. ★★★ CH 78 79 80 CS 78 79
> Tiny winery using NAPA grapes to make first-rate CHARDON-
> NAY and CABERNET..

Heitz   Napa. ★★★★ CH 74 75 76 78 80 CS 74 75 76 77 78
> An inspired individual wine-maker who has set standards for
> the whole industry. His CABERNETS (esp. "Martha's Vine-
> yard") are dark, deep and emphatic, his best CHARDONNAYS
> peers of Montrachet.

Hoffmann Mtn. Ranch   Cen. Coast/San Luis Obispo. ★★★
> Small winery in new area near Paso Robles. CHARDONNAY and
> PINOT NOIR are promising.

Hop Kiln   Sonoma/Russian River. ★★
> Small winery. Individual, tasty PETITE SYRAH, ZIN, GEWÜRZ.

Inglenook   Napa and San Joaquin.   ⟨*⟩   → ✦✦✦ CS **74 76** 77 **78 79**
One of the great old Napa wineries recently much changed by new owners: Heublein Corp. Special Cask CABERNET SAUVIGNON remains best wine. Inglenook Vintage is a second label, Inglenook Navalle a third and the best value: good cheap RUBY, ZINFANDEL and FRENCH COLOMBARD.

Iron Horse Vineyards   Sonoma. ✦✦✦ CH **79 80** CS 79
Stylish Russian River property with CHARDONNAY, CABERNET, P. NOIR and SAUV. BLANC of vivid flavours. To watch.

(Italian Swiss) Colony   San Joaquin and Sonoma. *→ ✦✦
Honourable old name from Sonoma transferred to San Joaquin by new owners: Heublein Corp. Adequate standards. Lejon is a second label.

Jekel Vineyards   Central Coast/Monterey. ✦✦→ ✦✦✦ CH **80 81** CS **78 79**
Outstandingly well-made RIESLING and CHARDONNAY. CABERNET SAUVIGNON has recently caused a stir.

Johnsons of Alexander Valley   Sonoma. ✦✦
New small winery with good v'yd. land. CABERNET best.

Jordan   Sonoma.   ✦✦✦✦ CH **80 81** CS 77 **78** 79
Extravagant winery specializing in CABERNET modelled on Bordeaux. First CHARDONNAY in 1979.

Keenan, Robert   Napa. ✦✦✦ CH 77 **78 79** 80
Newcomer with very good first CHARDONNAY and CABERNET. V'yds. on Spring Mountain; wine-maker ex-CHAPPELLET.

Kenwood Vineyards   Sonoma. ✦✦→ ✦✦✦ CH **79 80** CS **78** 79
Steady small producer of increasingly stylish reds, esp. CABERNET and ZIN. Also good CHARDONNAY and CHENIN BLANC.

Kistler Vineyards   Sonoma. ✦✦ CH 79 81 CS 80
New small winery in hills. First CHARDONNAY (79) was overwhelming. Now also CABERNET and PINOT NOIR.

Korbel   Sonoma.   ⟨✦✦✦⟩
Long-established sparkling wine specialists. "Natural" and "Brut" are among California's best standard "champagnes".

Kornell, Hanns   Napa.   ⟨✦✦→ ✦✦✦⟩
Fine sparkling wine house making excellent full-flavoured dry wines: Brut and Sehr Trocken.

Krug, Charles   Napa. *→ ✦✦✦ CS 74 **77 78**
Important old winery with reliable range, incl. good CABERNET SAUVIGNON, sweet CHENIN BLANC and very sweet Moscato di Canelli. C.K. is the jug-wine brand.

La Crema Vinera   Sonoma. ✦✦✦→ ✦✦✦✦ CH **79 80** 81 PN **79** 80
Founded in 1979 at Petaluma for table and sparkling wines. CHARDONNAY and P. NOIR are both excellent.

Lambert Bridge   Sonoma. ✦✦
Small 1975 winery nr. Healdsburg has made promising CHARDONNAY; also CABERNET.

Lamont, M.   San Joaquin.   ⟨*⟩
New name for old Bear Mountain co-op, now owned by Labatt brewery. Well-made varietals, incl. FRENCH COLOMBARD.

Landmark   Sonoma.   ⟨✦✦⟩ CH **80** CS 79
New winery nr. Windsor with sound CHARDONNAY and CABERNET tending to improve.

Laurent Perrier   Central Coast/San Jose.   ⟨✦✦✦⟩ CH 81
Almaden-linked branch of the French Champagne firm started in 1981 with excellent dry still CHARDONNAY.

Lawrence Winery   Central Coast/San Luis Obispo.
Ambitious new mid-size winery in the Edna Valley.

Leeward Winery   Central Coast/Ventura. ✦✦✦ CH **80 81**
CHARDONNAY from Monterey and San Luis Obispo grapes started this new venture near Santa Barbara well in 1980.

Long Vineyards Napa. ★★→★★★ CH 78 79 80
New small winery in eastern hills nr. CHAPPELLET. So far good CHARDONNAY and late-harvest RIESLING.

Lytton Springs Sonoma. ★★
Small specialist in Russian River ZIN; thick, heady, tannic.

Mark West Sonoma ★★→★★★ CH **80**
New winery in cool sub-region starting well with whites: GEWÜRZ, RIESLING, CHARDONNAY.

Markham Napa. ★★(?)
New winery with 200 acres. Early releases show promise.

Martin Ray Central Coast/S. Cruz Mts. ★★★ CH 81
Eccentric small winery famous for high prices.

Martini, Louis Napa. ★★→ ★★★ CS 74 75 76 77 78 79 Z 77 78 79
Large but individual winery with very high standards, from jug wines (called "Mountain") up. CABERNET SAUVIGNON one of California's best. BARBERA, PINOT NOIR, ZINFANDEL, GEWÜRZ, FOLLE BLANCHE and Moscato Amabile are all fine.

Martini & Prati Sonoma. ★★
Important winery selling mainly in bulk to others. Uses the name Fountaingrove for a small quantity of good CABERNET.

Masson, Paul Central Coast. ★→ ★★
Big, lively and reliable middle-quality winery with good-value varietals, incl. CHARDONNAY, ZINFANDEL. Also Emerald Dry (EM. RIES.) Rubion (RUBY), good cheap sparkling and very good Souzão port-type.

Matanzas Creek Sonoma. ★★★ CH 78 79 80 CS 79
First wines were GEWÜRZ and very good PINOT BLANC. CHARDONNAY even better, though very alcoholic.

Mayacamas Napa. ★★★★ CH 76 77 78 79 CS 74 75 76 77 78
First-rate very small v'yd. and winery offering CABERNET SAUVIGNON, CHARDONNAY, ZINFANDEL (sometimes).

McDowell Valley Vineyards Mendocino. ★★
Big new development using old-established v'yd. to make wide range. To watch.

Mill Creek Sonoma. ★★
1974 winery near Healdsburg with pleasant, easy-going CHARDONNAY, MERLOT, CABERNET.

Mirassou Central Coast. ★★→★★★
Dynamic mid-sized growers and makers, the fifth generation of the family. Pioneers in SALINAS v'yds. Notable ZINFANDEL, GAMAY BEAUJOLAIS, GEWÜRZ and sparkling.

Mondavi, Robert Napa. ★★→★★★★ CH 76 77 78 79 80 CS 74 75 76 77 78 79
Fifteen-year-old winery with a brilliant record of innovation in styles, equipment and technique. Wines of character incl. CABERNET SAUVIGNON, SAUVIGNON BLANC (sold as Fumé Blanc), CHARDONNAY, PINOT NOIR. Also useful table wines.

Monterey Peninsula Central Coast/Salinas. ★★→ ★★★ CH 78 CS 78
Very small winery near Carmel making chunky chewable ZINFANDEL and CABERNET from SALINAS and other grapes.

Monterey Vineyard Central Coast/Salinas. ★★
The first big modern winery of SALINAS, opened 1974. Now owned by Coca Cola. Good ZINFANDEL, GEWÜRZ and SYLVANER and fruity feather-weight GAMAY BEAUJOLAIS.

Monteviña Amador. ★★ CS 79 Z 75 76 77 78 79
Pioneer small winery in revitalized area: the Shenandoah Valley, Amador County, in the Sierra foothills. ZINFANDEL, BARBERA and SAUVIGNON BLANC.

J. W. Morris North Coast (Oakland). ★★★
Small specialist in high-quality port-types, both vintage and wood-aged. Mainly SONOMA grapes. Good CHARD., CAB. S., ZIN.

Mount Eden Vineyards Central Coast. ★★★ CH 78 79 80
Company owning a major share of what were MARTIN RAY Vineyards. Expensive wines. M.E.V. is a second-line label.

Mount Veeder Napa. ★★★ CS 74 75 77 78
Ambitious little 1973 winery. High prices but good CABERNET.

Napa Wine Cellars Napa. ★★ CH 80 CS 78 79
Small Yountville winery with steady record, esp. for CABERNET and ZIN.

Navarro Vineyards Mendocino. ★★
Small specialist in GEWÜRZ in cool Anderson Valley.

Nichelini Napa. ⬚★
Old-style family winery. Sound varietals at the cellar door.

Novitiate of Los Gatos Central Coast. ★★
Jesuit-run altar-wine-orientated unrevolutionary winery with some adequate varietals, inadequately distributed.

Papagni, Angelo San Joaquin. ⬚★★
Grower of an old family with a technically outstanding modern winery at Madera. Dry coastal-style varietals incl. ex. ZIN, good CHARDONNAY, light "Moscato d'Angelo".

Parducci Mendocino. ⬚★★ → ★★★ CH 80 CS 74 75 78
Well-established mid-sized winery with v'yds. in several locations. Good sturdy reds: CABERNET SAUVIGNON, PETITE SYRAH, ZINFANDEL, Burgundy. Also pleasant slightly sweet CHENIN BLANC and FRENCH COLOMBARD.

Pecota, Robert Napa. ⬚★★ CH 81
New small cellar of ex-BERINGER man with high standards. Wines are CABERNET, SAUVIGNON BLANC, good light GAMAY.

Pedroncelli Sonoma R-R. ⬚★★ CH 80 CS 78 79
Long-established family business with recent reputation for well-above-average ZINFANDEL, GEWÜRZTRAMINER and CHARDONNAY in a ripe rural style.

Phelps, Joseph Napa. ⬚★★★ → ★★★★ CH 77 78 79 80 CS 74 75 76 77 78 79
De-luxe mid-size winery and v'yd. Late harvest RIESLING exceptional. Very good CHARDONNAY, CABERNET, SYRAH and ZIN. Second label Le Fleuron. "Insignia" is CABERNET/MERLOT.

Piper-Sonoma Sonoma. ★★★
A joint venture between Piper-Heidsieck of Champagne and Sonoma Vineyards released its first (very good) sparkling cuvée in 1980.

Preston Sonoma. ★★★
Tiny winery with very high standards in Dry Creek Valley, Healdsburg. So far SAUVIGNON BLANC and ZINFANDEL.

Rafanelli, J. Sonoma. ⬚★★
Tiny local cellar specializing in outstanding ZIN; also CABERNET SAUVIGNON.

Raymond Vineyards Napa. ⬚★★★ → ★★★★ CH 77 79 80 81 CS 77 78 79
Small 1974 winery near St. Helena with experienced owners. ZIN, CHARD, CHENIN BLANC and CABERNET all excellent.

Ridge Central Coast S. CRUZ. ★★★★ CS 74 75 76 77 78 79 Z 76 77 78 79
Small winery of high repute among connoisseurs for powerful concentrated reds needing long maturing in bottle. Notable CABERNET and very strong ZINFANDEL from named v'yds.

River Oaks Sonoma. ★→★★
Sound commercial wines from same winery as CLOS DU BOIS.

Roudon-Smith Santa Clara/Santa Cruz. ★★→ ⬚★★★ CH 79 80
New small winery. Really stylish CHARDONNAY.

Round Hill Napa. ⬚★★ CH 80 81 CS 79
Consistent good value, esp. GEWÜRZ and FUMÉ BLANC, from St. Helena. Second label: Rutherford Ranch.

Rutherford Hill Napa. ★★★ CH 77 78 79 80 CS 76 77 78
Recent larger stable-mate of FREEMARK ABBEY. Good early GEWÜRZ, MERLOT, ZIN. Better CHARD. and CABERNET.

Rutherford Vintners Napa. ★★→★★★ CH 80 CS 77 78
New small winery started in 1977 by Bernard Skoda, former LOUIS MARTINI manager.

St. Clement Napa. ★★★ CH 78 79 80 81 CS 77 78 79
Small production. Good CABERNET powerful CHARD.

St. Francis Sonoma. ★★ CH 80 81
New small winery to use excellent CHARD, CABERNET, GEWÜRZ grapes from older v'yd.

Saintsbury Napa. ★★★ CH **81** PN **81**
New winery with encouraging first wines.

Sanford and Benedict Santa Barbara ★★★
New winery whose first CHARDONNAY and PINOT NOIR (1976) caused a stir. Uneven quality.

San Martin Central Coast. ★★→ ★★★ CS 78
Restructured old company using SALINAS and SAN LUIS OBISPO grapes to make clean, correct varietals. "Select Vintage" is top label. Also pioneers in "soft" (low-alcohol) wines.

San Pasqual S. California. ★→★★
New winery near San Diego with pleasant whites, esp. CHENIN BLANC, SAUVIGNON BLANC. Also GAMAY.

Santa Cruz Mountain Winery Central Coast. ★★→★★★ CS 78 79 PN 79
Small winery in the hills with hopes for fine PINOT NOIR.

Santa Ynez Valley Winery Santa Barbara. ★★★ CH 79 80 81
Promising white wines, inc. SAUVIGNON BLANC.

Sausal Sonoma. ★★
Small specialist in stylish ZIN, etc.

Schramsberg Napa. ★★★★
A dedicated specialist using historic old cellars to make California's best "champagne". Now also brandy.

Schug Winery Napa. ★★★(?)
New (1982) enterprise of PHELPS' brilliant winemaker.

Sebastiani Sonoma. ★→ ★★ CS 78
Substantial and distinguished old family firm with some robust appetizing wines, esp. BARBERA. Top wines have SONOMA appellation. Big improvement recently.

Shaw, Charles F., Vineyards and Winery Napa. ★★
Off-beat St. Helena specialist in GAMAY light red.

Silver Oak Napa. ★★→★★★ CS 78
Small 1972 winery succeeding with oaky CABERNET.

Simi Alexander Valley. ★★→★★★ CH 79 80 CS 77 78
Restored old winery with expert direction. Notable wines incl. racy GEWÜRZ, gentle ZIN, delicate CABERNET.

Smith-Madrone Napa. ★★→★★★ CH **81** CS 79
New v'yd. high on Spring Mountain made good RIESLING in '77. PINOT NOIR and CABERNET look promising.

Smothers Santa Clara/Santa Cruz. ★★★
Tiny winery owned by T.V. comic made remarkable first wines, esp. late-harvest GEWÜRZ.

Sonoma Vineyards Sonoma R-R. ★★ →★★★ CS 78
Quick-growing business, well-regarded for varietals, esp. RIES. and CHARD. Range includes single-v'yd. wines, esp. Alexander's Crown CABERNET. See also Piper-Sonoma.

Souverain Alexander Valley. ★★ CH 81 CS 78
Luxurious new mid-sized winery with highly competent wines, both red and white, if no great ones.

Spring Mountain Napa. ★★★ CH 79 80 CS 75 77 78 79
Renovated small 19th-century property with winery noted for good CHARDONNAY, SAUVIGNON BLANC and CABERNET.

Stag's Leap Wine Cellars   Napa. ***→ **** CH 77 78 79 CS 74 75 76 77 78 **79**

New small v'yd. and cellar with high standards. Excellent CABERNET and MERLOT, fresh GAMAY, fine CHARDONNAY.

Sterling   Napa. *** CH 77 78 79 CS (Reserves) 74 76 77 78

Spectacular mid-sized winery, now owned by Coca-Cola. Strong, tart SAUVIGNON BLANC and CHARDONNAY; fruity CABERNET and MERLOT.

Stonegate   Napa. **→ *** CH 79 80 CS 78 79

Small privately-owned winery and v'yd. making CABERNET, SAUVIGNON BLANC, CHARDONNAY.

Stony Hill   Napa. **** CH 74 75 76 77 78 79 80

Many of California's very best whites have come from this minute winery over 30 years. Owner Fred McCrea died in 1977; his widow Eleanor carries on. Stony Hill CHARDONNAY, GEWÜRZ and RIESLING are all delicate and fine.

Stony Ridge Winery   Livermore. **→ *** CH 79 80 PN 79

Recent revival of an old Pleasanton winery making a wide range, including dessert and sparkling wines, at fair prices.

Sutter Home   Napa. ** Z 77 78 79 80

Small winery revived, specializing in ZINFANDEL from Amador County grapes: excellent heavy-weight.

Swan, J.   Sonoma. ** Z 74 75 76 77 78

Young one-man winery with a name for rich ZINFANDEL.

Trefethen   Napa. ***→ **** CH 77 78 79 80 CS 74 76 77 78 79

Growing family-owned winery in Napa's finest old wooden building. Good RIESLING, CABERNET. Brilliant CHARDONNAY and a notable low-price blend, Eshcol.

Trentadue   Sonoma R-R. **

Small v'yd. and smaller winery making sound big-flavoured wines, incl. some from unorthodox varieties.

Tulocay   Napa. **

Tiny new winery at Napa City. First wines are good PINOT NOIR and CABERNET.

Turgeon & Lohr   Central Coast. **

Small winery in San Jose with its own v'yds. in SALINAS. Reliable RIESLING and CABERNET rosé

Ventana   Central Coast/Monterey. ** CH 78 79 80 81

New in '78 with flavoury PINOT BLANC and CHARDONNAY.

Vichon Winery   Napa. **→ *** CH 80 81

Founded 1980; original and ambitious. Fine CHARDONNAY and blended (50/50) SAUVIGNON/SEMILLON "CHEVRIER BLANC".

Villa Mount Eden   Napa. *** CH 78 80 81 CS 74 75 77 78 79

Small Oakville estate with excellent dry CHENIN BLANC, good CHARDONNAY, and CABERNET outstanding.

Weibel   Central Coast and Mendocino. *→ **

Veteran mid-sized winery without high ambitions. specialist in own-label sparkling wines.

Wente   Livermore and Central Coast. *→ ***

Important and historic specialists in Bordeaux-style whites. Fourth-generation Wentes are as dynamic as ever. CHARDONNAY, SAUVIGNON BLANC and RIESLING are all successful commercial wines. Now also sparkling.

William Hill Winery   Napa.

Huge new plantings in the Mayacamas mountains and a new winery will soon yield something worth watching.

Zaca Mesa   Central Coast/Santa Barbara. ** CH 78 79 81 CS 79

Santa Ynez Valley pioneer most successful with CHARDONNAY and RIESLING.

Z-D Wines   Napa. *** CH 80 CS 78

Very small winery (moved from Sonoma to Rutherford) with a name for powerful PINOT NOIR and CHARDONNAY.

The Pacific North-West

Vineyards have now been planted in at least half of the States in the Union — Texas included. So far the only ones that present a palpable challenge to California (for quality; not quantity) are Oregon and Washington in the north-west and their inland neighbour, Idaho.

Oregon's vineyards lie in the cool-temperate Willamette and slightly warmer Umpqua valleys between the Coast and Cascades ranges. Those of Washington and Idaho are mainly east of the Cascades in the semi-arid Yakima Valley and Columbia basin areas, with very hot days and cold nights. Oregon-grown wines are consequently more delicate, Washington's more intensive in flavour. Several wineries use both. Whites are in the majority, though Oregon has high hopes for Pinot Noir.

The principal current producers are:

Amity Vineyards Oregon
> Established 70-acre Willamette winery; uneven results but PINOT NOIR from Oregon and Washington grapes is promising.

Associated Vintners Washington
> A Washington pioneer at Redmond, nr. Seattle. CABERNET, SEMILLON, RIESLING and dry spicy GEWÜRZTRAMINER have all been successful. Good value. Now good Chardonnay.

Château Ste. Chapelle Idaho
> The only Idaho winery, near Boise. CHARDONNAY or RIESLING with exceptionally intense flavours are very promising.

Château Ste. Michelle Washington
> The largest north-west winery, with 2,600 acres, very modern equipment and a wide range of labels. Best wines are CABERNET, SEMILLON and RIESLING. Sparkling wines to come.

Elk Cove Vineyards Oregon
> Very small new winery. Good CHARDONNAY and RIESLING. PINOT NOIR. Reserve '79 was very good.

The Eyrie Vineyards Oregon
> Early (1965) Willamette Valley winery with Burgundian ideas; remarkable oak-aged PINOT NOIR and CHARDONNAY. Also Pinots Gris and Meunier.

HillCrest Vineyard Oregon
> Early (1961) Umpqua Valley winery. Inconsistent, but RIESLING, CABERNET and PINOT NOIR can score well.

Knudsen Erath Oregon
> Willamette Valley vineyards with reliable good-value PINOT NOIR, RIESLING. CHARDONNAY and GEWÜRZTRAMINER can also be good. Oregon's biggest winery.

Ponzi Vineyards Oregon
> Tiny family winery near Portland. RIESLING and CHARDONNAY are best. "Oregon Harvest" is a CHARD/PINOT BLANC blend.

Preston Wine Cellars Washington
> Rapidly growing new Yakima Valley winery already acclaimed, especially for SAUVIGNON BLANC and MERLOT. Also CHARDONNAY, RIESLING, GEWÜRZTRAMINER.

Sokol Blosser Vineyards Oregon
> New Willamette Valley winery with wide range, including CHARDONNAY, SAUVIGNON BLANC, Müller-Thurgau, highly rated PINOT NOIR, MERLOT and (slightly sweet) RIESLING.

Tualatin Vineyards Oregon
> Consistently good specialist (hitherto) in whites, west of Portland. Known for RIESLING, GEWÜRZTRAMINER and dry MUSCAT. Recently promising PINOT NOIR.

New York

New York State and its neighbours Ohio and Ontario make their own style of wine from grapes of native American ancestry, rather than the European vines of California. American grapes have a flavour known as "foxy"; a taste acquired by many easterners. Fashion is slowly moving in favour of hybrids between these and European grapes with less, or no, foxiness. The entries below include both wineries and grape varieties.

Aurora
> One of the best white French-American hybrid grapes, the most widely planted in New York. Formerly known as Seibel 5279. Good for sparkling wine.

Baco Noir
> One of the better red French-American hybrid grapes. High acidity but good clean dark wine.

Benmarl
> Highly regarded and expanding v'yd. and winery at Marlboro on the Hudson River. Wines are mainly from French-American hybrids, but European vines also make good wine.

Boordy Vineyards
> The winery which pioneered French-American hybrid grapes in the USA. Started by Philip Wagner in Maryland in the '50s.

Brights
> Canada's biggest winery, in Ontario, now tending towards French-American hybrids and experiments with European vines. Their CHELOIS and BACO NOIR are pleasant reds, respectively lighter and more full-bodied.

Bully Hill
> New (since 1970) FINGER LAKES winery using both American and hybrid grapes to make varietal wines.

Château Gai
> Canadian (Ontario) winery making European and hybrid wines, incl. successful GAMAY and PINOT NOIR.

Catawba
> One of the first American wine-grapes, still the second most widely grown. Pale red and foxy flavoured.

Chautauqua
> The biggest grape-growing district in the e., along the s. shore of La. Erie from New York to Ohio.

Chelois
> Popular red French-American hybrid grape, formerly called Seibel 10878. Makes dry red wine with some richness, slightly foxy.

Concord
> The archetypal American grape, dark red, strongly foxy, making good grape jelly but dreadful wine. By far the most widely planted in New York (23,000 acres).

Delaware
> Old American white-wine grape making pleasant, slightly foxy dry wines. Used in "Champagne" and for still wine.

De Chaunac
> A good red French-American hybrid grape, popular in Canada as well as New York. Full-bodied dark wine.

Finger Lakes
> Century-old wine district in upper New York State, best-known for its "Champagne". The centre is Hammondsport.

Fournier, Charles
> The top quality of "Champagne" made by the GOLD SEAL company, named for a former pioneering wine-maker.

Frank, Dr. Konstantin
> A controversial figure in the FINGER LAKES: the protagonist of European vinifera vines. See Vinifera Wines.

Gold Seal
> One of New York's biggest wineries, makers of Charles FOURNIER "Champagne" and the HENRI MARCHANT range. Known for high quality and readiness to experiment.

Great Western
> The brand name of the PLEASANT VALLEY WINE CO'S "Champagne", one of New York's best wines.

Hargrave Vineyard
> Trend-setting winery with 50 acres on North Fork of Long Island. Very promising CHARDONNAY, PINOT NOIR.

Henri Marchant
> Brand name of GOLD SEAL's standard range of mainly traditional American-grape wines.

Inniskillin
> Small new Canadian winery at Niagara making European and hybrid wines, incl. good MARÉCHAL FOCH.

Isabella
> Old CONCORD-style red grape making strongly foxy wine.

Phylloxera is an insect that lives on the roots of the vine. Its arrival in Europe from North America in the 1860s was an international catastrophe. It destroyed almost every vineyard on the continent before it was discovered that the native American vine is immune to its attacks. The remedy was (and still is) to graft European vines on to American rootstocks. Virtually all Europe's vineyards are so grafted today. Whether their produce is just as good as the wine of pre-phylloxera days is a favourite debate among old-school wine-lovers.

Maréchal Foch
> Promising red French hybrid between PINOT NOIR and GAMAY. Makes good burgundy-style wine in Ontario.

Moore's Diamond
> Old American white grape still grown in New York.

Niagara
> Old American white grape used for sweet wine. Very foxy.

Pleasant Valley Wine Co.
> Winery at Hammondsport, FINGER LAKES, owned by TAYLOR'S, producing GREAT WESTERN wines.

Seibel
> One of the most famous French grape hybridists, responsible for many successful French-American crosses originally known by numbers, since christened with such names as AURORA, DE CHAUNAC, CHELOIS.

Seyve-Villard
> Another well-known French hybridist. His best-known cross, no. 5276, is known as Seyval Blanc.

Taylor's
> The biggest wine-company of the Eastern States, based at Hammondsport in the FINGER LAKES. Brands incl. GREAT WESTERN and LAKE COUNTRY. Most vines are American.

Vinifera Wines
> Small but influential winery of Dr Frank, pioneer in growing European vines, incl. RIESLING, CHARDONNAY and PINOT NOIR, in the FINGER LAKES area. Some excellent wines.

Widmers
> Major FINGER LAKES winery selling native American varietal wines: DELAWARE, NIAGARA, etc.

South America

The flourishing vineyards of Argentina (the world's fifth largest) and Chile are known to the world chiefly as a source of cheap wine of sometimes remarkable quality. Most of it is drunk within South America. Brazil also has an expanding wine industry in the Rio Grande do Sul area, but as yet no exports.

ARGENTINA
> The quality vineyards are concentrated in Mendoza province in the Andean foothills at about 2,000 feet. They are all irrigated. San Raphael, 140 miles s. of Mendoza city, is centre of a slightly cooler area. San Juan, to the north, is hotter and specializes in sherry and brandy.

Andean Vineyards
> Widely distributed brand of adequate quality from PEÑAFLOR.

Bianchi, Bodegas
> Well-known premium wine producer at San Raphael owned by Seagrams. "Don Valentin" CABERNET and Bianchi Borgogna are best-sellers. "Particular" is their top CABERNET.

Castell Chandon Excellent fresh white from a Moët offshoot.

Cooperation San Raphael
> Enormous co-operative for bulk wines and concentrated grape juice.

Crillon, Bodegas
> Brand-new (1972) winery owned by Seagram's, principally for tank-method sparkling wines.

Esmeralda Producers of a good Cabernet, St Felician, at Cordoba.

Furlotti, Angel
> Big bodega at Maipu, Mendoza. 2,500 acres making its best red wine from a blend of CABERNET, MERLOT and Lambrusco, white from PINOT BLANC and RIESLING.

Giol The enormous State co-operative of Maipu province. Mainly bulk wines. Premium range is called "Canciller".

Gonzales Videla, Bodegas
> Old-established family firm re-equipped for modern methods. Brands include "Tromel" and "Panquehua".

Goyenechea, Bodegas
> Basque family firm making old-style wines, including Aberdeen Angus red.

La Rural, Bodegas
> Family-run winery at Coquimbito making some of Argentina's best Riesling and Traminer whites and some good reds.

Lopez, Bodegas
> Family firm best known for their "Château Montchenot" red and white and "Château Vieux" CABERNET.

Norton, Bodegas
> Old firm, originally English now owned by Seagrams, at Perdriol. "Perdriel" is brand-name of 10-year-old premium Cabernet in flask-bottles. Also good whites, incl. Riesling and Chardonnay.

Orfila, José
> Long-established bodega at St. Martin, Mendoza. Top export wines are Cautivo CABERNET and white Extra Dry (PINOT BLANC).

Peñaflor
> Argentine's biggest wine company, with four v. modern bodegas and 3,000 acres in San Juan and Mendoza. Range includes Andean and Trapiche brands of CABERNET, CHARDONNAY and PINOT BLANC; also good-value red in cans. Tio Quinto is their popular medium sherry.

Proviar, Bodega Producers of "champaña" (sparkling wine) under contract with MOËT ET CHANDON. Premium brands are "Baron B", Castell Chandon, Valmont and Valtour.

Santa Ana, Bodegas
> Small, old-established family firm at Guaymallen, Mendoza. Wide range of wines include good Syrah Val Semina.

San Telmo
> Large modern bodega on the California model. Apparently good 'varietals'.

Suter, Bodegas
> Swiss-founded firm best-known for "Etiquetta Marron" white and "Juan Suter" reds. Owned by Seagrams.

Toso, Pascual
> Old Mendoza winery at San José, making one of Argentina's best reds, Cabernet Toso. Also RIESLING and sparkling wines.

Trapiche
> Top quality range of wines from PEÑAFLOR designed for export.

Weinert, Bodegas
> New winery producing crisp, fruity, modern-style white.

CHILE
> Natural conditions are ideal for wine-growing in central Chile, just south of Santiago. But political conditions have been very difficult, and the country's full potential still has to be explored. The Cabernets are best. The principal bodegas exporting wine from Chile are:

Canepa, José
> A modern establishment at Valparaiso handling wine from several areas. Very good French-style CABERNET from Lontüé, Talca, 100 miles south; dry SEMILLON, sweet Moscatel.

Concha y Toro
> The biggest and most outward-looking wine firm, with several bodegas and 2,500 acres in the Maipo valley. Remarkable dark and deep CABERNET, MERLOT, Verdot. Brands are St. Emiliana, Marques de Casa Concha, Cassillero del Diablo.

Cousiño Macul
> Distinguished estate near Santiago. Very dry "green" SEMILLON and CHARDONNAY. Don Luis light red, Don Matias dark and tannic, are good CABERNETS.

Santa Carolina
> A bodega with pleasant widely available dry wines mainly consumed in S. America.

Santa Helena/San Pedro
> Brands now controlled by RUMASA (see Spain), long established at Lontüé, Talca. Range of good wines sold all over S. America, esp. Bordeaux-like CABERNET.

Santa Rita
> Bodega in the Maipo valley s. of Santiago. Pleasant soft wines including the "120" brand. Casa Real is the best wine.

Tocornal, José
> Considerable exporter to Venezuela and Canada.

Torres, Miguel
> New enterprise of Catalonian family firm (see Spain). Viña Santa Digna CABERNET and light gassy SAUVIGNON white.

Undurraga
> Famous family business; one of the first to export to the U.S.A. Wines in both old and modern styles: good clean SAUVIGNON BLANC and oaky yellow "Viejo Roble". "Gran Vino Tinto" is one of the best buys in Chile.

Viña Linderos
> Small family winery in the Maipo valley exports good full-bodied CABERNET.

Australia

It is only 20 years since modern wine technology revolutionized Australia's 150-year-old wine industry, ending the dominance of fortified wines and making table wines of top quality possible. Already the results are as impressive as California's. The Australians know it: little is left for export.

Traditional-style Australian wines were thick-set and burly Shiraz reds or Semillon or Riesling whites. The modern taste is for lighter wines, especially Rhine Rieslings, and for Cabernet reds, but the best still have great character and the ability to age splendidly.

Australia's wine labels are among the world's most communicative. Since Australians started to take their own wine seriously they have become longer and longer winded, with information about grapes, soil, sunshine, fermenting periods and temperatures, wine-makers' biographies and serving hints. Little of this is pure salesmanship. It is intended to be, and really is, helpful. Bin-numbers mean something. They need to be noted and remembered. Prizes in shows (which are highly competitive) mean a great deal. In a country without any sort of established grades of quality the buyer needs all the help he can get.

Wine areas

The vintages mentioned here are those rated as good or excellent for the reds of the areas in question. Excellent recent vintages are marked with an accent, e.g. 80'.

Adelaide   66 67 70 71 72 73 75 76 77 79 80' 81
    The capital of South Australia had the state's first v'yds. A few are still making wine.

Barossa   66 68 72 73 75 76 77 79 80' 81'
    Australia's biggest quality area, of German origin, specializing in white (esp. Riesling; best from the Eden Valley at 1,500 feet), good-quality reds and good dessert wines.

Clare-Watervale   66 68 70 71 72 75 76 77 78 79 81
    Small cool-climate area 90 miles n. of Adelaide best known for Riesling; also planted with Shiraz and Cabernet.

Central Victoria   66 68 71 73 74 76 79 80
> Scattered v'yds. remaining from vast pre-phylloxera plantings include GT. WESTERN, CH. TAHBILK, AVOCA and BENDIGO.

Coonawarra   66 68 70 71 72 73 74 75 76 77 79 80 81
> Southernmost v'yd. of South Australia, long famous for well-balanced reds, recently successful with Riesling.

Franklin River/Mount Barker ·
> Promising new cool area of W. Australia.

Hunter Valley   66 67 70 72 73 74 75 76 77 79 80' 81
> The great name in N.S.W. Broad deep Shiraz reds and Semillon whites with a style of their own. Now also Cabernet and Chardonnay. Recent expansion at Wybong, etc., to the w.

Keppoch/Padthaway   75 76 77 78 79 80' 81'
> Large new area in southern S. Australia being developed by big companies as an overspill of Coonawarra. Cool climate and good potential for commercial reds and whites.

Langhorne Creek   See Southern Vales

N.E. Victoria   66 70 71 72 73 75 76 80'
> Historic area incl. Rutherglen, Corowa, Wangaratta. Heavy reds and magnificent sweet dessert wines.

Margaret River/Busselton
> New area of great promise for fine wines, s. of Perth in W. Australia.

McLaren Vale and S. Adelaide   See Southern Vales

Mudgee   73 74 75 77 78 79'
> Small traditional wine area in a N.S.W. fruit-growing district. Big reds of considerable colour and flavour and full coarse whites recently being refined.

Murray Valley   N.V.
> Important scattered v'yds. irrigated from the Murray river, incl. Swan Hill, Mildura, Renmark, Berri, Loxton, Waikerie. Largely sherry, brandy, "jug" and dessert wines.

Riverina   N.V.
> Fruit- and vine-growing district irrigated from the Murrumbidgee river. Mainly jug wines, but good light "varietals".

Southern Vales   66 67 70 71 72 73 75 76 77 79 80' 81
> General name for several small pockets of wine-growing s. of Adelaide of which McLaren Vale is the most important. Big full-blooded reds and rather coarse whites.

Swan Valley
> The main v'yd. of Western Australia, on the n. outskirts of Perth. Hot climate makes strong low-acid wines.

Upper Hunter   69 73 75 76 79 80 81'
> New region 60 miles N.W. of Hunter Valley, N.S.W. with more extreme climate, specializing in white wines, lighter and quicker-developing than Hunter whites.

Yarra Valley ('Lilydale')   77 78 80' 81
> Historic wine area near Melbourne fallen into disuse, now being redeveloped by enthusiasts with small wineries. A bewildering range of varieties and styles.

Wineries

All Saints   N.E. Vic. Full range ★→★★
> Big old family-run winery in dessert-wine country. Sturdy reds. Sweet brown MUSCAT is sometimes exceptional.

Angove's   S.A. Table and dessert ★→★★
> Family business in Adelaide and Renmark in the Murray Valley. Sound traditional wines.

Arrowfield   N.S.W. Table   ★★
> The largest Upper Hunter vineyard, on irrigated land. Light Cabernet and succulent Chardonnay.

Bailey's   N.E. Vic. Table and dessert ★★→★★★
Small concern making rich old-fashioned reds of great
character, esp. Bundarra Hermitage and dessert MUSCAT.

Balgownie   Vic. Table   ★★★★
Specialist in fine reds, particularly straight CABERNET. Also
exceptional CHARDONNAY.

Basedow   S.A. Table   ★★★
Small top-class Barossa winery buying grapes for excellent
Sharaz, etc.

Berri Coop.   S. Aus. full range   ★→★★
Aus's largest winery, selling mostly to other companies. Now
developing own name with success; esp. robust oaky reds.

Best's   Central Vic. Full range ★→★★
Conservative old family winery at Great Western with good
strong old-style claret, hock and sparkling wines.

Bilyara   N. Barossa. S. Aus. Table and sp. ★★→★★★
Wolf Blass is the ebullient German wine-maker with dazzling
products and propaganda. His oaky wines are not for keeping.

Bleasdale   Langhorne Creek, S.A. Full range ★→★★
Small family business making potent wines of many kinds.

Bowen Estate   S.A. Table ★★★
Small Coonawarra winery; intense CABERNET SAUVIGNON,
good Riesling. Sparkling Chardonnay on the way.

Brand   Coonawarra, S.A. Table   ★★★
Small family estate. Outstandingly fine, bold and stylish
CABERNET and SHIRAZ under the Laira label.

Brokenwood   N.S.W. Dry red.   ★★★
New small winery owned by lawyers blends Hunter wine with
Coonawarra from BRAND. Exciting quality of CABERNET
SAUVIGNON and SHIRAZ since 1973.

Brown Brothers   Milawa, N.E. Victoria. Full range   ★→★★★
Old family firm with new ideas, wide range of rather delicate
wines, including several well-made varietals from various
districts, a refreshing change from the blood-and-guts style of
the area. CHARDONNAY and dry white muscat outstanding.

Buring, Leo   Barossa, S.A. Full range ★→   ★★★
"Château Leonay", old white-wine specialists, now owned by
LINDEMAN. Outstanding "Reserve Bin" RHINE RIESLING.

Campbells of Rutherglen   N.E. Vic. Full range ★★→★★★
Impressive new whites and authentic regional reds.

Chambers' Rosewood   N.E. Vic. Full range   ★★   →★★★
Good cheap table wines and very good dessert wines, esp.
Flame Tokay.

Château Tahbilk   Central Vic. Table ★→   ★★★
Family-owned wine-estate making CABERNET, SHIRAZ, RHINE
RIESLING and Marsanne. "Special Bins" are outstanding.

Château Yaldara   Barossa, S.A. Full range ★
A showpiece of Barossa, popular with tourists. Sparkling
wines are a speciality.

Conteville   W. Aus. Table   ★★
New winery north of Perth. Richly flavoured reds and light
dry muscat table wines, also experimentals from Mt. Barker
in the south.

Craigmoor   N.S.W. Table and Port ★→★★
The oldest Mudgee winery. Robust reds and whites, and port
matured in rum barrels. Also CHARDONNAY.

d'Arenberg   McLaren Vale, S.A. Table and dessert ★→★★
Small-scale old-style family outfit s. of Adelaide. Strapping
rustic reds; CABERNET, SHIRAZ and Burgundy.

Drayton   Hunter Valley, N.S.W. Table   ★★
Traditional Hunter wines, Hermitage red and SEMILLON
white, from the old Bellevue estate.

Elliott's Oakvale   Hunter Valley, N.S.W. Table ★★
>   Long-established grower. "Tallawanta" reds and "Belford" whites are in the bosomy, deep-flavoured Hunter style.

Enterprise Wines   S.A. Table ★★→★★★
>   Tim Knappstein, ex-Stanley, concentrates on RHINE RIESLING and CABERNET SAUVIGNON, made in an old brewery in Clare.

Evans and Tate   W. Aus. Table ★★→★★★
>   Big, soft, Rhônish reds from both the Swan Valley of W.A. and the Margaret River.

Gramp's Orlando   Barossa, S.A. Full range ★→★★★
>   Great pioneering company, now owned by Reckitt & Colman. Range includes sweet fizzy "Barossa Pearl", good standard Jacob's Creek Claret, etc., and some of Australia's best RHINE RIESLING: Steingarten. William Jacob is a low-price line.

Hamilton's   S. Adelaide and Barossa, S.A. Full range ★
>   Mildara have just bought this firm with popular light wines, e.g. Ewell Moselle and Springton Riesling.

Hardy's   Southern Vales, S.A., Barossa, etc. Full range ★→★★
>   Famous wide-spread family-run company using and blending wines from several areas, incl. a CABERNET, reliable light St. Thomas Burgundy and good Old Castle Riesling. Hardy's recently bought HOUGHTON and REYNELLA.

Henschke   Barossa, S.A. Table ★★
>   Family business known for sterling Shiraz.

Houghton/Valencia   Swan Valley, W.A. Full range. ★→ ★★
>   The most famous old winery of W. Australia. Soft, ripe "White Burgundy" is the top wine. Now also excellent CABERNET.

Hungerford Hill   Hunter Valley, N.S.W. Table ★→★★
>   Big new winery with over 1,000 acres and modern ideas, using Hunter and Coonawarra grapes.

Huntingdon Estate   N.S.W. Table ★→★★
>   New small winery; the best in Mudgee. Fine award-winning reds and clean SEMILLON and CHARDONNAY.

Kaiser Stuhl   Barossa, S.A. Full range ★→★★★
>   The Barossa growers' co-operative. A fine modern winery with high standards. "Individual v'yd." Rieslings are excellent. So is "Special Reserve" CABERNET.

Krondorf Wines   S.A. Table
>   Rejuvenated old winery in Barossa Valley, S.A.

Lake's Folly   Hunter Valley, N.S.W. Table ★★★★
>   The work of an inspired surgeon from Sydney. A new style for the Hunter Valley: CABERNET and new barrels to make rich complex California-style reds. Also excellent CHARDONNAY.

Leeuwin Estate   W. A. Table ★★→★★★★
>   New Margaret River estate leading Australia with superb Chardonnay and developing reds.

Leconfield   S.A. Table ★★★
>   Coonawarra CABERNET and oak-aged Riesling of great style.

Lindeman   Orig. Hunter, now everywhere. Full range ★→★★★
>   One of the oldest firms, now a giant owned by Phillip Morris Corp. Its Ben Ean "Moselle" is Australia's best-selling wine. Owns BURINGS in Barossa and Rouge Homme in Coonawarra. Dessert-wine v'yds. at Corowa, N. Victoria. Many inter-state blends. Pioneers in modernizing wine styles.

McWilliams   Hunter Valley and Riverina, N.S.W. Full range ★→★★★
>   Famous family of first-rate Hunter wine-makers at Mount Pleasant and Lovedale (HERMITAGE and SEMILLON). Pioneers in RIVERINA with lighter wines, incl. sweet white "Lexia" and fine varieties.

Mildara   Murray Valley, S.A. Full range ★→★★★
>   Sherry and brandy specialists at Mildura on the Murray river also making fine CABERNET and RIESLING at COONAWARRA.

Mitchelton   Central Vic. Table   `*→ ***`
>   Big modern winery. A wide range incl. v.g. Marsanne.

Morris   N.E. Vic. Table and dessert `**→ ****`
>   Old winery at Rutherglen making Australia's best brown "liqueur" muscat. Now owned by Reckitt & Colman.

Moss Wood   W. Aus. Table `***`
>   Tiny 2-acre v'yd. on Margaret River. CABERNET SAUVIGNONS with rich fruit flavours not unlike the best Californians.

Mount Mary   Central Vic. Table `****`
>   Small v'yd. nr. Melbourne. A top "boutique" winery for CHAR-DONNAY, PINOT NOIR and CABERNET.

Orlando   See GRAMP

Penfold's   Orig. Adelaide, now everywhere. Full range `*→ ****`
>   Ubiquitous and excellent company: in BAROSSA, HUNTER VALLEY, RIVERINA, COONAWARRA, etc. Grange Hermitage is `****`, St.Henri Claret not far behind. Bin-numbered wines are usually outstanding. "Grandfather Port" is sensational.

Petaluma   S.A. `****`
>   A recent rocket-like success with (N.S.W.-grown) CHARDON-NAY and RIESLING, now centred around new winery in ADELAIDE HILLS using Coonawarra and Clare grapes.

Piper's Brook   Tasmania Table `***`
>   Cool-area pioneer with highly promising Riesling, P. Noir, etc., from near Launceston.

Quelltaler   Clare-Watervale, S.A. Full range `*→ **`
>   Old winery n. of Adelaide known for good "Granfiesta" sherry and "hock". Recently good Rhine Riesling and SEMILLON.

Redman   Coonawarra, S.A. Table `***`
>   Small new winery making only COONAWARRA claret of SHIRAZ and CABERNET of top quality.

Reynella   Southern Vales, S.A. Full range `*→ ***`
>   Red-wine specialists s. of ADELAIDE. Highly esteemed rich CABERNET and "Vintage Reserve" claret. Now owned by Hardy's.

The Robson Vineyard   N.S.W. Table `**→ ***`
>   Tiny HUNTER VALLEY winery. Wide range of varietals; CHAR-DONNAY and HERMITAGE consistently show winners.

Rosemount   N.S.W. Table `*→ **`
>   Bustling newcomer in Upper HUNTER. Agreeable RH. RIESLING and Traminer/Riesling blend.

Rothbury Estate   Hunter Valley, N.S.W. Table   `***`
>   Important syndicate-owned wine estate concentrating on traditional HUNTER wines: "Hermitage" and long-lived SEMIL-LON. New plantings of CABERNET, CHARDONNAY, PINOT NOIR.

Saltram   Barossa, S.A. Full range `*→ ***`
>   Seagram-owned winery making a notable "Metala" Cab/Shiraz, good CABERNET, "Mamre Brook" and good "Selected Vintage" claret and RHINE RIESLING and Char-donnay.

Sandalford   W. Aus. Table   `*→ **`
>   Fine old winery with contrasting styles of red and white varietals from Swan and Margaret rivers.

Saxonvale   N.S.W. Table   `**`
>   Large newcomer at Fordwich, N.W. of Hunter. After early difficulties now making very good SEMILLON and CHARDON-NAY. Also CABERNET, SHIRAZ.

Seppelt   Barossa, S.A. Central Vic., etc. Full range `*→ ***`
>   Far-flung producers of Australia's best "champagne" (Gt. Western Brut), good dessert wines (from Rutherglen, the Murray Valley, Barossa), the reliable Moyston claret and some good private bin wines from Gt. Western in Victoria.

Seville Estate Victoria Table ★★★
> Tiny new Yarra Valley winery with exceptional Chardonnay, late-picked Riesling, Shiraz, etc.

Smith's Yalumba Barossa, S.A. Full range `★→★★★`
> Big old family firm. Best wines incl. Carte d'Or Rhine Riesling from Pewsey Vale above Barossa, good "Galway Vintage" claret, "Galway Pipe" port and Chiquita sherry.

Stanley Clare, S. Aus. Full range ★→★★
> Important medium-size quality winery owned by Heinz. Among Aus.'s best RH. RIESLING and CABERNET and complex Cabernet-Shiraz-Malbec blends under Leasingham label.

Stanton & Killeen N.E. Vic. Table & dessert ★★
> Small old family firm with fine Moodemere reds and rich muscats.

Stonyfell Adelaide, S.A. Full range ★→★★
> Long-established company best known for "Metala" CABERNET SHIRAZ from Langhorne Creek.

Taltarni Victoria. Table ★★★
> Dominique Portet, brother of Bernard (Clos du Val, Napa), son of André (Château Lafite), produces huge red wines near Avoca. Sparkling wines on the way.

Taylors Wines S.A. Table ★★
> Large new red wine producing unit (CABERNET and HERMITAGE) turning to whites (RHINE RIESLING).

Tisdall Wines Victoria. Table ★★→★★★
> Exciting young winery in the Echuca river area, making local wines plus finer material from central ranges (Mount Helen CABERNET SAUVIGNON, CHARDONNAY, RHINE RIESLING).

Tollana Barossa, S.A. Full range `★→★★`
> Old company famous for brandy, has latterly made some remarkable CABERNET and RHINE RIESLING.

Tulloch Hunter Valley, N.S.W. Table ★★
> An old name at Pokolbin, with good dry reds and "Riesling".

Tyrrell Hunter Valley, N.S.W. Table ★★→ `★★★`
> Up-to-date old family business at "Ashman's". Some of the best traditional Hunter wines, Hermitage and RIESLING, are distinguished by Vat Numbers. Also big rich CHARDONNAY and delicate PINOT NOIR becoming known in Europe.

Valencia see Houghton/Valencia

Vasse Felix W. Aus. Table ★★
> The pioneer of the Margaret River. Elegant CABERNETS that have been compared to St. Julien.

Westfield W. Aus. Table `★★`
> Perhaps the best table wine in the Swan Valley. CABERNET and Verdelho show finesse.

Wolf Blass see **Bilyara**

Woodleys Adel, S. Aus. Table ★★
> Well-known for Queen Adelaide label claret and Riesling.

Wyndham Estate Branxton, N.S.W. Full range ★→★★
> A very large new Hunter group. Some fine Hunter varietals occasionally emerge from a very mixed range. Geo. Wyndham's original estate is now a tourist attraction.

Wynns S. Aus. and N.S.W. Table ★→★★★
> Large inter-state company, originators of flagon wines, with winery in RIVERINA and vineyards at Coonawarra, making exceptional CABERNET. Owned by Toohey's Brewery (which also owns the former Seaviews, now a sparkling wine cellar).

Yellowglen Vic. Sparkling ★★★
> Owners Holm and Landragin intend to make Australia's best sparkling wine. The omens are good.

New Zealand

An infant wine industry already making an international impact with fruity and well-balanced table wines from the classic grape varieties. Progress has accelerated since new vineyard areas were planted in the early '70s on both North and South Islands. There are now over 10,000 acres. White grapes predominate. Müller-Thurgau ("Riesling-Sylvaner") is the most planted variety.

The general style of wine is relatively light with fairly high acidity. The distinctive flavours of grape varieties are well marked and critical opinion sees a very bright future for the industry. The principal producers are:

Cooks
> Progressive new company at Te Kauwhata nr. Auckland. Fine light CABERNET, CHARDONNAY and GEWÜRZ: also CHENIN BLANC, SAUVIGNON BLANC, MÜLLER-THURGAU.

Corbans
> Old-established firm at Henderson, nr. Auckland, now owned by Rothman's. Emphasis on whites and sherry.

Delegat's
> Impressive Gisborne whites and Auckland-area reds.

Gisborne
> Major white-grape district in n.e. of N. Island.

Glenvale
> Old-established fruit company with 250 acres of vines at Napier, HAWKES BAY. Table wines improving.

Hawkes Bay
> The biggest vineyard area on the east coast of North Island.

Marlborough
> Recently developed vineyard area at north end of South Island, now with over 2,000 acres.

Matawhero
> Small POVERTY BAY producer with high-quality GEWÜRZTRAMINER, CHARDONNAY.

McWilliams
> Winery at HAWKES BAY. Related to the major Australian company. Wines include Baco Noir (see New York), Cresta Doré, CABERNET and good CHARDONNAY.

Montana
> The largest winery, originally at POVERTY BAY; pioneer with fine wines and in planting at MARLBOROUGH. MÜLLER-THURGAU and CABERNET both very successful. Also good Gisborne Chardonnay.

Nobilo's
> Yugoslav family firm, making some of N.Z.'s best reds at Huapai, n. of Auckland.

Penfolds
> Founded 1963 by the Australian company. V'yds. at Henderson, nr. Auckland. CABERNET, PINOTAGE, "Autumn Riesling".

Poverty Bay
> Important area near Gisborne, east coast of North Island.

Te Mata Estate
> Old Hawkes Bay property restored, making excellent CABERNET/MERLOT. Also CHARDONNAY, FURMINT.

Vidal's
> Highly proficient and atmospheric Hawkes Bay winery. Fine CABERNET and sparkling wine.

Villa Maria
> Yugoslav family winery nr. Auckland. Riesling-Sylvaner and CABERNET both successful.

South Africa

South Africa has made excellent sherry and port for many years, but has taken table wine seriously only in the last decade. Since 1972 a new system of Wines of Origin and registered "estates" has started a new era of competitive modern wine-making. Cabernet Sauvignon reds of high quality are already well established; the signs are that Chardonnay, Sauvignon Blanc and other superior grapes now being introduced will be similarly successful.

Allesverloren ★★
> Estate in MALMESBURY with over 325 acres of v'yds., formerly well known for "port", now specializing in ripe, powerful, deep reds, incl. CABERNET and TINTA BAROCCA. Distributed by BERGKELDER.

Alphen ★
> Winery originally at Constantia, owned by the famous Cloete family (see GROOT CONSTANTIA), now at Somerset West. Name is used as a brand.

Alto ★★
> STELLENBOSCH estate of 247 acres high on a hill, best known for massive-bodied CABERNET and a good blend: Alto Rouge. Distributed by BERGKELDER.

Autumn Harvest
> Popular low-price range from STELLENBOSCH FARMERS' WINERY.

Backsberg ★★
> Name formerly associated with commercial blends, now a prize-winning 400-acre estate at PAARL with notably good, relatively light, CABERNET. Also Sauvignon Blanc.

Bellingham
> Top brand name of UNION WINE. Reliable reds and whites, esp. SHIRAZ. The GRAND CRU is well known.

Benede-Oranje
> Newly demarcated wine region in the Orange River irrigation area. The northernmost region.

Bergkelder
> Big wine concern at STELLENBOSCH, member of the OUDE MEESTER group, making and distributing many brands and estate wines, incl. FLEUR DU CAP, ALTO, HAZENDAL, etc. Now combined with STELLENBOSCH FARMERS' WINERY. See Cape Wine and Distillers Ltd.

Bertrams
> Major wine company owned by Gilbeys with a wide range of well-made varietals, esp. CABERNET.

Blaauwklippen ★★
> Estate s. of STELLENBOSCH producing RHINE RIESLING, SAUVIGNON BLANC and light fruity reds.

Boberg
> Controlled region of origin for fortified wines consisting of the districts of PAARL and TULBAGH.

Bonfoi ★★
> Estate in STELLENBOSCH district. The CHENIN BLANC is marketed through the BERGKELDER.

Boschendal ★★
> Estate in PAARL area being developed on old fruit farm. Emphasis on white wines. Also a charming restaurant.

Breede River Valley
> Demarcated wine region east of Drakenstein Mtns.; hotter than coastal area. Being upgraded to produce good light wines, esp. at Robertson and Worcester.

Bukettraube
New German white-wine grape with acidity and muscat aroma, popular in S. Africa for blending.

Cabernet
The great Bordeaux grape particularly successful in the COASTAL REGION. Sturdy, long-ageing wines.

Cape Wine and Distillers Ltd.
The holding company for the reconstructed liquor interests of Oudemeester, STELLENBOSCH FARMERS' WINERY, etc.

Carlonet
See Uitkyk

Cavendish Cape   ★★
Range of remarkably good sherries from the K.W.V..

Chenin Blanc
Workhorse grape of the Cape; one vine in four. Adaptable and sometimes very good. Alias STEEN.

Cinsaut
Bulk-producing French red grape formerly known as Hermitage in S. Africa. Chiefly blended with CABERNET, but can make reasonable wine on its own.

Coastal Region
Demarcated wine region, includes PAARL, STELLENBOSCH, Durbanville, SWARTLAND.

Colombard
The "FRENCH COLOMBARD" of California. Prized in S. Africa for its high acidity and fruity flavour. An element in many "Steens".

Constantia
Once the world's most famous muscat wine, from the Cape. Now the southernmost district of origin See also GROOT CON-STANTIA.

Delheim   ★★→★★★
Winery at Driesprong in one of the best and highest areas of STELLENBOSCH, known for delicate STEEN and GEWÜRZ-TRAMINER whites and also light reds: PINOTAGE, SHIRAZ and CABERNET.

Drostdy   ★★
Range of sherries from BERGKELDER.

Edelkeur   ★★★★
Excellent intensely sweet white made with nobly rotten (p. 47) STEEN grapes by NEDERBURG.

Estate wine
A strictly controlled term applying only to some 60 registered estates making wines made of grapes grown on the same property.

Fleur du Cap   ★★
Popular and well-made range of wines from the BERG-KELDER, Stellenbosch. Particularly good CABERNET; RIESLING less good.

Gewürztraminer
The famous spicy grape of Alsace, successfully grown in the TULBAGH area.

Grand Cru (or Premier Grand Cru)
Term for a totally dry white, with no quality implications. Generally to be avoided.

La Gratitude
Well-known brand of dry white from the STELLENBOSCH FARMERS' WINERY.

Goede Hoop   ★
Estate in STELLENBOSCH district. Pleasant blended red bottled and sold by BERGKELDER.

Groot Constantia   ★★
> Historic estate, now government-owned, near Cape Town. Source of superlative muscat wine in the early 19th century. Now making CABERNET, PINOT NOIR, PINOTAGE and SHIRAZ reds. The CABERNET is best. Also a blend, Heerenrood.

Grünberger ★★
> Famous brand of not-quite-dry STEEN white from the BERG-KELDER, though flagrantly dressed up as a German Franconian "Steinwein".

Hanepoot
> Local name for Muscat of Alexandria, widely grown for sweet dessert wines.

Hazendal   ★★
> Family estate in w. STELLENBOSCH specializing in semi-sweet STEEN, marketed by the BERGKELDER.

Jacobsdal   ★
> Estate in STELLENBOSCH district, overlooking False Bay. PINOTAGE bottled and sold by BERGKELDER.

Kanonkop   ★★★
> Outstanding estate in n. STELLENBOSCH, specializing in high-quality and particularly full-bodied CABERNET, PINOTAGE and Pinot Noir. Paul Sauer Fleur is a Bordeaux-style blend.

Klein Karoo
> The easternmost S. African wine district, warm and dry, specializing in dessert and distilling wine.

Kerner   Flowery grape variety recently introduced from Germany.

Koopmanskloof   ★
> STELLENBOSCH estate making good dry Chenin Blanc "Blanc de Marbonne".

K.W.V.
> The Kooperatieve Wijnbouwers Vereniging, S. Africa's national wine co-operative (now independent) originally organized by the State to absorb embarrassing surpluses, now at vast and splendidly equipped premises in PAARL making a range of good wines, particularly sherries.

Laborie   N.Y.A.
> New K.W.V.-owned showpiece estate on Paarl Mtn. CABERNET and PINOTAGE-based Blanc de Noirs sparkling.

Landgoed
> South African for Estate; a word which appears on all estate-wine labels and official seals.

Landskroon   ★
> Family estate owned by Paul and Hugo de Villiers. Mainly port-type wines for K.W.V. but recently some good dry reds – Pinot Noir, TINTA BAROCCA and CABERNETS Sauv. and Franc.

Late Harvest   Term for a mildly sweet wine. "Special Late Harvest" must be naturally sweet. "Noble Late Harvest" is the highest quality level of all.

Malmesbury
> Centre of the SWARTLAND wine district, on the w. coast n. of Cape Town, specializing in dry whites and distilling wine.

Meerendal   ★★
> Estate near Durbanville producing robust reds (esp. SHIRAZ) marketed by the BERGKELDER.

Meerlust   ★★★
> Beautiful old family estate s. of STELLENBOSCH making outstanding CABERNET marketed by the BERGKELDER. Now adding Merlot, etc. for balance and complexity.

Monis   ★→★★
> Well-known wine concern of PAARL, with fine "Vintage Port", now merged with the STELLENBOSCH FARMERS' WINERY.

Montagne ★★
> Relatively new but successful estate of 320 acres near STELLENBOSCH. Wines incl. CABERNET, SHIRAZ and PREMIER GRAND CRU. Owned by Gilbeys. Name may change soon.

Montpellier ★→★★
> Famous pioneering TULBAGH estate with 370 acres of v'yds. specializing in white wine. Produced the first two whites to be officially designated SUPERIOR (RIESLING and GEWÜRZTRAMINER), also CHENIN BLANC and sparkling wine.

Muratie ★
> Ancient estate in STELLENBOSCH, best known for its port and Pinot Noir. 110 acres of v'yds. also grow CABERNET, RIESLING, STEEN and CINSAUT.

Nederburg ★★→★★★★
> The most famous wine farm in modern S. Africa, now operated by the STELLENBOSCH FARMERS' WINERY. Its annual auction is a major event. Pioneer in modern cellar practice and with fine CABERNET, "Private Bin" blends and EDELKEUR. Also good sparkling wines and RIESLINGS.

Olifantsrivier
> Northerly demarcated wine region with a warm dry climate. Mainly distilling wine.

Oude Libertas
> Popular range of mid-quality wines from STELLENBOSCH FARMERS' WINERY. The STEEN and CABERNET are best.

Overberg
> Demarcated wine district in the Caledon area, Coastal Region.

Overgaauw ★→★★★
> Estate w. of STELLENBOSCH making good STEEN, very good CABERNET, and Tria Corda, a CABERNET/MERLOT blend.

Paarl
> South Africa's wine capital, 50 miles n.e. of Cape Town, and the surrounding demarcated district, among the best in the country, particularly for white wine and sherry. Most of its wine is made by co-operatives. See also Boberg.

Paarlsack ★
> Well-known range of sherries made at PAARL by the K.W.V.

Pinotage
> South African red grape, a cross between PINOT NOIR and CINSAUT, useful for high yields and hardiness. Its wine is lush and fruity but never first-class.

Piquetberg
> Small demarcated district on the w. coast round Porterville. A warm dry climate gives mainly dessert and distilling wine.

Premier Grand Cru
> See Grand Cru

Riesling
> South African Riesling makes some of the country's better white wines, but is not the same as Rhine Riesling, which has only recently been planted in any quantity in S. Africa.

Rietvallei ★★
> New ROBERTSON estate. Fortified Muscadel, table wines to come.

Robertson
> Small demarcated district e. of the Cape and inland. Mainly dessert wines (notably MUSCAT), but red and white table wines are on the increase. Includes Bonnievale.

Roodeberg ★★
> High-quality brand of blended red wine from the K.W.V. Has good colour, body and flavour and ages well in bottle.

Rustenberg `***`

Effectively, if not officially, an estate red wine from just n.e. of STELLENBOSCH. Rustenberg Dry Red is a good Cabernet/Cinsaut blend. The straight Cabernet is outstanding. Also promising Pinot Noir.

Schoongezicht *

Partner of RUSTENBERG, one of S. Africa's most beautiful old farms and producer of agreeable white wine from STEEN, RIESLING and Clairette Blanche. Now registered as an estate.

Shiraz

The red Rhône grape, recently gaining in popularity in S. Africa for rich deep-coloured wine.

Simonsig `**→***`

Estate owned by F.J. Malan, Chairman of the Cape Estate Wine Producers' Association. Produces a wide range, incl. WEISSER RIESLING and a successful "Méthode Champenoise".

Simonsvlei

One of S. Africa's best-known co-operative cellars, just outside PAARL. A prize-winner with both whites and reds.

Spier *

Estate of five farms w. of STELLENBOSCH producing reds and whites. The SHIRAZ is best.

Steen South Africa's commonest white grape, said to be a clone of the CHENIN BLANC. It gives strong, tasty and lively wine, sweet or dry, normally better than S. African RIESLING.

Stein

Name used for any medium dry white wine.

Stellenbosch

Town and demarcated district 30 miles e. of Cape Town, extending to the ocean at False Bay. Most of the best estates, esp. for red wine, are in the mountain foothills of the region.

Stellenbosch Farmers' Winery (S.F.W.)

South Africa's biggest winery (after the K.W.V.) with several ranges of wines, incl. NEDERBURG, ZONNEBLOEM, Lanzerac, OUDE LIBERTAS and the popular TASSENBERG. Also "Vinotas Light". See Cape Wine and Distillers Ltd.

Stellenryck

Good-quality BERGKELDER range, esp. for RIESLING and CHENIN BLANC.

Superior

An official designation of quality for WINES OF ORIGIN. The wine must meet standards set by the Wine & Spirit Board.

Swartland

Demarcated district around MALMESBURY. ALLESVERLOREN is the best estate.

Swellendam

Demarcated district of the s.e., with Bonnievale as its centre. Dessert, distilling and light table wines.

Sylvaner

Introduced variety. The only commercial wine from it comes from OVERGAAUW. Müller-Thurgau is often misnamed Sylvaner.

Taskelder *

Range of good value wines from the STELLENBOSCH FARMERS' WINERY, including CH. LIBERTAS, Lanzerac Rosé, LA GRATITUDE and Tasheimer.

Tassenberg *

Popular and good-value red table wine known to thousands as Tassie.

Tawny

As in Portugal means port-style wines aged in wood.

Theuniskraal ★★

Well-known TULBAGH estate specializing in white wines, esp. RIESLING and GEWÜRZTRAMINER. Also STEEN, Semillon. Distributed by the BERGKELDER.

Tulbagh

Demarcated district n. of PAARL best known for the white wines of its three famous estates, MONTPELLIER, THEUNISKRAAL and TWEE JONGEGEZELLEN, and the dessert wines of its co-operative at Drostdy. See also BOBERG.

Twee Jongegezellen ★★→★★★

Estate at TULBAGH. One of the great pioneers which revolutionized S. African wine in the 1950s, still in the family of its 18th-century founder. Mainly white wine, incl. RIESLING, STEEN and Sauvignon Blanc. Best wines: "Schanderl" and "T.J.39". The name means "two young friends". Exports via GILBEYS.

Uiterwyk ★★

Old estate w. of STELLENBOSCH making a very good CABERNET SAUVIGNON and pleasant whites.

Uitkyk ★★

Old estate at STELLENBOSCH famous for Carlonet (big gutsy CABERNET) and Carlsheim white. Now 400 acres. Distribution by BERGKELDER.

Union Wine

Company with HQ in Wellington, near PAARL. Brand names Culemborg, BELLINGHAM and Val du Charron.

Van Riebeck

Co-operative at Riebeck Kasteel, MALMESBURY, known for pioneering work in white wine technology.

Verdun ★

Estate w. of STELLENBOSCH, best known for its Gamay red, but also a good SAUVIGNON BLANC.

Vergenoegd ★★

Old family estate in s. STELLENBOSCH supplying high-quality sherry to the K.W.V. but recently offering deeply flavoured CABERNET and excellent SHIRAZ under an estate label.

Weisser Riesling

A fairly recent introduction from Germany. Considerably finer than the S.A. RIESLING, which it is replacing.

Weltevrede ★

Progressive ROBERTSON estate. Colombard and blended whites.

De Wetshof ★★★

Pioneering estate in ROBERTSON district. Prize-winning Riesling marketed by BERGKELDER. Also CHARDONNAY, SAUVIGNON BLANC and a sweet noble-rot white, Edeloes.

Wine of Origin

The S. African equivalent of Appellation Contrôlée. The demarcated regions involved are all described on these pages.

Worcester

Demarcated wine district round the Breede and Hex river valleys, e. of PAARL. Many co-operative cellars make mainly dessert wines, brandy and dry whites.

Zandvliet ★★

Estate in the ROBERTSON area marketing a light SHIRAZ through the BERGKELDER. Later will add a Cabernet-Merlot blend.

Zonnebloem ★★

Good-quality brand of CABERNET, RIESLING, PINOTAGE and PREMIER GRAND CRU from the STELLENBOSCH FARMERS' WINERY. The Cabernet is vintage-dated and ages well in bottle.

QUICK REFERENCE VINTAGE CHARTS FOR FRANCE AND GERMANY

These charts give a picture of the range of qualities made in the principal areas (every year has its relative successes and failures) and a guide to whether the wine is ready to drink or should be kept.

🍾 drink now   ▬ needs keeping   ✓ can be drunk with pleasure now, but the better wines will continue to improve

0   no good   **10**   the best

Combinations of these symbols mean that there are wines in more than one of the categories.

(Symbol key used below: ▬ = needs keeping, 🍾 = drink now, ✓ = can be drunk with pleasure now)

FRANCE

	Red Bordeaux		White Bordeaux	
	Médoc/Graves	Pom/St-Em.	Sauternes & sw.	Graves & dry
82	7–10 ▬	7–9 ▬	3–7 ▬	7–9 ✓
81	6–8 ▬	7–9 ▬	5–7 ▬	7–8 ✓🍾
80	4–6 ✓	3–5 ✓	5–8 ▬	5–7 ✓
79	5–8 ▬	5–9 ✓	6–8 ▬	4–6 🍾
78	6–9 ✓	6–8 ✓	4–6 ✓	7–9 ✓
77	3–5 ✓	2–5 ✓	2–4 🍾	6–7 🍾
76	6–8 ✓🍾	7–8 ✓	7–9 ✓	4–8 ✓
75	9–10 ✓🍾	8–10 ✓🍾	8–10 ✓🍾	8–10 ✓
74	4–6 ✓	3–5 🍾	0	4–6 🍾
73	5–6 🍾	5–7 🍾	0–4 🍾	7–8 🍾
72	2–5 🍾	2–4 🍾	2–4 🍾	4–5 🍾
71	5–8 ✓	6–8 ✓	8–9 ✓	8–9 ✓
70	9–10 🍾	9–10 ✓	9–10 🍾	9–10 🍾
69	1–4 🍾	0–3 🍾	5–7 🍾	8–9 🍾
67	5–7 🍾	6–8 🍾	7–10 ✓	8–10 🍾
66	7–9 ✓🍾	8–9 ✓	4–7 🍾	7–8 🍾

	Red Burgundy	White Burgundy		
	Côte d'Or	Côte d'Or	Chablis	Alsace
82	5–7 ✓	6–8 ✓	6–7 ✓	7–9 ✓🍾
81	3–5 ✓	5–8 ✓🍾	6–9 ✓🍾	7–8 ✓
80	4–7 ✓	4–6 ✓	5–7 ✓	3–5 🍾
79	5–7 ✓	6–8 ✓	6–8 ✓	7–8 ✓
78	8–10 ✓🍾	7–9 ✓	7–10 ✓	6–8 🍾
77	2–4 🍾	4–6 🍾	5	3–5 🍾
76	7–10 ✓🍾	7–8 ✓	8 ✓	10 ✓
75	0–5 🍾	4–8 🍾	8–10 🍾	9 🍾
74	2–5 🍾	5–8 🍾	6–8 🍾	6–7 🍾
73	4–7 🍾	8	7–8 🍾	7–8 🍾
72	4–9 🍾	5–8 🍾	1–4 🍾	3 🍾
71	8–10 ✓	8–10 🍾	7–9 🍾	10 🍾

Beaujolais: 81 and 82 are the vintages to buy and drink. **Mâcon-Villages** (white): 82, 81 and 79 are good now. **Loire:** Sweet Anjou and Touraine. Best recent vintages: 82, 79, 78, 76, 73, 71, 70. **Upper Loire:** Sancerre and Pouilly-Fumé 82, 81 and 79 are good now. **Muscadet:** D.Y.A.

GERMANY

	Rhône			Rhine		Moselle	
82	4–7 ✓		82	4–6 ✓		4–7 ✓	
81	5–7 ✓		81	5–8 ✓		4–8 ✓	
80	7–8 ✓🍾		80	4–7 🍾		3–7 🍾	
79	6–8 ✓🍾		79	6–8 ✓🍾		6–8 ✓🍾	
78	8–10 ✓🍾		78	5–7 ✓		4–7 ✓	
77	4–6 ✓		77	5–7 🍾		4–6 🍾	
76	6–9 🍾		76	9–10 ✓		9–10 ✓	
75	0–5 🍾		75	7–9 🍾		8–10 🍾	
74	4–7 🍾		74	3–6 🍾		2–4 🍾	
73	5–8 🍾		73	6–7 🍾		6–8 🍾	
72	6–9 🍾		72	2–5 🍾		1–4 🍾	
71	7–9 🍾		71	9–10 ✓		10 ✓	

N.B. Fully detailed charts will be found on pages 24, 25 (France), 77 (Germany).